# A FALSE SPRING

· · · · · · · · · · · · · · · · · · ·

## by Pat Jordan

A FIRESIDE BOOK
Published by Simon & Schuster Inc.
New York   London   Toronto   Sydney   Tokyo

First Fireside Edition, 1988
Published by Simon & Schuster Inc.
Simon & Schuster Building
Rockefeller Center
1230 Avenue of the Americas
New York, New York 10020
Published by arrangement with Dodd, Mead & Company
FIRESIDE and colophon are registered trademarks
of Simon & Schuster Inc.

Manufactured in the United States of America

10  9  8  7  6  5  4  3  2  1  Pbk.

Library of Congress Cataloging in Publication Data

Jordan, Pat.
    A false spring.

    (A Fireside Sports Classic)
    Reprint. Originally published: New York : Dodd,
Mead, 1975.
    "A Fireside Book."
    1. Jordan, Pat.    2. Baseball players—United States
—Biography.    I. Title.    II. Series.
[GV865.J67A34  1988]  796.357'092'4  [B]  87-36407

ISBN 0-671-65994-4 Pbk.

For Carol, who knows

WITH so many trees in the city, you could see the spring coming each day until a night of warm wind would bring it suddenly in one morning. Sometimes the heavy cold rain would beat it back so that it would seem that it would never come and that you were losing a season out of your life. . . .When the cold rains kept on and killed the spring, it was as though a young person had died for no reason.

Life had seemed so simple that morning when I had wakened and found the false spring. . .

Ernest Hemingway's *A Moveable Feast*

# A FALSE
# SPRING

# ...1

I SEE myself daily as I was then, framed in a photograph on the desk in my attic room. The picture was taken on June 27, 1959, at County Stadium in Milwaukee, Wisconsin, a few minutes before the Milwaukee Braves were to take the field against the Chicago Cubs, to whom they would lose that day 7-1.

I am standing midway between the firstbase line and the home team's dugout. To my back I see the stadium's half-filled bleachers. I am wearing a Braves' uniform. Although the photograph is black and white, I see all the colors. My cap has a navy crown, a white M and a red bill. My flannel uniform is the color of cream. It is trimmed—shirt and pants—with a half-inch-wide, tricolored stripe of black and red and black satin. The word "Braves" is scripted in red and outlined in black at a slight upward angle across the front of the shirt. The script is underlined by a black and gold tomahawk. Below the tomahawk, in the left-hand corner of the shirt is "24" in large block numerals, also red and outlined in black. Unseen in the photograph but clearly in my mind's eye is the small gold patch stitched onto the shirt sleeve below my left shoulder. It is the face of an Indian of indeterminate tribe, the face contorted by a war cry no less menacing for being inaudible.

To my right is Whitlow Wyatt, the Braves' 52-year-old pitching coach. Wyatt is smiling at me. My gaze, however, is directed to my left toward Warren Spahn, the Braves' great

1

left-handed pitcher. Both Spahn and I are perspiring. We have just finished running wind sprints in the outfield and are apparently on the way to the clubhouse to change our shirts when we stop to pose for this photograph. . . . For whom? For some faceless fan leaning over the dugout roof, imploring "Please!" whose good fortune it was to catch us in an obliging mood? So we stop, strike a pose, so casual, and wait for the camera's click. To pass this moment, as he has innumerable others like it, Spahn, hands on hips, turns to me with some bit of small talk, a phrase, meaningless, meant only to fill the instant. And I listen. Nonchalantly, hands on hips also, I listen to Spahn. To Spahnie. To Spahnie who is talking to me, so much younger, and yet with my amused smile looking so at ease—today amazed at how truly at ease I do appear, at how naturally I did fit, in that uniform, between those men, with Spahn, Spahnie and I, the best of friends, I, too, having done this small thing so often, having struck this obliging pose for so many fans, waiting only for the camera's click before tossing off a remark at which Spahnie and I would laugh on the way into the clubhouse to change our shirts.

I was 18 years old that day and the photograph had been arranged by the publicity department of the Milwaukee Braves, with whom I had just signed my first professional baseball contract. Of all the major league uniforms I wore that summer—and I wore many—none was so gaudy and none so impressive as the uniform of the Braves. That was one reason I signed with them rather than with one of the other 15 major league teams who had also offered me a contract. There were other reasons. The Braves had agreed to pay for my college education, to pay me a salary of $500 per month during each baseball season, and to deposit in my savings account every June 27 for the next four years a certified check for $8750. All told, my bonus amounted to more than $45,000 distributed

2

over a four-year period. It was one of the largest bonuses—if not *the* largest—any young player received from the Braves in 1959. For my part, I promised to leave Milwaukee the following morning on a flight to McCook, Nebraska, where I would begin my professional career as a pitcher with the McCook Braves of the Class D Nebraska State League.

I pitched in the minor leagues for three years, at towns like McCook, Davenport, Waycross, Eau Claire and Palatka, before I was given my unconditional release by those same Milwaukee Braves. I never did pitch a game in Milwaukee County Stadium, nor did I ever again speak to Warren Spahn. I did, however, keep the cash.

As I write this, confronted on my desk by that reminder of unfulfilled promise, 13 years have elapsed since I posed with Warren Spahn, and 10 years since my last professional game. I was married the year I left baseball (the phrase I always use) and now have five children. I also returned to college and graduated in 1965 with a Bachelor of Arts Degree in English. I taught English at a parochial all-girls high school for five years (the only male in a world of nuns and teeny boppers) and finally turned to writing. I have had little to do with baseball since my release by the Braves. Except for an abortive comeback attempt at 22 (at 22?), I have not pitched a game.

That "comeback" was a disaster. It had been urged on me by my brother, George, a lawyer, 13 years older than I, and who had had so much to do with my career, with my having had a career, that he could never reconcile himself to my having lost it. Years after I left baseball, he still kept on the wall of his law office that photograph of me at County Stadium. It was a constant embarrassment to me. Yet he never tired of explaining to his clients who that young player next to Spahn was, or what his promise had once been. I think he did this from a sense of loyalty to me, a brotherly duty not to abandon, and

3

also because he remembered me only as I had been before that publicity shot. He never saw me pitch in the minor leagues, especially that last year, and so never saw the roots of my failure, a failure that has always bewildered him. George remembered me only as I had been in high school, when there was little I could not do on a pitcher's mound. Or in Little League, when my successes, which he shared, were close to total. In those days I often pitched to him on the sidewalk in front of our house. Our parents sat on the front porch and watched. They applauded my efforts. After a fastball that cracked in his catcher's mitt, my brother would yank his hand out of the glove and shake it fiercely as if to shake off the hot pain. And they would applaud. My brother, tall, gangling, wearing a white button-down shirt, the sleeves rolled up past his elbows, would grimace in both mock and very real pain as he shook his burning hand. How I responded to that gesture!

One day when George couldn't "work with me," as he used to call it, I badgered my father into catching me. I was 11, I think, and already threw quite hard. My father, a lefty, had never been much of an athlete. He had been an orphan, and in his teens he turned to gambling for his satisfactions, and in later years for his livelihood. His interest in sports was less fervid than that of the rest of us. My mother was passionately devoted to Joe DiMaggio, and George and I were just as passionately devoted to my pitching, which we thought of even then as potentially a career. For my father, sports were never something to be played, but something to lay nine-to-five on. He was in his early forties then, and, although he'd ceased to gamble full-time, he was still a betting man. And occasionally he would deal cards in a late-night poker game. He was an excellent dealer and was paid handsomely for his efforts. It was in the hands, he said. His fingers were small and soft and plump; my mother said they were like the link sausages she

4

threw in the spaghetti sauce. But how they flashed when dealing cards! He used only his left hand. His fingers were pressed together in the shape of a trowel. They supported the deck. He dealt with a flick of his wrist, his thumb shooting cards around the table with such speed and precision one listened for clicks.

My father began to catch me with reluctance. He had to wear the catcher's mitt—meant for one's left hand—on his right hand. His little finger fit into the glove's fat thumb, which stuck out ridiculously. He grumbled as I threw. His mind was on the card game at which he would deal later that evening at a local Italian Athletic Club. "Fellow athletes," my mother used to say, and we'd all laugh. All except my father. He took his sport seriously, too. To impress him I cut loose with a fastball without telling him. Startled, he caught it on the middle finger of his left hand, the one without the glove. The finger split open and blood spurted out, spotting his shirt and pants. For just a second he looked at his finger in disbelief. Then he ran bellowing into the house. I was too terrified to follow. When I finally did get up the courage to go inside, I found him sitting at the kitchen table, his hand wrapped in a blood-soaked handkerchief. He was trying to deal a poker hand to my white-faced mother. With a glance she warned me to silence. The cards slipped in his bleeding hand. They began to spill, slide down his wrist. He tried to pin them to his side with his elbow. They scattered across the floor. He glared at them. Cursed their ancestry. Snatched them up with his good hand and tried to deal again.

Years later, we would all laugh at that scene—my mother and I terrified, my father dealing, the cards spilling, curses and blood-stained kings. It became one of those anecdotes for which families invent a significance which, at the time, eluded them but in retrospect grows to mythical proportions. The point became—my speed! I threw *that* hard! Hard enough, at

5

11, to break a grown man's finger, pink and vulnerable as it might have been. It seems, even then, we were attuned to such small evidences of my destiny. My parents, brother and I always had more than a premonition that my talent was something beyond the ordinary. It was a gift, we knew, and so it must be cultivated with the greatest care. For instance, my mother never asked me to do chores on a day I was to pitch, while my father spent all his spare money on the best equipment for me. (At 11 I had a $30 glove and $27 kangaroo-skin baseball spikes.) George, a struggling lawyer then, spent most of his lunch hours working out with me at the park near home. He would catch me for about 20 minutes, then make me run wind sprints from home plate to first base and back again. All the while I ran, he would remind me in long monologues just how badly I wanted a baseball career, and how hard I must work at it. This way, the entire family shared in the development of my talent. From the very first, I was aware that this talent I possessed must be treated with reverence because it was only partly mine, and partly my family's. My talent united my family in a way we have never been since I lost it.

When I was 12 years old and in my final season of Little League baseball, my name appeared regularly in headlines in the sports section of the Bridgeport, Connecticut, *Post-Telegram*. The stories varied only slightly. Another no-hitter. More strikeouts. My third consecutive no-hitter. My fourth. And so it went. A season of six games in which I allowed two hits and struck out 110 of the 116 batters retired when I was on the mound. I had been almost perfect. Just two hits all year. And in my last two games every single out made was, in fact, a strikeout (36 in a row, since Little League games last only six innings) with scarcely a walk, an error or a foul ball in between. After the fourth consecutive no-hitter, my parents were called by a reporter for Ripley's *Believe It Or Not.* He wanted to

6

verify certain facts. Possibly I would appear in one of their columns, he said. Where, I wondered? Alongside some Zulu tribesman who could fit an entire watermelon, lengthwise, in his mouth?

One night we received a call from Dick Young, the sportswriter for the New York *Daily News*. He interviewed my parents and me over the telephone. A few days later he wrote a column about me. In August the New York Yankees, with whom we were all enamored, invited my parents and me to appear on Mel Allen's television show prior to a Yankee–Red Sox doubleheader. We arrived at the Stadium properly awed —my mother wearing a corsage and my father and I dressed uncomfortably in suits and ties. We were treated royally. Pinstripes everywhere. Pictures of Ruth and Gehrig and Di-Maggio. My mother swooned. Yankee executives hovered over me, smiling. "So this is our little pitcher? Does he want to be a Yankee when he grows up?"

Needless to say, I did not think of myself as "a little pitcher." Nor did I think I had to "grow up" before I could pitch for the New York Yankees. I was ready then, and to prove it I had brought my glove in a brown paper bag. I expected Mel Allen to turn to me in mid-interview and say, "Well, Pat, why don't you throw a few? Show the fans your stuff." And I would step onto the field and proceed to astonish all the viewers and fans, but most importantly, the Yankees, with my blazing fastball. What an embarrassment it would be for Vic Raschi! How he would envy me, throwing in my suit and tie with more speed than he ever dreamed of having!

We sat in box seats along the thirdbase line. Television cameras were aimed at us from the field. The signal was given. Mel Allen, turning to his right, asked my parents a question. His lips peeled apart like an open wound. My father fidgeted; my mother touched her corsage. One of them answered. More

7

questions. Nervous smiles. Quick glances at the cameras and then back to Mel Allen. I sat at the end of the row, farthest away. I could barely hear. It did not matter. I just sat there waiting, my heart pounding, the brown bag at my feet. And when it was almost over, and I knew it was too late for me to throw, Mel Allen leaned across my parents and asked me a question. I was so disheartened I couldn't answer. He repeated it. I mumbled something and he returned to my parents. I sat there, glaring across the field at Vic Raschi, warming up with his pathetic fastball.

My brother remembered this. The no-hitters, the headlines, Dick Young, Mel Allen. He remembered it all so well that when I told him what I'd written about that day at Yankee Stadium, he said, "But you forgot Casey Stengel! Remember what he said when he found out about the strikeouts?" I didn't remember. "He said, 'I guess your fellas don't need no gloves when you pitch.' "

What I had been is still clear to my brother. It is a picture whose lines have been redrawn so often, retracing identical successes year after year, that it has become etched in his memory. He never saw those lines erased during my years in the minor leagues and then somehow redrawn, without his knowledge, until what they defined when I was released by the Braves in 1962 was something unrecognizable to him. That was why he urged me to make a comeback so soon after I had left baseball. He would not accept the fact that I had lost it all in only four years. It would take only a little practice, he said. We could work out on his lunch hour. He would have me throwing like my old self again. That was the phrase he used: throwing like my old self. Then, when I was ready, he would pick some Sunday afternoon and some team in the Senior City League, and would inform the newspapers and the scouts he knew that I would pitch that day. And after the game, after I had struck out 13 or 14 batters, the scouts would be only too eager to sign me again. "Maybe even another bonus," my brother said, only half-kidding. "But smaller, naturally."

The high school field where we threw was always deserted at noon. I would arrive first, to claim the field, then wait for George. I passed those agonizing minutes pacing from the pitcher's mound and back again, praying that no one else would show up, would intrude on this routine, our ritual, wishing my brother would hurry so we could get it over with and I could flee. He would then pull up in his new air-conditioned car. A successful lawyer now, approaching forty, with a touch of gray in his wiry hair, which he still wore in a crew cut. He had fleshed out a lot and was no longer gangling. Still, he was six feet, four inches tall and very sturdy looking. Unbreakable is the word that perhaps best described him, still describes him. He played sports mechanically, as if by memory but not instinct. He moved stiffly, his back a poker that seemed incapable of bending. *He* seemed incapable of bending, of ever breaking —as I had in the minor leagues. (His argument for my attempting this comeback was brief, "You aren't going to quit, are you?") He wore dark-rimmed glasses and a snazzy bow tie. He would take off his jacket, some Scottish plaid from the racks of J. Press in New Haven, and fold it neatly over a bench. Then he would roll up the sleeves of his shirt. Very carefully, fold after even fold, past his elbows, that same white, button-down shirt, the gesture suddenly calming me, reassuring me. Then we would begin throwing as we had so many times before.

But my comeback did not work out as my brother had planned. I have never again thrown like my old self. And on the day I finally took the mound in the same semi-pro league in which five years before I had struck out batters at will, I was unable to retire a single man. The fans loved it. They laughed

9

and hooted each time my poor catcher (some high school boy I have never seen again) scrambled back to the screen to retrieve another of my wild pitches. I wore my Braves' uniform that day, a further affront to those fans, many of whom had seen me pitch before and who had been burdened too long with my past successes. I left the game in the first inning. So many runs were scored, so many batters walked or hit, so many wild pitches bounced in front of the plate or flung over my catcher's up-stabbing mitt, that I have retained only fragments from that day. Jagged little pieces . . . the shouts of "has-been," "washed-up," "always a bum." The look of pity on my catcher's face as he walked out to reassure me for the tenth time. A look he is not easy with at his age. And I, feeling bad for him, too. He senses that something is eluding him beside my fastballs. The fans *so* vicious at this meaningless game? It frightens him. This exorcising of private devils. He crouches for another pitch. I begin my windup, rear back, and catch him shooting a look over his shoulder at the fans. The ball rattles the home-plate screen. The runner on third trots home, and with a little jump lands on the plate with both feet. I sigh, exhausted, feeling empty. Truly empty. Without insides. Filled only with air. Floating above things for a change. Not caring now. Untouchable. Not a bad feeling. Nice, really. New to me. At ease now, I wait for the ball. Look around. Catch sight of my brother. All else dissolves—fans, players, noise, heat, exhaustion, time—is gone. I see only him. Standing beneath a tree along the firstbase line. Wearing dark glasses. Watching and not seeing. He clenches his fist, makes a short, pistonlike punch into an invisible gut. Mine! He still believes! Amazing! It doesn't matter if I don't believe. He does. In spite of me, it can still be done. Merely by an act of his will. Another punch. But the niceness remains. I shrug.

*      *      *

I think often about that day. And about the others, too, the good ones. Baseball was such an experience in my life that, 10 years later, I have still not shaken it, will probably never shake it. I still think of myself not as a writer who once pitched, but as a pitcher who happens to be writing just now. It's as if I decided at some point in my life, or possibly *it* was decided, that of all the things in my life only that one experience would most accurately define me. It hardly matters whether this is a fact or a private delusion. It matters only that I devoted so great a chunk of my life to baseball that I believe it's true. I believe that that experience affected the design of my life to a degree nothing else ever will. Yet it never seemed to end properly, neatly, all those bits and pieces finally forming some harmonious design. It just stopped, unfinished in my memory, fragmented, so many pieces missing. Over the years I have begun sorting and resorting those bits and pieces—delicately, at first —finding every now and then a new one to further flesh out that design, finally discovering the pieces had always been there and that what had been missing was in me. This book, then, is an attempt not to relive that experience but to resee it, once and for all, as it truly was, somehow frozen in time, unfragmented, waiting only for me to develop the perception needed to see it whole.

# ...2

THE bird dogs came first. They appeared one spring day in my sophomore year of high school, drawn by the odor of fresh talent and sweet young grass. I knew about bird dogs even then, at 15, and had been waiting impatiently for them to appear. It was a sign. On that day baseball ceased to be just a game for me; it also became my career.

They were called bird dogs because they sniffed out talent, although the name does not do justice to the men. They were kindly, stooped old men in plaid shirts and string ties. They had once owned taverns or hardware stores, and in their youth had possibly played ball with Kiki Cuyler or Georgie Cutshaw. Now, retired, they measured out their weekday afternoons at a succession of high school baseball games. They were always easy to spot, even from the pitcher's mound, since few adults ever bothered to attend the meaningless games my coach let me pitch as a sophomore; and because they always stood behind the homeplate screen, as if they were ill-at-ease unless viewing life through a maze of wire triangles. Their job was to unearth talent for the major league team with which they were affiliated. It was a loose affiliation, really. In most cases it consisted simply of their friendship with some organization's full-time scout. Most bird dogs never got paid a cent for their efforts, although occasionally one might be slipped a hundred dollars if his discovery reached the major leagues. But they were so old (in their seventies and eighties) and the gestation period of a professional ballplayer so long (often more than six years in the minor leagues) that few bird dogs lived long enough to see their judgments confirmed. That wasn't the reason they spent the time and effort, anyway. They did it to pass the time, for one thing, and because they loved the game. But most of all they did it because they appreciated talent. Just discovering it and watching it develop was satisfaction enough for these old men.

One day in my sophomore year at Fairfield Prep, a Jesuit-run high school in Fairfield, Connecticut, I struck out 19 apprentice plumbers, bricklayers and carpenters from nearby Bullard-Havens Technical High School. That night, Johnny Barron, an aged Cincinnati bird dog, telephoned our house. He spoke first with my father and then my mother, as if, like some Victorian suitor, he was seeking permission to court me—which, in a way, he was. Finally, I took the receiver with trembling hands. His voice surprised me. It was ragged and halting, yet somehow at ease, as if we were old friends. And in his mind we were old friends since he'd just seen me pitch.

Johnny did most of the talking that night. He took much for granted. He detailed my strengths and weaknesses (weaknesses?) with a familiarity that would have annoyed me were it not for the warmth in his voice. He said of my fastball, "And when you do make the big leagues, it'll be your fastball that takes you there. It's a beautiful fastball!" It was a strange word to use, I thought, one reserved for a painting or statue or some other work of art. He was a strange man, too. He took such delight in just talking to me that it embarrassed me, even though I'd been aware from the first that my talent, with which I was so familiar as to be no longer awed by it (just as I was no longer awed by my ability to walk), was to others so extraordinary as to inspire a respect that approached adoration. Its presence could lead a dignified old man like Johnny Barron to lose his composure when merely talking to its possessor, a 15-year-old boy. However, the fact that this respect was for the talent, not its possessor, escaped me then.

Johnny concluded his talk a little breathlessly, saying, "I wish we could sign you now. But we can't until you graduate high school. By that time most of the other clubs will be bidding a lot of money for you. I'll be out of the picture then. Our scouts and front-office people will have taken over. But I hope you'll remember me, that I was the first to appreciate your gift. It will mean a lot to me." Although I was not sure what he wanted or why, I promised, and he hung up satisfied. I seldom pitched a game that year without spotting him behind the backstop. Often I would not feel comfortable on the mound until spotting him, and would spend long moments rubbing up a baseball until I did. Strangely enough, I never talked to Johnny again, although he often spoke with my parents during the games I pitched. When I did sign a professional baseball contract in 1959 it was with the Braves, however, not the Reds. But I kept my promise and had the local newspaper insert a small paragraph near the bottom of the article that told of my signing. The paragraph mentioned how John Barron, Sr., of Haddon Street, Bridgeport, Connecticut, had been the first bird dog to notice me.

I pitched four one-hitters in my sophomore year of high school, and the following year my reputation as a major league prospect was firmly established. The bird dogs, like Johnny, were gone by then. They had been replaced by full-time scouts who moved in quickly, like carpetbaggers, to take advantage of the friendships cultivated by the bird dogs. The scouts were younger men, in their fifties usually, and their appreciation of talent was more professional than esthetic. They were not unkind men, although they were certainly not so lovable as the bird dogs. But maybe when I caught my first whiff of that bonus money I was not so lovable either, and perhaps it was a good thing that bird dogs like Johnny Barron could not see me then.

When my brother George was 12 years old, my father took him along on a gambling foray into Canada. In Montreal my father won ten thousand dollars in an all-night poker game. The game broke up after dawn, and my father went directly to a bank where he exchanged the large bills for singles, which he stuffed into an old valise. He returned to the hotel as my brother was waking. He made him sit up in bed and put his hands over his eyes. Then he emptied the contents of the valise over his head. The bills fluttered about my brother like falling leaves. They both began to laugh idiotically and to toss the bills into the air until the room was littered with them. For the rest of the day, while my father slept, my brother counted and stacked the bills. And he played with them daily over the next few weeks, although each day their number diminished, until finally none were left. Then he and my father returned to Connecticut. If George and I inherited any legacy from our father, who in a lifetime of gambling let over a million dollars slip through his fingers, it was this ironic disregard for money. Money was never something one saved in our home (there were no piggy banks), nor was it something one learned the value of (no stern lectures on lost dimes). Nor was it an evil. It was simply something one needed a minimum of in order to live. Any amount beyond that should be acquired as effortlessly as possible and consumed just as effortlessly. My father was a master at both, although his mastery of the former was surpassed by the latter. My brother and I still cherish this legacy, however, and it has greatly affected our lives. Yet during

15

1958 and 1959 the anticipation of a large amount of money became our common obsession in a way it never has, before or since.

It began during my junior year of high school. I had won 12 consecutive games over a two-year period and had averaged almost two strikeouts per inning. I'd been equally successful pitching in the Senior City League, a nearby semi-professional circuit filled with ex-minor leaguers in their twenties and thirties. In my first appearance with them, at the age of 15, I pitched a one-hit shutout. But beyond such achievements and my obvious physical talent, I had the look of a finished pitcher. I was big for my age. At 16 I stood six feet tall and weighed 175 pounds. My pitching delivery, so painstakingly cultivated by my brother, was smooth and natural and all of a piece, unlike other young pitchers whose deliveries are composed of distinct and conscious stages. My mannerisms on the mound were those of a professional. My brother had taught me how to shake off a catcher's sign with a flick of my glove; how to landscape the dirt on the mound with my spikes; how to hold a runner to first base with the barest of peeks over my left shoulder; and how to receive my catcher's return throw with such a disdainful snap of the glove that the batter could not help but feel my contempt for him. My brother and I left no detail unperfected. We discussed the proper way for a pitcher to wear his uniform, and we decided that a fastball pitcher, like myself, should let his pants' legs fall well below his knee before fastening them. Only infielders and pitchers without "stuff" wore their pant legs fastened at the knees. "Besides," my brother said, "it'll make you look taller in the eyes of the scouts."

I'd been able to master these peripheral details because for 10 years I'd done little else but pitch. I had never really liked the rest of the game, for it was filled with too much dead time.

Only the pitcher, isolated on a small rise, seemed constantly in motion. He was the catalyst about whom the fans, the players and the game itself revolved. I liked this feeling of power, of being the center of the action, of controlling things. When not pitching I had no desire to play shortstop or left field or even take my turn at bat. I was solely a pitcher—and in my mind's eye, I am still one today. I often go to the small park near home and, when the field is deserted, take the mound and begin to pitch baseballs into the screen behind home plate. It relaxes me. The pump, the kick, the follow through. No longer the center of the action, no longer controlling things, feeling often powerless, I take comfort only in the act as it has finally become for me, divorced from all externals. I am at home with it because it was the first thing in my life that I could do well and others couldn't. At eight, this discovery was my first hint that I was a distinct and separate entity with potentials and abilities entirely my own. I stood out, both in my own eyes and to those around me. Because I owed my first distinctness to this talent, I mistook it for the only distinctness I would ever have. I *was* my talent. Its loss would be a loss of self. So I played to it. I polished it at the expense of everything else. And I could do it so well, naturally, almost without effort, that it became increasingly easy for me to neglect any other potential whose luster would have demanded a strenuous effort.

But at 16 I knew none of this. I knew only that I loved to pitch. And it was this strong affection for my talent as much as the talent itself that drew the dozen or so major league scouts to each game I pitched as a high school junior. Unlike the bird dogs, who had appeared alone and inconspicuously, the full-time scouts entered the park in garrulous clusters. They carried aluminum deck chairs in one hand and fat little black note-books in the other. They were always deeply tanned from their recent spring training with "the big club" in Florida or

Arizona, while we in New England were not even pink from our faint and fleeting spring sun. They dressed with the flamboyance of traveling men who seem always to be anticipating warmer climates. They wore bright Banlon jerseys and golf sweaters and gold slacks and black-and-white loafers with tiny tassels and, even on the most sunless of days, dark glasses. And yet, despite this flamboyance, their clothes were in a way quite nondescript, of indefinable origin, a wardrobe of brand names that could have been pieced together anywhere across the country. Those Haggar slacks might have been picked up in a Sears Roebuck in Stockton, California, on the hot, dusty day they saw that farm boy strike out 17, or at a J.C. Penney's in Fayetteville, North Carolina, on the muggy evening they watched that good nigra boy hit four home runs. The scouts' origins were as indefinable as their clothes'. Those men had been worn thin by years of travel, then rewoven with remnants from all their stops so that even a native New Yorker might now chew tobacco and speak with faint threads of a Southern drawl.

The scouts unfolded their deck chairs in the grass behind the homeplate screen and watched the game with what seemed to be barely passing interest. They talked mostly among themselves. Their conversation seldom touched on what was happening before their eyes. They paused only infrequently to pull out a stopwatch and time a runner to first base, or maybe to ask a neighbor about that last putout, which they then recorded in the notebooks they had to turn in to the front office as proof they were doing their job. But these pauses were merely interruptions in their perpetual talk about good restaurants nearby where they would meet after this, their third game of the afternoon; or about too much bourbon consumed last night in a motel room in Naugatuck, Connecticut, and how they couldn't handle it like they used to, or women either for that

18

matter, and they'd all laugh; or finally about that good Polack boy they'd given a $40,000 bonus a few years ago and was now hitting .227 in the Three-I League, but still was saving their hide with the front office by showing a little power, and thank God for small blessings. Their conversation touched rarely on the progress and doings of "the big club" for which they worked—that world, although in the same universe, was just too many light-years removed from their own, from this moment and the high school game they were only half-watching. Inevitably, during the course of these games, their talk drifted to mutual friends in baseball, old friends who were doing well financially or physically, or maybe not so well, who were actually broke, or maybe sick, or dying even of the Big C, or worse than that, who were out of baseball. There was nothing worse than being out of baseball for men who'd spent their lives in it. It was like being out of the mainstream of all that really mattered in life, the good life. And it was so unnecessary, stupid even, to be out of baseball. There was always a place for those who kept their noses clean. "Don't ever make enemies," they were taught on becoming professionals. "You never know who you might be playing for someday." The scouts had listened and survived. They had played for 15 years in the minor leagues and never moved higher than the Sally League. And when they got hurt one day and kept on playing for the good of the organization and in so doing had sacrificed their careers (a smart sacrifice really, for by then they had no careers), they were rewarded on their fortieth birthday with a job as manager of Mayfield, Texas, in the Kitty League. And at fifty, when they could no longer take the pressure of the 6-hour bus rides from Mayfield to Corpus Christi, which had begun to get to their kidneys, they were rewarded further with a job as fulltime scout for the Eastern Seaboard, or maybe the West Coast, or the Southwest Territory. They breathed easily now, a little more easily anyway. As long as they didn't do anything foolish, they would never be out of baseball. They would never have to join that "lunch bucket brigade" which they feared and which they joked about as they watched from their deck chairs behind the homeplate screen.

But it wasn't all the good life for the scouts. There were hazards. And in those days before the advent of the free-agent draft, they could be treacherous.* It was easy for the bird dogs. They simply pointed to the talent. It was the scouts who had to then bring it down on the wing. They needed good reflexes and strong insides and a quick mind and plenty of endurance, even at their age. Without these qualities, too much talent might escape them and they'd find themselves out of baseball, just as they might if they got trigger-happy and bagged too many $100,000 bonus babies who never made it past the

• • •

*The free-agent draft was initiated by the major leagues in 1965. Prior to it, all amateur players were free to sign with any club of their choice the moment their high school class was graduated. By the 1950s, when baseball, like most sports, had become a vastly more lucrative business than ever before (thanks primarily to television), major league teams began offering large sums of money to untried youngsters in order to outbid their rivals for his services. The result was a bidding war that reached its peak when Rick Reichardt, a Madison, Wisconsin, teenager, was given a $175,000 bonus by the California Angels. The free-agent draft eliminated such excesses by eliminating the open market on players. It made all free agents susceptible to two major league drafts, one held in June and the other in January. If a player was drafted by a club in one phase, he was unable to sign with any club but that one for six months. Then, if still unsigned, he was returned to the draft pool and could be drafted by a club in the next phase. The process repeated itself until a player either signed with a club that drafted him; enrolled in a four-year college, in which case he could not be drafted until his class was graduated or he had turned 21; or was no longer drafted. At no point, however, was a player free to bargain with or sign with any club other than the one that owned his current draft rights. Players could no longer auction themselves off to the highest bidder, so bonus demands plummeted. Now, in order to sign a draft choice, a major league club had only to make its offer tempting enough to convince a player it would be foolish to waste six months hoping he might be drafted by a new club that would offer him more money. In fact, usually when a player was redrafted he was offered less money than before.

Three-I League. And always there was the competition squatting right there beside them, eating and drinking and laughing with them, but nevertheless scheming against them, just as they, too, were scheming. It was a risky business and that's what appealed to them. It was exciting; it kept them young. To do it well they had to retain at least remnants of those physical attributes that had meant to much to them in their playing days. They had been physical men in their youth, and their values and pleasures had remained physical beyond middle age. As long as they remained in baseball, no matter how peripherally, they would never completely lose that physicality, would never grow too old to function in the only way that had ever mattered. Even approaching 60, it would still be possible for them to consume large quantities of bourbon, or have an occasional woman in their motel room, while other men their age were going on errands for their wives or tending an orange tree in the backyard of their home in St. Petersburg, Florida.

But the competition *was* fierce. The scouts needed all the weapons they could carry. Money was the most powerful. If they were sufficiently impressed with a prospect, they simply offered him more money than anyone else. Few prospects could refuse. But such offers were rare and a little too risky for most scouts, who treated bonus money as if it were fished dollar by dollar from their own pockets. It was safer for them to equal a rival's offer and then bring up other weapons. A scout for the Yankees, for instance, might inform a prospect, some thickly muscled outfielder from Sioux City, that Mickey Mantle's legs were starting to go. The Yankees would need someone soon to carry on that pinstriped tradition of great outfielders that began with Babe Ruth and continued through DiMaggio and Mantle. If the prospect still wavered, the scout had only to point to those World Championship pennants flying above Yankee Stadium. There was a great deal of money to be made

21

playing for the Yankees in New York, money that no ball-player, no matter how talented, would ever see in Pittsburgh.

That may have been true once, a scout for the Milwaukee Braves might say to that same prospect, but don't forget, the Braves defeated the Yankees in the 1957 World Series and were forging a new and more powerful dynasty of their own. Ah, yes, a scout for the lowly Washington Senators might say, the Yankees and Braves are powerful teams. They have extensive farm systems loaded with much talent. The Senators, however, have finished in last place three years running and their farm system is a mere skeleton of most clubs', and sorely lacking in talent. Of course, this means that a young prospect signing with the Senators would move rapidly through their system to the major leagues, whereas he might languish unnoticed in the more corpulent systems of the Yankees and Braves. That's all very nice, a scout for the recently transplanted Dodgers might respond, but what happens when a ball game is over? A ballplayer has to live in the city in which he plays. After a strenuous day at the ball park he needs to fall back on a lifestyle conducive to relaxation. Such a life-style can be found only on the Coast. The West Coast. L.A. And that scout would spin tales of eager starlets and perpetual sunshine that few boys from Sioux City ever dreamed existed, except between the covers of *Playboy,* and which few could resist. But some did. And if a scout could not bring down a prospect with money or such arguments, he brought him down with the force of his own personality. Or what purported to be a personality. Most scouts had discovered early in their careers that they possessed certain attributes useful in capturing young talent. And so they traded on them, just as in their playing days they had traded on their hustle, which for a while had obscured their inability to hit. They traded so heavily on these attributes that eventually they became vivid parts of themselves, which, like their

22

clothes drew one's attention but revealed nothing of the man.

With each new success my junior year, the scouts lavished more and more attention on my parents, my brother and myself, until there was barely a moment when their presence was not felt. On a night before I was to pitch, for instance, a scout would telephone our home. Once he had identified himself as a scout, he would be turned over to my brother, to whom we had entrusted my career (I was not allowed to talk to scouts). While he gave directions to the ball park or accepted or refused a dinner invitation, I would be upstairs sleeping, trying to sleep anyway, actually just lying perfectly still, catching bits of the conversation below—the names of famous men like Paul Richards or George Weiss, who were making a special trip from New York or Baltimore to see me pitch.

In school the next day as I daydreamed through my classes, strange men in bright clothes wandered the corridors in search of my classroom, or waited for me in the school parking lot when I went outside to eat lunch. Those same men reappeared later in the afternoon as I warmed up far down the left field foul line. At first I could distinguish them only as middleage men carrying deck chairs and black notebooks, but as the year progressed and I saw the same faces game after game, I began to distinguish one scout from another. I never really got to know them personally, except for one or two, and so I remember them only vaguely as possessors of a certain eccentricity. And yet, to this day, I *see* them quite clearly, as in snapshots that have been perfectly preserved. I retain a memory filled with such snapshots taken at various moments as I paused on the mound between pitches.

Rubbing up a baseball before I throw my first pitch of the ball game, I catch sight of my brother standing on the small rise that runs along the thirdbase line. He is typically impassive,

23

arms folded across his chest, nodding faintly to the words of the two scouts on either side of him. To his right stands Frank McGowan, a distinguished-looking man with thick white hair, a florid complexion and a booming politician's voice. McGowan has just spread his arms wide in a gesture meant to reassure my brother of the sincerity of his latest promise concerning my future with the Baltimore Orioles. The man to my brother's left is built like a fireplug. His neck hangs in folds over the collar of his shirt. He is Ron Northey, a recently retired major leaguer in his first year of scouting for the Chicago White Sox. Northey's left cheek is swollen with chewing tobacco, a habit from his playing days that he has been unable to shake. Possibly he is unwilling to shake it since it serves as an excellent reminder to prospects and their families of his recent big-league career. Northey has just told my brother that if *he* doesn't know a major league pitching prospect when he sees one, then who does? To punctuate this he turns his head away from my brother and, at the same moment McGowan is spreading his arms, spits tobacco juice over his shoulder.

One cold drizzly afternoon I am kicking my spikes against the pitching rubber to dislodge some mud when I look up to see Ray Garland, a scout for the New York Yankees, standing on the sidelines beside my mother. Ray is a slick little man who speaks out of the side of his mouth as if distrusting what even he has to say. He is wearing a black double-breasted topcoat with velvet lapels. The coat is wet from the rain and gives Ray the appearance of a drowning rat. Yet he looks perfectly composed, as always. He just stands there in the drizzle, unprotected, his left arm extended away from his body, his hand clutching an umbrella which is protecting my mother, sitting dryly in Ray's deck chair and watching me pitch.

*     *     *

On the hottest day of the spring, when for the first time the sun's rays have become oppressive, I bend over to pick up the resin bag and see, inverted, Jeffery Aloysious Jones talking to my father behind the home team's bench. Old Jeff, as he refers to himself, is a scout for the Milwaukee Braves. He is a large man built like an egg. His face is also egg-shaped and just as smooth, though its smoothness is marred by two eyebrows grown wild as unpruned shrubs. Because of his size, Jeff stands slightly hunched over, as if his entire life were spent talking down to men like my father, much smaller than himself. He speaks in a soft voice distinguished by a pronounced stutter and a Yankee accent. His posture and speech combine to lend him an endearing air of self-deprecation. That, too, is how old Jeff sees himself, a humble Yankee treading daily in a field of vipers. On this hot day Jeff has surrendered his straw hat to my father, whose bald head was falling prey to the sun's rays. Jeff, equally bald but for a friar's tuft, has spread a white handkerchief over his gleaming pate.

There were other scouts, too. John Pollodoro, a wizened Italian, spoke through badly fitted false teeth. When John got excited, which was often, his teeth began to click out of joint with his lips, so that from a distance he looked like a poorly dubbed foreign film. Jack Clark, a scout for the Cincinnati Reds, was a confirmed bachelor who always smelled of bourbon. He was the first scout to arrive at each ball game and the last to leave. From the moment he arrived, he talked aimlessly to anyone who would listen. The stories he told had neither point nor end. Their purpose seemed only to retain an audience for as long as possible. To reassure himself of their presence (although their attention was not required), he would repeatedly lay his hand on each person's forearm. Jack had no permanent residence. His life was lived within the borders of each game he attended. It was peopled by scouts and prospects and parents and coaches and umpires, all of whom were his only respite from the motel room where he was then staying. As prodigal as Jack Clark was with his words, Whitey Pjurek was miserly. Whitey treated each word from his lips as if it were one of the dollar bills he might someday have to pay a prospect. He despised large bonuses going to untried youngsters, and, whenever he did speak, it was always to bemoan the loss of "the good old days," when prospects were signed for the price of a oneway bus ticket to Pancakesville, Georgia.

Of all the scouts I met, the two I still see most clearly are Ray Garland and Jeff Jones. They had the highest regard for my talent and, accordingly, spent the most time, as Jeff would put it, "romancing" me and my family. Ray, a shrewd little man from the Bronx, sensed quickly the great power my brother would ultimately wield over my signing. He talked only with him at games. When he learned that George was about to begin his first season as head basketball coach at Fairfield University he persuaded his nephew, a much sought-after high school player from New York City, to enroll there. Four years later that nephew would captain my brother's team. Jeff Jones, on the other hand, found my parents more susceptible to his charms than my less impressionable brother. He frequently invited them out to dinner to discuss my possible future with the Milwaukee Braves. I attended such a dinner only once, yet I remember it distinctly even though I took no active part. It was one of those awkward affairs in which everyone at first talked around the subject they'd come to discuss—me. Throughout the entrée I was the recipient of fond glances and faint smiles that seemed to arrive whenever I put a forkful of shrimp to my lips, and seemed to require from me a response of which I was ignorant. On occasion Jeff would reach across the table and pat my right arm fondly, although to my mind,

26

a little too delicately, as if it were a dozing cat he did not entirely trust. When my parents ordered cocktails, Jeff ordered a large glass of orange juice without comment.

"Oh, you don't drink, Mr. Jones," said my mother.

"Not really," said Jeff, "although it isn't entirely my own choosing." Only when he was pressed by my parents would Jeff consent to tell the story of his forced sobriety, a story he told as only he could, with that faint and endearing Yankee stutter.

"When I was a boy," he began, "my parents were very strict Yankee Protestants. We're from Maine, you know. They followed the old-fashioned "Blue Laws" to the letter. One of those laws prohibited us boys from playing baseball on the Sabbath. I was a pretty fair ballplayer in those days. It was my one true pleasure. I pleaded with my mother to let me play on the Sabbath, and she finally consented, only if I would promise never to drink hard liquor or smoke tobacco as long as I lived." Jeff paused, and those great shrublike eyebrows tangled together. "When she died, I promised on her deathbed that I'd never break that vow."

There was a prolonged silence at the table after that story, due, I'm sure, to the fact that my parents felt suddenly as unworthy as I did in the presence of such a man as Jeff Jones. Jeff broke the silence after an appropriate pause. "I don't tell that story to everyone," he said. "But I knew you'd understand, being New Englanders yourselves. We New Englanders have the same old-fashioned values, don't we? That's important. Especially for a growing boy like Pat." Smiles all around. "If he plays baseball for the Braves he'll be surrounded by good people with just such values. You know, when the Braves moved to Milwaukee from Boston, they took most of those fine Boston employees with the team. The whole organization is filled with devout Irish Catholics like yourselves."

"Excuse me?" my mother said.

"I said," repeated Jeff, " 'If Pat signs with the Braves you can rest assured he'll be looked after by good Irish Catholics like yourselves.' "

"Oh, we're not of the Irish extraction, Mr. Jones," said my mother. "We're Catholics, but we're certainly not Irish."

Jeff pointed a finger at me and said quite distinctly, "But Patrick—Micheale—Jordan? I thought . . ."

"It was Giordano a generation back," said my father.

Jeff nodded. "I see," he said, and then lowered his head to his plate and began to eat. I remember him eating strangely, like a huge rabbit. He picked up a sprig of parsley that garnished his plate and popped it into his mouth. He nibbled it with his front teeth. His nose twitched. The tiny parsley leaves protruded from his lips as he nibbled the stalk. Then suddenly they were gone. Finally, Jeff looked up, smiling, and began to speak again about the advantages of my signing with the Braves. He reassured my parents, particularly my mother, that the entire organization, from the lowest minor league manager to the vice-president, took a fond interest in all its players.

"You know, it comes from above," said Jeff, pointing to the ceiling of the restaurant. My parents and I looked up, as if expecting to see God. Jeff then added as an afterthought, "Why, Mr. Perini wouldn't have it any other way. He treats his players as if they were his own boys."

"Mr. Perini?" said my mother.

"Yes, Mrs. Jordan. Louis Perini, the owner of the Milwaukee Braves, you know."

After dinner, which Jeff paid for out of a black change purse that my father later referred to as "a pinch poke," we had to stand by the table for a few minutes while Jeff recorded the price of the dinner and a 10 percent tip in his black book. While he wrote I couldn't help but notice a large diamond ring on his pinkie. The incongruity of such ostentation startled me. To this day, whenever I think of Jeff I first think of that ring, and I wonder if it was not the one true glimpse we got of him.

Beyond the mere details of that dinner, I have retained an overwhelming impression from it: an awareness, for the first time, that I could be superfluous to a discussion of myself. My parents and Jeff spent the evening talking about me, around and over me, but never to me, the way adults do when they are considering your best interests, which are of such importance as to preclude your being consulted. I'd know this feeling many times over the next months, until it became quite pleasurable. Whenever my parents or brother were discussing my future with a scout or a farm director, I'd look around the office or stadium or wherever we were and daydream. My mind would take effortless flights to a world of no-hitters and World Series triumphs. During such trips I would feel disembodied, secure in the knowledge I had been relieved of the burdens of my future. It was with a certain disquietude that I found myself recalled from such trips by a voice intruding, "Isn't that so, Pat?"

In 1958, however, I was not the only high school pitcher in New England to receive such attention from major league scouts. The scouts who appeared at my games also appeared at those of John Papa, a pitcher from nearby Stratford. In fact, the scouts were about equally divided as to which of us was the better prospect. John, a senior and a year older, threw harder than I did. But he suffered from bouts of wildness and sorely lacked those pitching graces my brother had cultivated in me. What John achieved by brute force, in a flurry of arms and legs, I achieved using force as well as finesse, in a smooth and effortless delivery. Whether John would ever attain a measure

29

of my polish or I his speed, was the question that divided the scouts.*

Memorial Day, 1958. John and I faced each other in a high school game to decide the District Championship. That game drew 16 scouts (one from each team then in the major leagues) and 4000 fans. It was perhaps the largest crowd ever to watch a high school baseball game. The fans and scouts had come not to see the District Championship resolved, but to determine in their own minds the relative abilities of John Papa and myself. Since John was a senior and would be free to sign a professional contract within a few days, this game meant a great deal more to him than to me. All season long he had pitched under the shadow of his impending bonus. Every well-pitched game meant thousands of dollars added to that bonus, while every poorly pitched one was money lost. I did not feel such pressures since I would not be able to sign a contract until graduation the following spring. Baseball was still a sport for me, and, although this game was important, it was just one of many I had pitched since I was eight years old. I felt little

• • •

*Our respective lack of polish and speed was not what eventually prevented us from becoming the major league pitchers our potential had indicated, although John Papa did pitch a total of two innings for the Baltimore Orioles. He allowed five hits and four bases on balls, and struck out three batters. His earned run average was 22.50. What those statistics don't reveal, however, is the manner in which John's brief career was terminated. He was pitching for the Orioles with two runners on base and two outs. Ted Kluszewski, a former home-run slugger for the Cincinnati Reds and now finishing out his career with the Los Angeles Angels, was at bat. John's manager, Hank Bauer, walked out to the mound and told his nervous rookie that Kluszewski's reflexes were gone and he would never be able to hit a good Papa fastball. "But whatever you do," said Bauer as he left the mound, "don't throw him a change-of-speed." John nodded and promptly threw two fastballs past the slow-swinging Kluszewski. Then, for reasons known only to himself (possibly to exhibit the finesse he had been reminded so often that he lacked), John tossed Kluszewski a change-up, which he propelled into the upper deck of the right field bleachers. The following morning John Papa was riding a Pullman car from Baltimore to Rochester, New York, of the International League, from where he would never return to the major leagues.

30

anxiety. If anything, the vast crowd and the scouts and the District Championship that hung in the balance exhilarated me.

With John it was different. During batting practice I sat in the dugout and watched curiously as he played an exhausting game of pepper. He started warming up down the left field foul line a full 30 minutes early, whereas I did not begin my warm-ups until 12 minutes before game time, as was my custom. When his team took the field, John leaped up the dugout steps so hastily that he tripped and fell onto the playing field. As the dust rose about him my teammates laughed at him. I can still see John Papa sprawled in the dust, looking so ridiculous that I, too, laugh at him, begin to laugh, fall silent, suddenly see myself in John, feel for the first time a flutter in my stomach.

Although I beat John 2–1 in extra innings, the outcome of the game was irrelevant since we both pitched superbly. Only style distinguished our performances. "Jordan *looks* like a pitcher," said one scout. However, nothing much was resolved in the minds of the fans or scouts except that each of us, in our own distinctive way, was an outstanding prospect. Thus no one was surprised a week later when John Papa signed a $35,000 bonus contract with the Baltimore Orioles. In the newspaper accounts of John's signing, more than one scout ventured the opinion that by my senior year I would be a better prospect. If so, wondered Whitey Pjurek, how much of a bonus would I demand?

My brother and I spent the winter of my senior year thinking of little else but the size of my impending bonus, which until Papa's signing had been only a pipe dream. The scouts contributed to our common obsession by hinting daily that if I continued to improve I might be worth as much as $100,000. Whenever I called George at his law office that winter, he was always conferring with an accountant, or else computing by himself various tax setups for bonuses ranging from $50,000 to $100,000. For my part, I passed the school year talking off-handedly to my classmates about bonuses of $100,000. Yet, despite our obsession, neither my brother nor I craved money. Our father's legacy had taken root. Our family, neither rich nor poor, needed no vast sums of money to pay off heavy debts. There were no *things* any of us desired. Then why did we continue to concern ourselves with the size of my bonus to the exclusion of practically everything else?

I think partly we were infected by the ease with which the scouts tossed about these figures. It was like a game. Once begun, we found the tossing effortless, too. Yet, like a game, there was also an unreality about it. Figures such as $100,000 were beyond our comprehension. They were merely abstractions. A $20 bill in one's pocket had weight. But a $100,000 bonus was like a Frisbee that we could frivolously toss into the wind. Its lightness, however, did not alter the fact that my brother and I desperately wanted that $100,000 bonus. After years of hard work we saw it as the ultimate testimony to his coaching and my talent. At the time (1959), $100,000 was the largest bonus ever paid a young pitcher. If I received that figure it would be proof, in our minds, that I was the greatest young pitcher in the country. It was a shallow reason, I see now. But not the only one. Over the years I have pieced together another that clarifies my brother's obsession with the size of my bonus, and his almost fanatic dedication to my career. Unlike myself, he is the son of our mother's first husband. Yet I can only think of him as my brother. Whenever someone, in passing, refers to him as my step-brother or half-brother, I am momentarily jarred. This is a credit to our father, who raised us both with such natural affection that I never questioned our having different last names until well into my teens. My brother, however, must always have been aware of his special relationship. He

32

reveres our father for having raised him as one would a natural son. In his mind, this will remain a kindness that deserves his deepest gratitude and love. For instance, our house was mortgaged in the late 1940s to send my brother to Georgetown University, then mortgaged more heavily in the early 1950s to send him to Georgetown Law School. Such sacrifices must have weighed heavily on my brother. In one of his letters from Law School he wrote: "Don't ever worry, Dad, I have great plans for Patty's future." I was eight years old at the time, and when I was 18 my bonus would be the culmination of George's plans. The money would give me security and our parents peace of mind, since further mortgages to pay for my education were out of the question. But more important, it would give my brother peace of mind. It would represent a small portion of his gratitude to our father, and therefore its size was extremely important to him. It would be directly proportionate to the depth of his gratitude.

Did I know any of this at 18? I'm not sure. I sensed that my bonus had a significance for George that was beyond logic or my understanding. What it was I had no idea. But the mere fact of it being so important to him was enough for me. It must be important, and I would do anything he wished in order to bring it about. When, in the early spring of my senior year, he suggested that money, not affection for a scout or a team, be our only consideration, I agreed. To ensure the largest bonus possible, he said, he had devised a plan.

By that time George had taught me everything he knew about pitching from his limited experience. There was nothing more we could do to improve on my talent. We could certainly not push it beyond its natural limits. However, to impress the scouts, we could camouflage those limits. If I could not throw a baseball any faster, I could at least give the appearance of doing so. Before a game, instead of warming up far down the left or right field foul line, as I used to, I would throw from beside home plate toward the screen, against which my catcher crouched, and behind which sat the scouts. Only a few feet away, the scouts were afforded an umpire's eye-view of my pitches, which seemed to be coming directly at them until the last-second intercession of my catcher's glove. I warmed up slowly. After 10 minutes I would be throwing with great effort but at only half-speed. The scouts would be lulled into believing they were seeing my best fastball, when suddenly I would cut loose with a pitch so much faster than my previous ones as to stun them. The disparity between the speed of the two pitches lent my true fastball an illusion of speed greater than it possessed. To sharpen this illusion, I'd occasionally fire a fastball beyond my catcher's reach. Instinctively, the scouts would throw up their arms in self-defense just as the ball hit the screen and fell harmlessly to the grass. I'm sure the illusory threat of that errant fastball etched on their minds an additional image of speed I did not actually possess.

Once on the pitcher's mound I concentrated not on winning the ball game but on accumulating the greatest number of strikeouts. Scouts were more impressed with a pitcher's ability to strike out batters than they were by his ability to win games or pitch no-hitters. The latter were contingent on too many factors beyond a pitcher's control (teammates, parks, umpires, luck, etc.) while the former was dependent only on his natural skill. Each batter became only a potential strikeout victim. I worked them accordingly. I'd learned that the most impressive strikeout results from a high fastball through which the batter swings and misses. The image of a batter swinging fiercely at a ball tucked safely in a catcher's glove leaves in the minds of fans and scouts alike a sense of the pitcher's overwhelming power.

I spent my senior year throwing nothing but high fastballs.

34

The difficulty with such a pitch, however, comes when a batter doesn't swing at it (it's a ball), and when he does swing and connects (it travels a long way). In one game I found myself pitching with the bases loaded (due to three walks) and the opposing team's eighth batter at the plate. He was a burly, free-swinging hitter who seldom made contact with the ball. When he did, however, he had the power to put it into orbit. With two strikes on him, I knew instinctively that I could strike him out with a curveball, but to impress the scouts I threw a high fastball. He swung, and a few seconds later the ball returned to earth on the tennis courts 400 feet down the left field line. People who were at that game, and their number seems to grow every year, still ask me about "Carson's home run." I smile and say, sure I remember it. I should. It cost me about $40,000.

My obsession with strikeouts became comical after awhile. I even rooted for my teammates to make errors behind me so I would get another opportunity for a strikeout. I remember one game in which a batter, with two strikes on him, lofted a fly ball in foul territory along the firstbase line. My catcher threw off his mask and circled under it. The first baseman raced in and he, too, began circling under the ball. I came off the mound shouting, "I've got it! I've got it! I've got it!" Both teammates backed off, and I let the ball drop at my feet. They looked at me in disbelief. I smiled. What did they know, anyway? It was only a game to them. For me, it was business. Now I had a second chance for a strikeout.

In another game I was hit in the chest with a line drive off the bat of the first hitter. I staggered to the ball, picked it up, threw him out and collapsed. When I regained consciousness in the dugout my first thought was of all those strikeouts still to be got. I told the coach I was fine. I can still pitch, I said. It wasn't until I was led out to the pitcher's mound that I realized I couldn't see. Everything was a blur to me. "I can't see! I can't see!" I began screaming. My coach grabbed me and said, "Don't worry, Pat. I'll bring in someone else." I was suddenly calmed. "That's all right, Coach," I said. "I can pitch. Just point me toward home plate."

My sight returned after two warm-up pitches, both of which landed against the homeplate screen 20 feet above ground. The opposing team was so terrified that, once up at the plate, they began to dive for safety the moment I went into my delivery. I easily recorded 14 strikeouts in that game and learned a valuable lesson as well. From then on, whenever a fresh batter stepped into the batter's box to start an inning, I fired my last warm-up pitch 10 feet over his head.

The result of all this should be obvious. In trying to create the illusion that my talent was greater than it was, it ceased to be as good as it was. I won five games and lost three my senior year. A few of those games were disasters. I averaged one less strikeout per game than I had in my junior year, and four more bases on balls. I expended so much energy worrying about the size of my bonus and trying to impress the scouts with my deceptions that I had little energy left for pitching. What had always been simply an end in itself had become a means to greater ends. In my obsession with those ends, I had lost the finesse and smoothness that distinguished me from a thousand other 17-year-old pitchers a year before. The scouts, far from being impressed, were now disenchanted with my potential. When I graduated from high school in May 1959, finally free to sign a bonus contract, the first few offers I received were for less than $40,000. My brother and I were crushed. How disdainfully we looked on those first offers. Frank McGowan, sitting in an easy chair in our living room, suggests $35,000, then sits back and smiles. George stands up and stalks out of the room as if personally insulted. McGowan's smile disappears and he looks from my mother to my father to me. "What'd I say?" he fairly shouts. "What'd I say?"

At the time George was being insulted by offers of $35,000, he was supplementing his lawyer's income at night by washing and waxing the gymnasium floor of a local Boys' Club for the sum of $25. Having a wife and five children, I know what $35,000 would mean to me today. Yet, at 18, I saw it, as did George, as an insult. After his initial dismay had worn off, however, my brother was determined to get me at least a $50,000 bonus. He arranged a series of special workouts at the major league stadiums of the three teams still most interested in me—the New York Yankees, Chicago White Sox and Milwaukee Braves. I would throw at each stadium under the scrutiny of that team's pitching coach, farm director, general manager and head scout, all of whom would be sufficiently impressed, we hoped, to offer me a $50,000 bonus. My first workout would be at Yankee Stadium.

While Ray Garland led my brother on a tour of Yankee Stadium, in which everything, even the walls of the Stadium Club, seemed to be done in white with navy pinstripes, I was led to the Yankees' dressing room where I was given the uniform I would wear for my workout. The dressing room was unlike any I had ever seen. It was brightly lighted, spacious and spotless. The walls were white enamel and the floor was covered with a thick carpet. The players' lockers lined the walls. Each was an open-faced stall filled with polished black spikes, fresh-smelling new gloves and smartly pressed pinstriped uniforms. Yogi Berra, squat and homely, was sitting in his underwear on the tiny stool in front of his stall. He was hunched over reading his mail. Elston Howard, with a long pockmarked face the color of light coffee, was sitting in front of his stall talking softly with muscular Moose Skowron. Other players, in various stages of undress, moved about the room or sat by their stalls methodically putting on their uniforms. In the center of the room was a large picnic table with benches on either side. Two fully-uniformed players sat across from one another, heads down, intently autographing the 18 new baseballs in the box between them. They signed each ball with a flourish, dropped it back into the box with a "plunk," and then plucked out another as if a piece of fancy fruit. After a while one of the players got up and left and another slid into his place and began autographing the same balls. Each player had a specific spot on the balls where his signature must go. And the size of his signature usually was proportionate to his fame—the largest flourishes belonging to Mickey Mantle and Yogi Berra and the smaller ones to Bob Grim and Johnny Kucks.

To the left of the dressing room was a small, dark lounge with a leather reclining chair, a sofa, a coffee table and a television set. Whitey Ford, in full uniform, was stretched out in the chair smoking a cigarette and reading the *Wall Street Journal.*

To the right of the dressing room was the trainer's room. Even more spotless and brightly lighted than the dressing room, it fairly gleamed with stainless steel instruments and yards of white gauze and tape. Mickey Mantle was straddling the aluminum whirlpool machine. His left leg was outside the machine's small tub, while his right leg was plunged into the hot, churning waters that had turned his flesh a glowing pink. He used his left leg to balance himself on the floor, making a few awkward little hops every few seconds to retain that balance. He was amazingly short, I noticed, and tightly muscled. His shoulders and chest, and the thigh and calf of his left leg, were wrapped in bandages. He was grinning as I passed. It was

38

a wide, blank grin that lent his puffy face an air of boyish dissipation.

I found an empty stall and began to undress among men who had been my idols since youth and whom I'd known only as names in newsprint and blurred images on a television screen. They did not look so imposing as I had imagined. I was bigger than most of them. As I undressed and put on my pinstriped uniform, I began to feel increasingly at ease. The uniform fit perfectly. I laced my spikes and stood up. I was indistinguishable from the players around me. I could have been any rookie just recalled from Denver or Richmond. I was truly at ease now and unbelievably confident, just as I had been on my last visit to Yankee Stadium as a 12-year-old on Mel Allen's television show. I was positive it was my destiny to be a teammate of these famous men.

I left the dressing room and began walking through the darkened runway that led underneath the concrete stands. Above me, I heard a faint rumbling. The runway became darker and darker as the stands above me graded lower and lower, and then suddenly I stepped through a doorway into the Yankee dugout and was momentarily blinded by the flash of sunlight and cloudless sky and immense expanse of field spread out before me. It took me a minute to catch my breath and for my eyes to adjust to the sudden brightness. Then, I traced the towering, triple-decked stands that surrounded the playing surface everywhere except in centerfield. As the stands rose they curved away from, then out over the field, casting a huge shadow, like the wings of a prehistoric bird, across the dark grass. The centerfield stands were open to the sun and seemed miles away. Behind them on an elevated track a train passed slowly. Only much later would I notice that the paint on those towering stands was faded and peeling, and that the grass which had looked so green was actually rather yellowish and did not cleanly outline the base paths as it should have. Yankee Stadium, as I remember it from that day, was not the most beautiful stadium I would visit. But it was the most majestic, and the memory of that day still chills me.

The playing field was deserted when I stepped onto the grass. The stands were empty also, except for the seats behind each dugout. It was hours before game time. I moved to a pitching rubber alongside home plate and was immediately tossed a baseball by a catcher in a Yankee uniform. I learned later he was Johnny Blanchard, an occasional substitute for Yogi Berra. Blanchard trotted back to the homeplate screen, crouched in front of it and gave me a target. I began to throw. As I did, I saw my brother, Ray Garland, the Yankee pitching coach Jim Turner and two men in business suits, whom I did not know, take seats directly behind the screen where Blanchard crouched.

As I threw, the Yankee and Kansas City players began to emerge from their dugouts like stragglers from a routed army. They started leisurely games of catch and pepper along the firstbase and thirdbase lines. They joked back and forth across home plate while I threw, unnoticed, between them. I was too scared to look either left or right, so I just continued to throw harder and harder until finally I cut loose with my first full-speed fastball. The sound of the ball hitting Blanchard's glove echoed around the stadium. The moment the ball left my hand I knew it was traveling faster than any ball I had ever thrown. I threw another fastball, and another, and another, each one a small explosion of its own. Those tiny explosions so exhilarated me that I failed to notice the Yankee and Kansas City players had stopped their banter. Nor did I notice when they also stopped their games of catch and pepper to just stand quietly and watch me throw. I was not aware of anything, really, except that the ball in my hand was as weightless as styrofoam and my motion had slipped into a groove so natural and smooth and mechanically perfect that it required no effort.

Even as I threw I saw it all—my arm passing above my head at precisely the same angle on each pitch. It was as if I, too, were standing outside myself, watching me throw. I imposed nothing on my talent. It had a will of its own, and all I could do was watch in amazement. This moment, then, was what it was all about. My talent, afterall, was simply a diversion. It existed as an end in itself, with no purpose beyond being perfected and enjoyed. Money, victories, strikeouts, batters even, were meaningless. The men evaluating it from behind the screen and the players paying homage to it beside me were also meaningless. Nothing mattered but the simple act of throwing. And since it was only a diversion, once completed it, too, lost all meaning.

I would have gone on like that forever if Blanchard had not stood up and turned to say a few words to the men behind the screen. As he did, he slipped a sponge into his glove. I was suddenly aware of being watched and was momentarily flustered by such attention. The players went back to their games of pepper and I was alone again. I did not wonder what Blanchard was saying about me, but only wished he'd return to his crouch so I could begin throwing again. I feared the moment had been lost.

After showering and dressing, I met my brother and Ray Garland in the office of Johnny Johnston, the Yankees' Farm Director and one of the men who had been watching me throw. The walls of his office were hung with huge blackboards that contained the names, birthdates, records and present teams of every player in the Yankee farm system. When a player was moved from one team to another, his name was moved accordingly. Ray sat on the sofa along the wall and motioned my brother and me to two chairs in front of Johnston's desk. Johnston, a pudgy, bland-looking man with thinning blond hair, sat across from us, his white face expressionless. Unlike the scouts, and like most front-office personnel, Johnston possessed no extensive baseball-playing experience. Nor did he possess any of their warmth, manufactured though it might be. He was a businessman. He leaned forward and clasped his hands. "Impressive," he said in a voice that did not sound impressed. "Very impressive. But you can't tell much from just watching him throw. . . . Still, we liked what we saw. We'll give him three tens. Thirty thousand spread over three years. That's the largest bonus we've offered anyone since Frank Leja."

"I'm sure," my brother said. "But the kid won't sign for a penny less than forty. We know we can get that from any club."

"Maybe," said Johnston. "But the Yankeees are not 'any club.' "

Ray Garland stood up. "He's right, ya know. Jeesus Christ, this *is* the Yankees! Most kids would sign with us for nuthin', much less thirty grand." Johnston nodded and motioned for Ray to sit down.

"It's got to be at least forty," said my brother. "And at that we're willing to take less than we could get from other clubs."

Johnston was silent for a moment and then said, "Three twelves. Thirty-six thousand dollars, and that's our final offer. If you leave here without signing, it'll go down to thirty again."

Ray jumped out of his seat. "Jeesus Christ, he's not kiddin'! That's the way he works. That's more money than even I thought he'd offer!" He turned suddenly toward me and said, "What do you think, Pat? Don't you want to be a Yankee?"

"What?" I said.

"Don't you want to be a Yankee?" Ray asked. Everyone was

staring at me. My brother and Johnston had surprised looks on their faces. Johnston said, "Well?"

"I don't know," I said. "I want to play for the Yankees, but . . ." I looked to my brother, who made an almost imperceptible shake of his head. ". . . It's up to my brother." He winked. (Years later when I would remind George about that day in Johnston's office, he'd say to me, "You know, I really wanted to take their final offer. But I knew it wasn't what you wanted." I said, "But it was! It was what I wanted!" He shook his head. "No, it wasn't," he said. "It would have hurt your pride to take less than we'd planned on.")

My brother turned to Johnston and said, "I don't see why the kid's worth thirty-six but not forty right now. I tell you what, we'll compromise. Throw in four years of college tuition and we'll sign." (At the time four years of tuition would have amounted to about $2800.)

Ray Garland smiled and looked to Johnston. Johnston shook his head no. My brother stood up to leave. I stood up. Ray jumped up and ran to the door. He spread his arms across it and said in an ominous voice, "I won't let you leave this room until Pat becomes a Yankee!" The gesture was a grand one, and my brother and I laughed over it on the way back to Connecticut. This was further proof, he said, that the entire proceedings had been carefully orchestrated by Johnston and Ray Garland, and that it was now only a matter of time before they acceded to our wishes.

A week later, we returned to Yankee Stadium only this time it was for a special workout for Hank Greenberg, the former homerun slugger of the Detroit Tigers and, at that time, a vice-president of the Chicago White Sox. Ron Northey, the White Sox scout in our area, had wanted me to work out in Chicago, but George had convinced him it would be more convenient for all of us to wait until the White Sox came to

New York. He also figured that if Ray Garland and Johnny Johnston saw me throwing for Greenberg, it would persuade them to produce the additional money we wanted. We had not heard a word from them since that day in Johnston's office. My brother had also formulated a theory that virtually assured me of at least a $50,000 bonus. If the notoriously tight-fisted Yankees offered me $36,000, he said, then freer-spending teams like the Braves or White Sox would almost surely offer more. What neither of us knew at the time, however, was that 1959 was the first year the Yankees began to offer large bonuses. They had lost too many fine prospects to teams like the Braves and White Sox over the past years, prospects who were no longer swayed by Yankee pinstripes. On that day I dressed in Chicago's gray traveling uniform, however, I was still very much impressed by those pinstripes. I had no desire to sign with any team other than the Yankees, and secretly I hoped that Hank Greenberg would not offer the $50,000 my brother now demanded.

The visiting team's dressing room in Yankee Stadium was much smaller and drabber than the home team's. It looked as I'd originally expected a major league locker room to look. Even the White Sox players appeared less impressive than had the Yankees. Many of their names were unfamiliar to me—Barry Latman, Norm Cash, Ray Moore, Earl Battey. Only Early Wynn, barrel-chested and scowling, was recognizable. The rest suffered in comparison to Mantle, Ford and Berra. So did the atmosphere of their locker room. It was raucous and profane, with none of that self-contained and muted efficiency so evident in the Yankees' dressing room. At one point as I dressed, Norm Cash, wearing a towel around his waist, began to prance about the room and yell in a shrill voice, "Call for Mr. Levy! Call for Mr. Levy! Call for Mr. Levy!" He stopped only when Barry Latman, the team's Jewish pitcher, lunged at him. The

44

two men grappled and fell to the floor. It took five of their teammates to separate them. I prayed that Hank Greenberg would not offer me $50,000.

I wanted to throw beside home plate as I had a week before, but Northey said it would be better for me to throw in the left field bullpen. "More privacy," he said. He smiled. "Ray Garland won't get a free peek at you out there." I threw well that day, and would have thrown even better if Greenberg had not stood behind my catcher and unnerved me. When I was sufficiently warmed up, he leaned over my catcher's shoulder like an umpire and said, "Let me see if you got a fastball." He was a huge man with a long, horsey face and bulbous nose. As I began my delivery I was tempted to use his nose as a target. After the pitch he straightened up. "Not bad," he said. "Fair enough for a kid." He spoke with a Bronx accent in a whiney voice that seemed ludicrous coming from such a big man. He continued to call for various pitches and to comment on them throughout the workout. He would have unnerved me even more if I had not caught sight of Ray Garland peeking over the wall that separated the bullpen's occupants from the fans. Ray's furtive looks made me smile, and I relaxed considerably. I began to throw almost as well as I had the week before, and nothing Hank Greenberg said or did could stop me.

Later, I met my brother, Northey and Greenberg in box seats along the thirdbase line. Greenberg was telling George what a great city Chicago was and what a great bunch of guys the White Sox players were. Cash and Latman, too, I was tempted to ask? Finally, he offered us $36,000. I was relieved. I didn't like him much. Maybe it was just his voice that did not seem to fit a man who once hit 58 home runs in a single season. I was disappointed in the same way all those silent film fans must have been the first time they heard John Gilbert in a talkie. Maybe, too, it was the way he had upset me while I was throwing. I suspected it had been deliberate on his part. Or perhaps it was simply my fault. Maybe I expected too much from a man who was no better and no worse than a lot of other men who never hit 58 home runs in one season.

After hearing Greenberg's bid we began to wonder if higher offers would come from other teams. So far we had received but three—$35,000 from the Orioles, $36,000 from the Yankees and $36,000 from the White Sox. Nothing indicated the Milwaukee Braves would offer more. George asked me if I was willing to sign with the Yankees for $36,000 and cancel our flight to Milwaukee. I said yes. That afternoon he called Ray Garland and told him we were ready to sign. We met Ray at the stadium and went directly to Johnston's office. Johnston was in conference, according to his secretary, so we took seats and waited. Ray was unusually quiet. It was almost an hour before Johnston came out of his office. He had his arm around the shoulders of a husky blond youth about my age, and he was congratulating the boys' parents. "You won't be sorry," he said and shook their hands. After they left, Johnston motioned us into his office.

"You win," my brother said with a smile. "The kid wants to sign for thirty-six."

"That's out of the question," said Johnston. "Did you see that boy who just left? His name is Hub King. We just gave him your $36,000. I'm afraid the best we can offer now is $24,000."

"What the hell do you mean?" shouted my brother. "The kid was worth $36,000 a week ago! What makes him worth less than that now? He hasn't gotten worse overnight, has he?"

Johnston didn't say anything for a few minutes. Ray was looking down at the floor. Finally Johnston said, "Well, $24,000, take it or leave it."

We left. On the way to our car Ray said, "I'm sorry about

this. There's nothing I can do." Then he shook my hand and wished me luck. It was then, finally, that my brother and I realized that of all the scouts we had known, Ray Garland was probably the most sincere. If only he hadn't been so slick-looking and hadn't talked out of the side of his mouth.

By the time George and I flew out to Wisconsin in late June 1959, we were both secretly convinced that I should sign with the Milwaukee Braves no matter what their offer. This would be my last such workout, I vowed to myself. The excitement I had felt upon dressing in a major league uniform and then throwing among major leaguers had palled. Nor was George any longer titilated by the large sums of money over which he bargained. At first he had enjoyed the entire process of matching his wits with men like Johnny Johnston. It had appealed to his legalistic and somewhat Machiavellian mind. He has always taken great pride in his ability to dissuade or persuade and ultimately achieve a desired result. It is not the result that appeals to him, though, but rather the process of manipulation. It may sound callous to say such a thing about a brother, but it isn't. For, unlike myself, George is always redeemed by his intentions. Our experience with the Yankees, however, had soured him on such manipulating, and possibly had shaken his confidence as well. He must have realized that somewhere along the way we had outwitted ourselves in our quest for the largest bonus, and that our only redemption lay in my signing a contract as quickly as possible and rising swiftly to the major leagues.

Milwaukee was a new-looking, freshly scrubbed city that reminded me more of a small town that had just kept branching out than it did any city I'd ever seen in the East. The esplanades dividing the downtown traffic were lined with neatly pruned trees and shrubs. County Stadium, home of the

Braves, was located on the city outskirts and seemed only recently to have been scooped from the reddish Wisconsin clay. The parking lot, as yet unpaved, was surrounded by dirt cliffs rising about 100 feet to plateaus that were thick with trees. Inside, the stadium was all shining aluminum and fresh orange and green paint. The stands rose away from the playing field and then terminated. They did not curve back over the field, nor were they roofed, and so they cast no shadows over the rich dirt and thick grass. There were small temporary stands in left and right field, and nothing in center field except a few trees. The entire stadium was open to the sun and elements and reminded me more of a high school diamond than a major league park. It seemed a natural setting for baseball and was in marked contrast to Yankee Stadium, a stately dowager of tattered dignity while County Stadium will always be the fresh-faced and inviting ingénue.

I threw well that afternoon, and while I showered and dressed in a deserted Milwaukee dressing room (the team would return from a road trip the next day) my brother bargained with Jeff Jones, Braves' farm director John Mullins and team vice-president Birdie Tebbetts. George did not reveal their offer to me until we had returned to our hotel. Then he told me that the Braves had offered us $35,000. However, if I stayed in Milwaukee and worked out with their pitching coach, Whitlow Wyatt, for a week, and Wyatt was impressed with me they would increase their offer. Unlike the Yankees, however, the Braves promised that nothing I showed or did not show during that week would cause them to lower their offer.

"The only difficulty," he said, "is that I have to be back home tomorrow to be in court the next day. If you decide to stay you'll be on your own."

I said I would stay. He agreed it would be best. And at the end of the week I would sign no matter what. The next morning I saw him off at the airport. I was alone! For as long as I could remember George had been there beside me, shaping my talent and my life, and now he was gone. So suddenly! Just like that. It was both a desolate and exciting feeling. At times over the next few years, when things went sour, I would call him and, holding back the tears, would ask what was going wrong with my career, what *had* gone wrong with it. I'd be standing in a telephone booth across the highway from an all-night diner where our team bus had stopped on its way back from Keokuk or Aberdeen or Leesburg. I never used the telephone in the diner because my teammates might overhear our conversation about my most recent performance. The connections were always poor in those roadside booths, and the noise of passing diesel trucks so loud that I would have to shout into the receiver—*"What should I do?"* But he could never answer me. For by then we had been separated by too much distance and too many places, and above all time. It must have been frustrating for him on the other end of the line; all that noise, my strident shouting, pleas almost, and he not knowing what was wrong or what to say. It was a new experience for him to be so helpless, to be so unable to influence the result of my career as he had always done, to know it was slipping away and yet not to know why. "If I could only have been there," he has said to me so many times over the years. "I know I could have straightened things out."

I worked out at County Stadium each day for a week. I would throw under the tutelage of Whitlow Wyatt in the right field bullpen, then run wind sprints before showering and dressing. Later I'd watch the evening's game from a box seat beside the Braves' firstbase dugout. Although the Milwaukee players were not my idols as the Yankees had been, they were every bit as famous in their own right. At the time they had won the National League pennant two years running and had defeated the Yankees in the 1957 World Series. They were easily recognizable to me as they emerged from their dugout to start each game. There was Eddie Mathews, with startling good looks and thick black brows and arms like hams that stuck out from his body; Red Schoendist, incredibly old and wrinkled looking, with washed out hair the color of his faded freckles; Joe Adcock, barrel-chested, block-jawed, as silent and immobile as a log; Hank Aaron, with his slender waist and hips and skin the flat black tone of latex paint; Frank Torre, as dark and sinister-looking as a Mexican villain from a Grade B movie; Carlton Willey, long-jawed, timid in appearance, with sunken cheeks and sad gray eyes that mirrored his luckless career; and finally, of course, Warren Spahn and Lew Burdette. Of all the players on the 1959 Milwaukee team, I was most drawn to these two famous pitchers. Spahn, at 37, had won 20 games in a single season nine times and would accomplish this feat four more times before his retirement. Burdette, lesser known at 33, had won 20 games only once, in 1958, but it was he who had won three games for the Braves in the 1957 World Series, and for that moment, at least, overshadowed his more illustrious teammate.

Spahn was a quick-gestured man with leathery skin, a beakish nose and darting eyes, like a bird. He exhibited none of that cool and heroic aloofness I'd expected from the greatest left-handed pitcher in baseball history. He was, if anything, effusive and kidlike, even at 37. He was smaller and squarer than I'd imagined, and he walked like a duck. Burdette, on the other hand, was tall and lanky and long-necked, and he moved in fits, like a turkey fleeing the axe. He had a kind of falling-apart stride in which his arms fluttered out from his body and his shoulders rose and fell about his neck, which clucked forward as he moved. Burdette had reddish hair, freckled skin and unblinking blue eyes that did not seem to absorb images so much as reflect them. Looking into them I'd see only myself. Burdette had an air of ironic—one is tempted to say, maniacal —detachment from things around him, all of which he seemed to view, his head listing toward one shoulder, from a perspective that was perpetually askew. Except for a faint and unalterable grin, he was as silent as Spahn was talkative. His humours were different from ours. He once threw a curveball at a batter's head and yelled, "Duck!" the moment the ball left his hand. His next pitch, a fastball in the same spot, was delivered with a stony silence and a flat grin.

Spahn and Burdette were inseparable that year, and it seemed Spahn's principal purpose to elicit something more from Burdette than that unalterable grin. One day as they ran wind sprints along the right field fence, Spahn spied two pretty girls in the stands. Without breaking stride, he leaped the fence and ran up an aisle after them. Spahn coaxed the girls out of the stands and posed for a photograph with his arm around each one. The photograph was taken by his grinning cohort, Lew Burdette.

Years later I would often hear the story about the day Spahn and Burdette posed for pictures to be used on cards placed inside packages of bubble gum. After they had finished, Spahn supplied the photographer, who was not a baseball fan, with pertinent information concerning the two famous pitchers. Shortly thereafter, when the cards appeared on the market, kids from all over the country let out a howl of protest upon discovering that Lew Burdette was a hook-nosed left-hander and Warren Spahn, a mad-eyed, grinning right-hander.

A few years after I left baseball I picked up a newspaper to read that Warren Spahn and Phil Roof, a rookie catcher, had been arrested in the early morning hours in a Milwaukee bar. Spahn was 41 and his drinking companion was 23. I was 23 at the time. I had a wife and three children. I was working the

51

night shift at a local newspaper while attending college during the day, and on reading that article I felt a certain loss. *I* should have been with Spahn in that bar! I put the newspaper down and saw exactly how it must have been. The next day in the clubhouse, Spahn and Roof laughing over their escapade. Their teammates kidding them about it. Eddie Mathews telling Spahn just how drunk he had been. Spahn laughing, kidlike at 41 as he was at 37, and would always be. He would never age, I thought. His body would age all right, nothing could stop that process. But what was inside it wouldn't. His interests and pleasures and amusements would always be the same, perfectly preserved by the game in which he lived.

Each day that I worked out at County Stadium, I waited until Spahn and Burdette began their wind sprints along the right field fence, and then I began jogging about 20 yards behind them. I jogged behind them daily for a week, and if they noticed, they never let on. I never spoke a word to Lew Burdette, and the only words I spoke to Warren Spahn were on my last day in Milwaukee when I signed my contract. I was called into the office of John Mullins, who handed me a telephone receiver. "Your brother," he said. My brother told me that Wyatt, a gracious old Southerner, had given me a glowing recommendation and that Mullins had increased his original offer of $35,000 to include a monthly salary of $500 and $1500 per year for my college education. "It's the best offer we've had," George said. "I think we should take it." I agreed and was about to hand the receiver back to Mullins when he asked, "You all right?" I said I was fine and then handed the receiver to Mullins. When he hung up he produced four identical contracts. I signed each one. They would all have to be signed by my parents, too, before they were binding since I was still a minor. I was 18 years old.

"Congratulations," said Mullins, and shook my hand. He told me I had been assigned to McCook, Nebraska, of the Class D Nebraska State League. It was a rookie league, he added, and so I would not be playing against experienced minor leaguers. I was to leave for McCook the next morning.

Later that afternoon, a few hours before game time, I dressed in my Braves' uniform and went down to the field where Wyatt and Spahn and a photographer were waiting for me. For the next 10 minutes we struck up various poses for the photographer along the firstbase line. Wyatt and Spahn and I. Spahnie and I, the best of friends. Spahnie, hands on hips, turns to me and says, "What's your name, kid?"

# ...3

I REMEMBER first the land. It was flat. Between it and the sky there was nothing—no buildings, no trees, no hills, no shadows—nothing as far as the eye could see but the sun and the sky and never-ending fields of wheat and corn and alfalfa. It was a land of horizons. Occasionally a thin black road parted the fields. The road went straight for miles. There was nothing on either side of it but the fields. As the road and the fields stretched ahead they grew closer and closer together until they converged at a point on the horizon. It was an illusory point that was never reached. It remained always the same distance ahead. Perpetually approaching it, one felt all movement was illusory, too. Only the fields moved, flashing by like scenery in a cheaply made movie. Finally, the illusion was broken by some scraggy trees growing alongside a water hole a few yards off the road. A cow, standing motionless in the shade of the trees, gazed blankly at the road. Beside her lay another cow, her tail switching off flies. Beyond the water hole was a dirt road that branched off from the paved road and led through the fields to a red barn and conical silo. Farther back from the barn, almost a mile from the paved road, was the farmhouse. It was small and white and cellarless. Each corner of the house rested on cinder blocks. From the paved road a passer-by, were he to look, could see underneath the farmhouse to the thin line of blue horizon visible on the other side.

*      *      *

I had been riding in the taxi for two hours and had seen nothing but an occasional farm and the fields. I had begun to lose all sense of place and direction, of where I'd come from and was going to, had become almost transfixed by the monotony of the land when I saw a sign flash by, *McCook City Limits* and another *Pop. 7687* then, one after another, the welcome-to-McCook signs put up by the Chamber of Commerce and the Masonic Lodge and the Kiwanis and Lions and Elks and Eagles and Rotary clubs. Then nothing for a while until the Calvary Cemetary and the Drive-In Theater, and then a little ways to the A-and-W Root Beer stand and the Phillips 66 Station and, quickly now, the wood-fronted pool hall, the bar, the M-and-E Diner and, turning left onto Main Street, the city of McCook. Inexplicably built on a hill. Main Street rose ahead of us at a 30-degree angle. It was a broad street on which cars were parked diagonally to the curb, still leaving plenty of room for traffic. It was lined on both sides by one- and two-story brick buildings—drugstores and shoe stores and hardware stores—and, moving up the hill, three- and four-story brick buildings—J.C. Penney's and Modrell's Cafe—and, almost at the top where I got off, the tallest building in McCook—the six-story Keystone Hotel. From its entrance I could see down the hill past the stores to the edge of the city about five blocks away. I could see beyond where Main Street stopped, too, out over the city to the surrounding plains. Main Street was a north–south road, and if it had not stopped at the edge of the city but had continued south for about 14 miles, it would have crossed into Kansas. Eighty miles west of Main Street was the Colorado State line. I had come to McCook by way of North Platte, Nebraska, which was 75 miles due north. North Platte was the only city of any consequence within 150 miles of McCook, and it possessed the only commercial airport within 230 miles.

55

A few yards up the hill from the Keystone, I could see the Fox Movie Theater, and a little further north the McCook YMCA. At the top of the hill was a small, tree-shaded park. There was an old band shell in the middle of the park. Beyond the park were houses. The business section of Main Street stopped at the park and the residential section fanned out east and north and west from there for about half a mile in each direction. Included among its white frame houses were a few churches, three grammar schools, a high school, McCook Junior College, St. Catherine's Hospital, the Municipal Swimming Pool, the McCook Fair Grounds where each July the Red Willow County Fair and Rodeo was held, the National Guard Armory that also served as a dressing room for the McCook Braves' baseball team and, about half a mile north of the armory, Cibola Stadium. The city's only lighted baseball park, it was part of the McCook County Fair Grounds. The fair grounds was a flat open field about one-quarter of a mile square located at the northern edge of the city. Beyond it, the plains began. Cibola Stadium was in the southern part of this field closest to the city. It faced north across the fair grounds toward the plains. Its playing surface was separated from the fair grounds only by an unpainted wooden picket fence that curved around the outfield. The field inside that fence was an extension of the field outside. It consisted of rock-hard dirt and scattered clumps of tall dried grasses. Surrounding the playing surface were about a dozen or so telephone poles, on top of which were 20 hooded light bulbs aimed down at the diamond. A 10-foot-high fence of chicken wire separated the field of play from the temporary stands along the firstbase line, behind home plate and along the thirdbase line. All told, the stands seated about 900 people. They were a mere skeleton of permanent stands, consisting of metal supports and 10 inclining rows of long wooden planks. The planks clattered and groaned when

56

stepped or sat on. They were warped and splintered from use and from constant exposure to the elements, the wind and rain and hail and snow, all of which could be seen, at times, forming across the fair grounds on the plains. There was a much smaller section of stands along the left field foul line directly behind a single picnic bench that served as the home team bullpen. Unlike seats in the other stands, which cost 75 cents, the left field seats cost only a quarter. They were reserved for the Mexican and Indian migrant workers who lived in shacks on the outskirts of McCook because they were prohibited from living in the residential section. Behind the left field stands was a small wooden building. This was boarded up during the day, but at night, with a game in progress, it became a refreshment stand on one side and rest rooms on the other. The rest rooms were directly below the highest part of the left field stands and so were always in shadows. The refreshment side was well-lighted and faced an open gravel space that was the stadium's parking lot. This could be entered and exited through only one gate, over which was strung a banner proclaiming Cibola Stadium the home of the McCook Braves of the Nebraska State League.

I have described McCook in detail, not because it was distinctive in any way but because it was distinctive in no way. There was nothing there, really, certainly nothing one couldn't find in hundreds of similar towns throughout the country. Over the next few years I would live in many such towns—Eau Claire, Waycross, Palatka, Bradenton—and for longer periods of time than the two months I spent in McCook. And yet, I remember none of those towns with the clarity of detail I do McCook. Even as I write this, I can see Main Street, the Keystone, the band shell, Cibola. Possibly because McCook was the smallest town in which I would ever play. Since I had no car, I walked everywhere, and within two months I knew every street and store, and even a few people, as one soon does in such a small, isolated town. And it was isolated. No matter where I walked, I came quickly to the town's limits. There was so much openness beyond those limits, so many horizons almost suffocating in their possibilities. The townspeople were confronted daily by this. It had intimidated them. There was too much out there; too many possibilities they would never grasp. And so for them there was nothing out there, nothing beyond the limits of their town, nothing to do, no place to go —except after a two-hour drive across the plains—to another town exactly like the one they'd left.

Living in their town, as I did, I got to know its limits very well. At times I felt, like the townspeople, bound by them. But only at times. Those horizons still had meaning for me, indicated direction. McCook was the first point on the map of my career. It would be a small but important part in my life that would be fulfilled someplace else, at a point further up ahead that would not elude me. I was as positive of this as only a self-absorbed 18-year-old can be. I knew that in years to come McCook would be important as the point where my career began.

Ironically enough, I was right, although for reasons other than I'd anticipated. McCook was a very important part of my life. It still is. In fact, its importance grows in my mind as I write this. It was the first place I lived alone. The life I built there was my own responsibility. I was confronted each day with myriad possibilities—when to eat, what to do, whom to befriend—from which I had to choose. For a brief time I made a pretense of looking to my past for help. I tried to remember what had been expected of me in similar situations. But sometimes the situations I met in McCook were new to me. Nothing from my past applied. So increasingly I turned out of desire and necessity to my own inclinations. What did I think? What

58

did I feel? What did I want? I began to see things—myself and others—through my own eyes. What I saw and what I was is still clear to me today. Much of it is what I am today. The person I was in McCook, however, bore little resemblance to the one I'd been under my watchful and protective family. And yet that new person, whether I liked it or not, was more consistent with my nature than the other had ever been.

It was a warm night, my first in McCook. From my seat on the top row of the stands behind home plate, I saw the McCook Braves run onto the field and the first batter for the North Platte Indians emerge from his dugout. Under Cibola's faint lights, each player was trailed by his shadow. There was a smattering of applause from the fans who filled almost every seat in the park.* It was exciting to know that tomorrow I would be part of this.

As yet, no one knew I was in town. Surrounded by strangers, my anonymity was exciting, too. It allowed me to watch the game with an objectivity that would soon be denied me. Sitting on the plank in front of me was a farmer in bib overalls. He wore a stiff, straw cowboy hat with a tightly curled brim. Through the crown of his hat I could see the curve of the top

• • •

*It was Tuesday evening in early July and almost 800 people had come to watch the McCook Braves in their third game of the season. (The NSL, being a rookie league, operated only in July and August of each year. It consisted of six teams: Holdrege (White Sox), Kearney (Yankees), Hastings (Giants), North Platte (Indians), Grand Island (Athletics), McCook (Braves). It was designed specifically for high school and college graduates who had not signed contracts until their classes had been graduated in June.) The Braves were the major source of entertainment for the townspeople and farmers alike. All of the Braves' weekday games were played at night to allow fans to put in a day's work, eat supper and still get to the ball park. Over the summer the Braves would have an average attendance of 700 people per game, about 10 percent of the town's population. This was comparable to the New York Yankees drawing over 700,000 people to each of their games.

of his head. Beside him sat his wife and two young sons, their hair dampened and flattened by their mother's hand. She, like her husband, was of indeterminate age. She wore her hair in a ponytail, and when she turned to speak to her husband I could see that the skin at the back of her neck was creased and leathery, like his, although whether from the sun and hard work or age was not clear. She wore a white sleeveless blouse and a long cotton skirt fluffed out by crinolines and resting high on her lap. Every so often she would fold her hands over it and press down gently. The stands were filled with such families, and with teenage girls in Bermuda shorts and teenage boys in Levis and football jerseys and prosperous-looking merchants in white shirts and ties and sharp-toed cowboy boots. Throughout the game the fans gossiped and talked business and crops and the teenagers flirted in the shadows behind the stands. Occasionally someone clapped at a fine play on the field or shouted at the umpire to the delight of their friends. People were constantly moving up and down the groaning planks, going to the rest rooms or returning from the refreshment stand with hot dogs and cokes.

From my high seat I could see into the left field corner where four Braves' relief pitchers were slouched on the picnic bench in the bullpen. Two of them had turned their backs to the playing field and were talking to some of the Mexicans in the left field stands. Behind those stands I could see the shadows of people waiting in line to get into the rest rooms. Others, mostly children, milled around the refreshment stand. The parking lot was filled with cars, older Fords and Chevys with fender skirts and lowered rear ends. There were some pickup trucks, too, and on their flat beds were dark bundles of dried alfalfa that gave off a sickly-sweet odor.

By the fifth inning the Braves were losing 8–6. It was a typical Class D minor league game, I would learn, filled with energetic but erratic play. A shortstop charged a ground ball and kicked it past the pitcher's mound, then followed with a diving catch in the hole of a line drive. An outfielder got down on one knee to field a ground-ball single and then turned around and ran wildly toward the outfield fence to retrieve the ball, which had rolled through his legs. On the next play that very same outfielder would catch a line drive over his shoulder after having run so deep into the centerfield corner, 420 feet away, that he had outrun the range of the lights and had momentarily disappeared into the darkness. The fans had to wait until the umpire, who had run into the darkness with him, emerged with his fist in the air before they could applaud the catch. The pitchers on both sides were wild and filled the night with bases on balls and wild pitches, and none of them, I noted with satisfaction, threw as hard as I did. When the Braves tied the game in the sixth inning, the fans cheered lustily.

In the seventh inning I felt a cool breeze and heard the sound of gears changing in the parking lot. I noticed that some of the fans had already left. Others were gathering their children, who had been playing underneath the stands, and were herding them toward the parking lot. Soon the breeze grew colder and more forceful, and with it came the hiss of gas escaping from a stove. The hissing came from the fair grounds and was, I discovered, only the rustling of the tall grasses in the wind. I looked out over the darkened fair grounds and saw on the plains an even darker swirling mass rising like a horn of plenty into the sky. The sky was a translucent purple, and the swirling mass was solid and black against it and seemed to be growing larger as it moved toward us. By the time it hit, the stands were all but descrted. Instantly, it rippled the players' uniforms, whirled dust everywhere. Batters stepped out of the box and turned their backs on it. Infielders flattened their gloves against their faces and peeked through the spread fingers until a split-second before the pitcher delivered the ball. At one point a pitcher reared back to throw and a gust of wind blew him off the mound. Both managers stormed out of their dugouts toward the homeplate umpire, and an argument ensued as to whether or not the pitcher should be charged with a balk. Such incidents must not have been rare in the Nebraska State League, for the umpire rendered his decision promptly and the game resumed in the midst of the wind and dust and it did not even stop when the first rain fell. Big, heavy, widely spaced drops, they hit the deserted planks in front of me with a loud splat. Dark splotches appeared in the wood.

In the ninth inning, with the score still tied, I heard a gunshot, and another, and still others coming quickly now, and it wasn't until I heard the tinkling of broken glass and saw thin ribbons of smoke unraveling from the lightpoles that I realized the bulbs were exploding. The growing number of black spaces in the rows of lights that ringed the field began to resemble missing teeth in a huge, gaping mouth. Each time a bulb broke there was a flash and a loud pop and a ribbon of smoke, and below the players shrugged their shoulders about their ears to avoid being cut by falling glass. By the tenth inning the field had darkened considerably, and in the darkness the Braves managed to push across the winning run and the game was over.

It wasn't until the following afternoon when I saw Cibola in the light of day that I realized how far I'd come from County Stadium in Milwaukee. Its shabbiness disheartened me. It was beneath me, I thought. I arrived at the park at noon after having walked almost a mile from town. The sun was high over the fair grounds and my teammates were in the midst of their afternoon workout. The pitchers were playing catch along the thirdbase line while the other players underwent fielding drills on the diamond.

They wore Milwaukee Braves' uniforms similar to the one I'd worn recently. Six years ago those uniforms had been worn by players on the Milwaukee Braves, five years ago by the Wichita Braves of the Triple-A American Association, four years ago by the Austin Braves of the Double-A Texas League, three years ago by the Jacksonville Braves of the Class A Sally League, and so on down the line until they'd settled, the thinned and yellowed residue of the system, on the backs of the McCook Braves. The uniforms were patched in spots where someone from Austin or Jacksonville or maybe even Milwaukee had broken up a double play or made a diving catch. Many of the tomahawks and numerals had been torn off and not replaced. All that remained to indicate a player's number was a dark shadow on his shirt where the numeral had been. Still, they *were* major league uniforms. Stitched inside the waistband of each pair of pants and on the tail of each shirt was the last name and number of the man who'd first worn them—Spahn 21, Aaron 44, Mathews 41. We always fought for the uniform of the major leaguer we most admired. It didn't matter whether an 18-year-old third baseman was a 40-extra-long and his idol, Eddie Mathews, a 46-stocky. The minor leaguer would tolerate the uniform's ill fit for the sake of whatever talent remained in those dark sweat stains that could never be laundered out. I was the last player to arrive in McCook and I would discover later that someone had mistakenly given Spahnie's uniform to a skinny left-handed pitcher named Dennis Overby. Vernon Bickford's uniform had been saved for me. It was in better condition than the others—almost new—and it fit perfectly.

I stood by the dugout for a while, aware of my teammates' curious glances, and watched my manager, Bill Steinecke, as he stood near home plate and hit ground balls to his fielders. He had been a catcher in the minors for years but had never made it to the major leagues. He had also played professional basket-ball with "The House of David," a touring team supposedly made up of Orthodox Jews but actually comprised of Gentiles, like Steinecke, who wore a false rabbinical beard for games.

Steinecke, who was in his late fifties, stood about five feet, five inches tall and weighed over 200 pounds, most of which had settled in his stomach and strained against his uniform shirt. He had a pink, shining, hairless face with small blue eyes devoid of eyebrows. He resembled Nikita Khrushchev except for the mouth, which, in Steinecke's case, was a lipless slit. His missing lipline had been redrawn with a brown stain, the result of 30 years of tobacco chewing. There were tiny tracks, like bird tracks, down the front of his uniform shirt. They were made by the tobacco juice that dribbled down his chin when-ever he got so excited during a game that he forgot to spit.

Steinecke stood at home plate with a fungo bat in one hand and a baseball in the other. He tossed the baseball into the air in front of him and, grunting fiercely, swung the bat. The ball landed, untouched, at his feet. The infielders, who had hunched forward in anticipation of a double play, relaxed, kicked dirt and resumed their stance. Steinecke's catcher, Joe Shields, picked up the ball and handed it to him. Shields, clean-cut and handsome, had recently been graduated from an Ivy League college and, in the fall, would begin his first year of medical school. For Shields, professional baseball was simply a summer job that would someday enable him to become a doctor. His back-up, who was catching one of the pitchers on the sidelines, was Elrod Hendricks, a black, very limber native of the Virgin Islands. He spoke a rhythmic calypso English that amused Shields, as it did most of the American players. But whereas Shields had received a $20,000 bonus from the Braves, who were ignorant of his future plans, Hendricks had got practically nothing from the Braves, and in fact was released by them within a year. Eventually, he signed with the Baltimore Orioles, for whom he played in two World Series. Shields became a doctor.

Steinecke tossed the ball into the air again, grunted and missed it. The infielders sighed. Steinecke glared at the ball at his feet. "Mother-fucker," he said to it. Shields attempted to pick it up, but Steinecke brushed him aside. Laboriously, the manager got down on one knee and picked up the baseball. He righted himself, using his bat for leverage. He threw the ball into the air again, only this time he swung timidly and the ball trickled toward third base. It stopped before Ron Hunt, a 19-year-old third baseman from St. Louis, Missouri, could reach it. Still, Hunt scooped up the dead ball with the great earnestness that would become his trademark and threw it toward second base. Chuck Carlin snatched it from the air and, in the same motion, flipped it across his chest to first base.

Carlin, a recent graduate of the University of Alabama, was pale and thin and unusually slow-moving off the diamond. He had fine yellow hair and the delicate features one associates with the decadent Southern aristocracy in a Faulkner novel. His wife, too, was pale and thin and slow, and only their four-month-old baby seemed to have flesh and vitality. Carlin came to McCook directly from his college campus, and the first person he saw in the Braves' locker room was Bill Stevens, a black outfielder recently graduated from the University of Connecticut. Carlin handed his spikes to Stevens and told him to polish them. "I didn't know," said Carlin later. "I'd never played with them or against them. The only ones I'd ever seen in a locker room were the clubhouse boys."

Carlin's relay was low and had to be scooped out of the dirt by Frank Saia, the 23-year-old first baseman. Saia, also married and a recent father, was a student at Harvard Law School in Cambridge, Massachusetts. Like Shields, he would play professional baseball this summer only as a means to furthering his education. Saia shook the dirt from his glove, spun toward home plate and threw the ball to Shields, who caught it and immediately threw to second. Carl Derr, a shy 20-year-old shortstop from Pennsylvania, caught the ball on the infield grass in front of second and returned it to Shields. Derr, a $22,000 bonus boy as was Hunt, would prove to be one of the most talented of the McCook Braves. And yet, like many such players, he never reached the major leagues, for reasons not apparent to anyone who'd seen him play.

When Steinecke finished with his infielders he waddled out to a spot between second base and the pitcher's mound and began hitting fly balls to his outfielders. Bill Stevens was in left field. He was a muscular, handsome, light-skinned black from Norwalk, Connecticut. Off the diamond he dressed in button-down shirts and crew-neck sweaters. He had been one of the most popular athletes at the University of Connecticut and had often dated white girls at college, which in the late 1950s was still something one took notice of at a movie theater or restaurant. When Stevens first arrived in McCook he had had difficulty finding a room to rent because of the town's ordinance prohibiting nonwhites from living in the residential section. An exception was made in his case, however, and he moved into an old house with five of his white college-educated teammates. Stevens played professional baseball for only two seasons. He decided to quit one night as he sat in an empty Trailways bus outside a roadside restaurant and waited for a teammate to bring his food.

Stevens' teammate at the University of Connecticut had been Ken Cullum, who, like Stevens, had been signed for a modest bonus by Jeff Jones. Cullum was now standing only a few yards away in center field. He was one of the most vicious

66

left-handed pull hitters I would ever see. Short and mildly stocky, he had piercing blue eyes, a broad, high forehead and wavy hair that he combed straight back. Cullum was an immaculate man who always smelled of cologne and often walked the streets of McCook wearing a paisley sportshirt, open at the throat, and a neatly pressed gabardine suit. His conversation was sparse and sprinkled with non sequiturs and sly grins. He spoke seriously and in comprehensible sentences only when discussing an article he'd read in *Playboy* magazine. He was reputedly a heavy drinker, and this fact had discouraged many major league scouts from offering him a bonus commensurate with his talent. Even Jeff Jones was not sure he'd done the right thing in signing Cullum, and he told me to avoid him when I reached McCook. "He's too mature for you," said Jeff.

Cullum was flanked in right field by two South Carolinians, Barry Morgan and Tim Strickland. Morgan, a $30,000 bonus baby, was only 18, but by virtue of his bonus he had been made the starting rightfielder. He was red-haired, freckle-faced and resembled a young Mickey Mantle. His batting swing was powerful like Mantle's, but as yet undisciplined. Over the years he would never quite discipline it enough to bring him to the majors, although he would have a fairly successful minor league career. Morgan was the youngest married player on the team. He'd married his high school sweetheart a few weeks before leaving for McCook. His wife had remained in South Carolina, however, and he never talked about her except to describe their wedding night.

Strickland, two years older than Morgan, stood almost six feet, four inches tall. He had a long nose stuck in the middle of a tiny head, an incredibly long neck and sloping shoulders. When he charged fly balls his elbows flapped like the wings of a terrified goose. In the midst of McCook's many bonus babies,

Strickland was self-conscious about having signed with the Braves for practically nothing.* He was also self-conscious about his meager education and the fact that the second and third fingers of his right had been fused together, like Siamese twins, since birth. He shook hands with his left hand, in the manner of an Italian film star, until two years later when minor surgery separated the two fingers. Strickland kept to himself in McCook, and the only words I remember him speaking were to an umpire who had called him out on strikes. With eyes bulging, he stuck his homely face against the umpire's mask and said, "You gook, you couldn't call a donkey fight!"

When Steinecke had concluded his outfield drills he dismissed everyone but his 10 pitchers. The other players returned to the armory in cars while the pitchers formed a line behind the mound and took turns fielding bunts. Each pitcher would step up on the mound, pantomime his motion without actually delivering a ball, and then wait in his follow-through until Steinecke bunted a ball down one of the baselines. Whenever Steinecke missed a bunt, the ball landing at his feet, he would kick it down one of the base lines. Occasionally, out of eagerness or maybe a desire to impress, one of the pitchers would charge the plate before Steinecke had bunted the ball. In response, Steinecke would surprise even himself with a vicious line drive at the pitcher's head. Such instances were rare but they seemed to delight the manager. While the offender lay quaking on the ground, Steinecke would cackle (a

• • •

*The McCook Braves were one of the wealthiest minor league teams in history, and certainly the wealthiest Class D team that ever existed. Its players had been given almost $500,000 in bonus money, and many of them were drawing monthly salaries in excess of $1500. True, there were those among us, like Hendricks and Strickland, who had received nothing and were drawing only $300 per month, but they were in the minority.

little madly, I thought) and tobacco juice would dribble down his chin.

Of the 10 pitchers on the mound that day, four were starters (I would be the fifth), and each of them had received a bonus between $30,000 and $40,000. The least impressive and yet the one who would be most successful during the season was Dennis Overby, a frail 18-year-old with a milky complexion and a seriousness beyond his years. Overby, a left-hander, delivered a baseball with such nonchalance it seemed to arrive at the plate simply by the force of his pulse. Because most of the bonus pitchers threw harder than Overby, we would watch in disbelief as he struck out batter after batter, achieving by savvy and pinpoint control what none of us could achieve by firing the ball with all our strength. The secret to Overby's success escaped me that year and I envied him. It was not fair, I thought, as I sat in the corner of the dugout and watched him coast from one victory to another, all of which he treated with a slighting indifference. Of course he was successful, he seemed to say. What else could he be? He never missed mass on Sunday, did he? And because I hungered for those achievements, I threw harder and harder, and still they came infrequently. And when they did come, they were muted in comparison to his. Secretly, I began to root against him. I had discovered, finally, that every victory he achieved, every strikeout, had been snatched irrevocably from my preordained allotment. Those were *my* successes! He was stealing them! It was unjust. I consoled myself with the knowledge that one day justice would prevail, things would right themselves as I'd been taught they always did.

And they did, for both of us. It began the following spring. I had been assigned to the Braves' minor league spring training camp at Waycross, Georgia, while Dennis had been invited to the major league camp at Bradenton, Florida. Each week I would pick up *The Sporting News* to read of his progress. In one intra-squad game he struck out Hank Aaron, Eddie Mathews and Joe Adcock in succession. He was the sensation of that camp, and the sportswriters at camp voted him the Braves' most-likely-successor to Warren Spahn. He was given a watch. Then one day after a heavy rain, he slipped on a muddy mound and tore the muscles in his left shoulder. Doctors who examined him said he would never pitch again. But because the Braves had given him a bonus whose payments were spread out over four years, they refused to let him quit.

If he quit before his contract expired he would lose his bonus money. Each spring Dennis would be assigned to Waycross and immediately put on the disabled list.* While the rest of us worked out with various teams in the system, Dennis remained teamless. His shirt bore no number. Often as I warmed up to start a game I would see him on some empty diamond running wind sprints in the outfield. He ran them in a half-hearted way, sensing, I'm sure, the idiocy of having to keep himself in shape for the game he'd never pitch. But still, it must have helped him pass the time—running from left field to center field and walking back again. Sometimes, too, I would see him throwing a baseball against a screen. Not throwing, actually, but pushing a ball in that funny, straining way a shot-putter does, his head inclining toward his left shoulder as if to hear the pain.

Whenever I passed Dennis that first spring, I saw in his eyes the dazed, unfathoming expression of an accident victim, one

• • •

*All of the Braves' minor league teams from Class AA to Class D trained at Waycross, Georgia. The camp was located on the outskirts of town and consisted of five army-type barracks, a recreation building, a large clubhouse and five baseball diamonds.

who has been struck down senselessly from the blind side. Each year his expression would change a little. It became one of resignation the following spring, an uncomprehending resignation touched with cynicism. But then that look changed, too. Resignation gave way to acceptance, and with it understanding. It was as if Dennis had been forced to acquire a certain knowledge very quickly, a knowledge the rest of us would acquire only much later, if at all. It was a knowledge whose acquisition became increasingly painful as it was prolonged. Seeing him then, I knew things no longer bothered him. He'd been the victim of an accident a while ago, but now he saw it all from a slight distance, standing on the curb with the others, looking at himself—the victim—with curiosity and understanding and even a certain amusement. There had been no blood, just a sudden jolt, more wrenching in its surprise than its injury. The pain had diminished considerably—not because the accident hadn't mattered, hadn't affected his life, because it had. Everything mattered. But with a little distance it didn't matter quite so much anymore. He knew if he could always be a spectator as he was being a victim, then he would not have to wait for time to pass. Even at the moment of impact he would know that the pain would be diminished with time, and so the pain would be diminished then, even as he was feeling it.

In my final season with the Braves, when things were going bad for me (not as bad as they'd gone for Dennis, but bad enough), I began to recognize in a most superficial way that look of his and I realized that what I was beginning to glimpse only as a faint shadow, he'd already seen in detail. One day at Waycross I asked him if he wanted to have a catch. We tossed the ball back and forth in silence for a while. I wanted to say something to indicate I sympathized, but I didn't know what to say. He was distracted, his mind elsewhere as he threw. I

71

thought he seemed indifferent to me, that he still remembered McCook.

Although Dennis Overby was the most successful pitcher at McCook in 1959, it was not by a wide margin. Paul Chenger, a 20-year-old physical education major from West Chester State Teachers' College in West Chester, Pennsylvania, was almost as effective and a great deal more impressive. Chenger possessed a superior fastball and a curveball of such speed and sharpness that Steinecke called it "the unfair one." Chenger was short and built like a weight lifter. He prided himself on the condition of his body and went to extremes to tap its resources. Between innings of a game he was pitching, he sucked honey from a plastic bottle. On the hottest nights he wrapped his arm in towels and wore a heavy windbreaker to ward off imaginary chills. Unlike Overby, who won effortlessly, Chenger's victories were carved from granite. On the mound he sweated and fidgeted and took deep breaths and stretched his arm overhead and twitched his shoulders and, in fact, seemed to feel his performance would be lacking unless he filled every second of it with a physical gesture. Work was his value and he cultivated it. With runners on base, Chenger simply worked harder, sweating more, twisting his arm a bit more strenuously for a sharper curveball. One day, a few years later, he twisted his arm a bit too strenuously and loosened bone chips in his elbow, ending his career.

One of Chenger's mound opponents in college had been Bill Marnie, a 20-year-old left-hander also from Pennsylvania. Marnie had signed a bonus contract with the Braves, too, and was one of McCook's starting pitchers. He was tall and gawky-looking, with a horsey, Lee Marvin face. He would have great success in the minors and within three years was pitching in the Double-A Texas League. However, he felt he should be pitching for Louisville of the Triple-A American Association.

So, to teach the Braves a lesson for not promoting him quickly enough, he enlisted in the Navy for four years—and never pitched again.

Bruce Brubaker, a 17-year-old right-hander from Harrisburg, Pennsylvania, was the youngest starting pitcher at McCook. He had a handsome face dominated by thick brows, and a large body that tended to baby fat. He was such a languid youth in both speech and movement that at times he seemed literally somnambulant. One spring training he was stricken with mononucleosis and continued to function for two weeks before he or anyone else discovered it. He treated his career with the same indolence and seemed to arouse enthusiasm only for such favorite pastimes as hunting deer and driving his souped-up Corvette. One day he wedded both pleasures when he gunned his Corvette to a speed of 126 miles per hour on a deserted road and ran straight into the stomach of a large deer who was crossing that road with an indolence equal to his own. Bruce stayed in professional baseball for 14 years. He reached the major leagues only once, in 1967, appearing in one game for the Los Angeles Dodgers before they returned him to the minors. In 1 1/3 innings he allowed three hits, struck out two batters and accumulated an earned run average of 20.25. He is still pitching in the minor leagues, and there is talk that someday he will be made a pitching coach.

Only Raymond Orlikowski, of all the relief pitchers, was occasionally given a starting assignment. Orlikowski, a 17-year-old southpaw from Stevens Point, Wisconsin, was as physically talented as any of the team's bonus pitchers. However, he had been cursed (blessed?) with an unbelievable naïveté that had permitted him to sign the first major league contract offered him. He had no conception of his talent, nor how to use it to bargain for a large bonus. So the Braves had acquired him for a few thousand dollars. Shortly after he signed with them, the

Cincinnati Reds offered him $30,000. Because he was not a bonus baby, the Braves treated Orlikowski with none of the pampered deference accorded the rest of us.* Ultimately this would embitter him and affect his career. He never became the major league pitcher his talent prophesied; instead, he returned to Stevens Point and became a baker.

Most of the remaining relief pitchers were considerably less talented than Orlikowski and few of them lasted longer than a season in professional baseball. Dennis Taijchman was a hulking Kansas farm boy with the square jaw and thick eyeglasses of a Clark Kent. He once single-handedly lifted a tractor out of a ditch to the amazement of his teammates. His strength disappeared magically whenever he tried to throw a baseball, however, and the following spring training he was released. Bobby Joe Wade, a 24-year-old Southerner, often boasted to his teammates that he would have sexual intercourse with a rattlesnake if only he could find someone to hold the snake. One day in the bullpen he offered to disclose the secret of his curveball if I would give him $10,000 of my bonus. A week later he was given his unconditional release.

Dave Breshnahan, a puckish, red-haired Northern Irishman, also failed to finish the season at McCook. During his stay, however, he delighted his teammates by reading to them from the erotic love letters of his 16-year-old sweetheart, who ex-

• • •

*The term "bonus baby" is usually applied to any player receiving more than $10,000 upon signing a contract. Naturally, whenever a team invests such money in a player they treat him more tenderly than they would a player in whom they invested little money. A bonus baby had only to hint at improvement in order to advance in the minors. But a non-bonus baby had to fashion a record of unquestionable success before he advanced. Les Bass, for example, a non-bonus pitcher, once won 15 games in a Class C league only to be returned to that league the following year. Tony Cloninger, a $100,000 bonus pitcher once finished with an 0–9 record in a Class B league and the following year pitched at Austin in the Double-A Texas League.

pressed a desire to resume their love-making at the bottom of her parents' swimming pool.

During the 1959 season more than 15 pitchers would appear in a McCook Braves' uniform, although never more than 10 at a time. Only one, Phil Niekro, a 20-year-old knuckleball pitcher from Blaine, Ohio, would ever have a major league career. In 1969 Niekro won 23 games for the Atlanta Braves and became the first knuckleball pitcher in major league history to win 20 or more games in a season. He is still the ace of the Atlanta staff. In 1959, however, the Braves had given him a $500 bonus and sent him to McCook as the tenth pitcher on the staff. At first he appeared only in the last innings of hopelessly lost games. He was ineffective because he could not throw his knuckleball over the plate and preferred, instead, to deal up one of his other pitchers, all of which were deficient. He seemed deficient. He was tall and blond and affected a deferential slouch. I dismissed him as a timid man. Years later I would realize that what I'd mistaken for timidity was actually a simple nature. Phil Niekro was the least complex man I'd ever met. He devoted his life to mastering a pitch. He had been taught that pitch by his father when he was six years old and had still not mastered it when he reached McCook. It is a capricious pitch. It has no logic. Even its name is illogical, since knuckles have nothing to do with its performance. To throw one, a pitcher digs the nails of his first two fingers into the seams of the ball and then pushes it toward the plate with the same motion he would use to close a door. Once released, the ball has no spin. It is caught immediately by air currents. (A spinning ball cuts through such currents and takes a direction of its own.) The vagaries of these currents may cause a knuckleball to rise or dip or flutter left and right, or maybe all these things at once, or just some of them, or none at all as it just floats lazily plateward. The ball's behavior is as erratic as the flight of a hummingbird. A knuckleball is as impossible to hit when thrown over the plate as it is to throw over the plate. A pitcher has no control over the pereginations of the ball. He imposes nothing on it but simply surrenders to its will. To be successful, a knuckleball pitcher must first recognize this fact and then decide that his destiny still lies only with the pitch and that he will throw it constantly no matter what. It was at McCook that Niekro first surrendered to the whims of this pitch and, shortly thereafter, where his first success began. It is a surrender a more complex man could never make, but one that eventually brought Niekro a success none of his teammates at McCook would ever approach.

I stayed to myself at first. I lived in a room at the Keystone Hotel. In the afternoons I walked to the Armory, where I dressed with my teammates and then sat in the back seat of one of their cars for the short ride to Cibola. I stared out the window and said nothing. Until I pitched my first game (and awed my teammates with my talent) I would not feel a part of the team. After the games I returned to town and sat on the bench in front of the hotel until midnight. I was fascinated by the cars "dragging main." It was a ritual I'd never seen back home and which, I learned, was indigenous to small, isolated towns like McCook. They were mostly older cars—rectangular Chevy Nomads and boxy Ford coupes with front ends indistinguishable from the backs and, occasionally, a low-slung and ponderous black Mercury with narrow windshield and hump back that crawled up Main Street looking as sinister as an alligator. The cars were filled with teenagers. They beeped their horns and gunned their motors and, half-hanging out of their windows, shouted recognition to passing cars filled with other teenagers they saw daily. Some of the cars were filled with girls in their early twenties who worked the night shift at the telephone company and who dragged main on their midnight lunch break. Others were filled with Mexicans who used the darkness and the obscurity of their moving cars to peer out at the town they seldom saw in the daylight. Even families dragged main, I noticed, and one night I saw the farmer and his wife whom I'd first seen sitting in the stands at Cibola. They were sitting in the cab of a pick-up truck, their two young sons between them, and staring out at the stores and the shouting teenagers and me. When they reached the bottom of the hill they turned right onto U.S. Highway 6 and returned to their farm somewhere beyond the city limits.

One night I was standing on the curb in front of the hotel when I saw Ron Hunt walking up the hill toward me. As he approached, a car filled with teenage girls drove by. I waved to them. They waved back and the car continued down the hill. Hunt noticed my gesture and came over to talk to me. He was a shy, earnest youth with a very short crew-cut that made his large ears look even larger. He was the first of my teammates with whom I'd had a conversation. We talked about our hometowns and our ambitions and hinted at the size of our bonuses. He seemed reticent to reveal the amount of his bonus but eager to discover mine. I told him off-handedly it was a lot more than $20,000. "Gosh!" he said.

While we talked the cars kept moving past us, and eventually the car with the girls came back up the hill. I stepped into the street and called out, "Hey, pull over!" The car slowed considerably, but when its occupants saw Hunt remain on the curb, his hands stuffed in the pockets of his khaki pants, it picked up speed again.

"Do you know them?" he asked.

"Of course not," I said, and yelled after the disappearing car, "Come on back!"

"Jeez!" He shook his head and smiled at my audacity. He

77

seemed impressed with it, as if it were a kind of sophistication he knew he lacked but, nevertheless, still admired from afar. He was a lot like a friend I had in Connecticut. Doug was shy, too, especially around girls. Whenever we saw two good-looking girls he would say, "Why don't you go talk to them?" I always did. While he hung back I would approach the girls and often make a fool of myself. Occasionally, though, I'd be warmly received and then I would turn and motion for Doug to catch up—which he did in his sheepish way. One day I approached two girls on the midway of an amusement park. After a little coaxing ("You can trust us, we're not dirty.") the girls agreed to go for a ride in the House of Horrors. Doug and his girl sat in the cart behind ours. It was pitch black inside, and when the first cardboard skeleton leaped out the girl beside me grabbed my arm. The darkened tunnel was filled with enough leaping skeletons and horrifying shrieks to keep her clinging to me throughout the ride. Near the end of it, however, I heard a loud slap that did not seem connected with any of the witches or skeletons popping up around us. When we finally emerged into the daylight, I looked back and saw Doug rubbing his cheek, his girl beside him, her arms folded tightly across her chest.

Ron Hunt reminded me of Doug, so when he asked me to be his roommate that night I gladly accepted. I moved in with him the following morning. We lived in a small gray house a few blocks north of the hotel. It was owned by a tiny, stooped lady with steel-gray hair. Ron first introduced her to me as "Mom," which momentarily confused me until I realized she wasn't actually his mother. She was a woman in her late sixties whose children had married and left McCook. She charged us eight dollars a week to sleep in a small room with two cots and one bureau. For another dollar she would serve us breakfast and allow us to watch television with her at night. I declined but

Ron didn't, although I'm sure she never got around to charging him that extra dollar. When I woke each morning I'd hear them in the kitchen. "Have another piece of toast, son," she would be saying. And he'd laugh in that boyish way of his and tell her that she treated him even better than his mother did. I always waited until they left the kitchen before I slipped out the door and walked downtown to eat my breakfast. After the games at night I continued to spend my time in front of the Keystone Hotel. I would stay there until midnight, by which time I knew both Ron and she had finished watching television and gone to bed.

I envied the easy intimacy they shared. I was alone for the first time in my life and would have been happy to find in McCook a remnant of the familial warmth I'd left behind. But I could never call her "Mom." It embarrassed me to do so. Their intimacy embarrassed me, too. It was too easily acquired, like a new glove broken in by someone else. No matter how comfortably it fit the hand, it would never feel quite right because it was someone else's glove. The oils that had softened and molded it had come from someone else's palm. Its comfort, then, was unearned. The intimacy Ron Hunt and that old woman shared was unearned, too, and actually not an intimacy at all. It was impossible to acquire such intimacy in only a week or even two months, and what they'd settled for were its superficial trappings. ("It's cold, son, don't forget your sweater.") Yet this simple manner would serve Ron Hunt well in the years to come. I did not have it, nor did I think it worth acquiring, although I know now it would have made things easier for me. I chose distance instead. I never spoke more than a few perfunctory words to her as I entered or left the house. She told Ron I was aloof, unfriendly. I do not remember what she was, other than an old woman in whose house I once slept for eight dollars a week.

Ten days after I arrived in McCook, Bill Steinecke told me I would pitch the second game of a night doubleheader against the Holdrege White Sox in Holdrege. The first game went 15 innings. In the eleventh Steinecke told me that if the game didn't end shortly there would be no second game. A town ordinance prohibited any game from beginning after 11 P.M., and it was already 9:30. "You'll get your chance some other day," he said. In the twelfth the White Sox got a runner to third base and I prayed he would score. He didn't, and in the following half-inning I prayed the Braves would score a run, but they didn't. My allegiance skipped back and forth between the two teams after each half-inning until finally the Braves won it in the fifteenth. It was 10:30 P.M.

"We'll start as soon as you're warmed up," Steinecke said to me. My warm-up catcher was Elrod Hendricks, who had caught all 15 innings of the first game and would sit out the second. He had just unbuckled his shinguards and was resting in the dugout when I told him I had to warm up.

"Oh, mon! Got plenty time," he said with a smile.

"I gotta start now," I said, and I walked down to the bullpen along the right field foul line. He followed, shaking his head sadly. He was very black, and in the dimly lighted bullpen I could barely see his face. I began to throw hard almost at once. Hendricks was standing, catching the ball with a carefree snap of his glove. Before he returned each pitch he spoke to the fans standing alongside the fence. I could see his white teeth as he smiled. "Hurry up," I shouted, but he did not seem to hear me. He lobbed the ball back in a lazy arc. He was still standing a few minutes later when I began to throw full-speed. I motioned for him to get down in a crouch and give me a target. He did so slowly, as if with great pain, and I heard the fans laughing. I fired the next pitch over his head. He made a half-hearted swipe at it with his glove. The ball rolled to the dugout.

"You coulda had that!" I kicked the dirt in front of me. "Shit!"

I saw his teeth again. "You don't like it, mon, get 'nother catcher."

"I will, goddamn it!" I ran to the dugout and got Joe Shields. When Hendricks saw me return with Shields he said, "Hey, mon, why you won do thot? Make Elrod like bod to moniger. Shouldn't do thot. We talk 'bout it in McCook, eh?" He was shaking his head sadly as he spoke, yet I could see his teeth so he must have been smiling, too.

My performance in that first game would typify my career. It was brief and resolved nothing. I pitched 2 1/3 innings before Steinecke relieved me with the score tied 2–2. I proved I had potential by striking out four of the seven batters I retired, but I also proved that that same talent was undisciplined by walking five batters in less than three innings. I allowed no hits and, in fact, refused to let the White Sox batters make contact with the ball. In the third inning, after I had struck out one man and walked two others in succession, Steinecke trotted to the mound.

"You're trying to throw the fuckin' ball by everyone," he said. "Relax, let the bastards hit it. We'll help you out." He looked over his shoulder at the next batter, a skinny, spectacled little infielder named Al Weiss (he would star for the New York Mets in the 1969 World Series, the same one in which Hendricks would star for the Baltimore Orioles.)

"This little bastard is gonna bunt the runners over," Steinecke said. "You let him. If he bunts toward first base, you go to first with the ball. But if he bunts down third, try to nail the lead runner. You understand?" I nodded, but as soon as he left the mound I decided to strike out Weiss. I walked him on four pitches, then walked the next batter to force in a run. This time Steinecke walked slowly out to the mound, and as he did so he

81

pointed to our bullpen where Orlikowski was warming up.

"That's it," he said and reached for the ball. I put it behind my back.

"What for?" I asked. "They're not hitting me."

"No, they're not," he said, smiling that maniacal smile of his. "But you're not gettin' the fuckers out, either." He spit tobacco juice and wiped the excess from his chin with the back of his hand. "No siree, Podner, you are certainly not getting them fuckers out, are you?"

I walked off the mound and sat in the dugout. I didn't know what to feel at that moment. I'd expected to strike out 18 batters and pitch a two-hit shutout or perhaps even be hit unmercifully. I had not precluded the second possibility. But this confused me. It was so inconclusive. What did it mean? I was still sitting there stunned when my teammates came in from the field at the end of the inning. As they did I heard Ron Hunt say to someone, "Man, my roomie throws bullets, don't he?" Then he lowered his voice a little and said, "He got a big bonus, you know. *Really* big!"

I relaxed considerably. It hadn't been a total loss after all. Thanks to Ron, they knew. That was enough to satisfy me, for at the time I still preferred those pure, isolated and transitory moments of success—a point proved—that stood out clearly and did not require the effort a more substantial success demanded.

The following morning I was sitting on the bench in front of the Keystone reading a newspaper when I heard a voice say, "Hey, mon, been looking for you." I looked over the paper to see Elrod smiling at me.

"What for?" I said. Still smiling, he hit me on the side of the head and I fell off the bench. I landed in a sitting position on the sidewalk, my legs spread out in front of me. I was still holding the newspaper, more dazed than hurt. I did not yet believe what had just happened. I looked around to see if there were any witnesses. But it was Sunday and the streets were deserted. Then I remembered the night before. Was that why Elrod had hit me? It was not enough, I thought, not enough for *me* to hit someone, anyway. There must be more. I had been shoved into the climax of this melodrama without having played the first act. And he was still smiling at me! I got up and he swung again. This time I blocked it with my arm. We circled each other warily. To the death, I wondered? But I wasn't even angry. I just hoped he would suddenly put down his arms and walk away and all would be forgotten. But he didn't. I decided to go out heroically. I lowered my head like a bull and charged his stomach. He grabbed me around the neck with one arm and began punching me in the stomach with his free hand. He punched me a number of times but none of the blows hurt; they just took my breath away in stages —punch by punch—until I had none left. When his arms got tired he let go and I fell down again. I took a deep breath but nothing came up. I took another but still nothing. My mind went into hysterics! I would never catch another breath! I would die here, on the streets of McCook, thousands of miles from nowhere! *My career!* It flashed before my eyes—2 1/3 innings? Was that *it?* I felt a little breath come and I gasped for it, then a bigger one and a still bigger one, until finally I was panting heavily on the sidewalk. Elrod must have decided I'd had enough, because when I looked up he was gone. I got up and sat on the bench for a few minutes. My stomach began to feel sore so I decided to walk home. By the time I reached the band shell in the center of the park my temple was throbbing and I could feel a large lump there. I walked faster, and when I reached my house my stomach began to convulse. I opened the front door and ran through the house. I passed

Mom in the kitchen. She looked over her shoulder at me just as I burst into the bathroom and began to dry-heave into the toilet. Nothing came up (I hadn't eaten yet), but every time I made a God-awful noise. When I finally stopped I was soaked with perspiration. I dried myself off and went into the bedroom and lay down. I slept through that afternoon's ball game and into the night. When I awoke it was dark. Ron was sitting on his bed in his underwear looking at me. He had a very serious expression on his face.

"You look terrible," he said.

"I don't feel so good," I replied. My stomach was sore and my temple was throbbing. I touched it. There was a large welt on the side of my head, as if I'd grown a frog's popeye while I'd slept.

"Mom's awfully upset," Ron said.

"I'll be all right."

"It's not that," he said. "She told me to speak to you. She said to tell you she won't tolerate no drinkers in her house. She never took in drinkers before and—"

"What? I wasn't drunk! I got into a fight with Elrod in front of the hotel."

"I know. I heard. I told Mom, but she just shook her head and said she wouldn't tolerate no drinkers and that's final."

"But I wasn't drinking!" I began to shout. "I don't even drink beer!"

"Shh! Mom's sleeping. She was so upset she went to bed early. She's not used to this kinda thing, you know? I think you oughta apologize anyway. Promise her you'll never do it again."

"Do what again?"

"Get drunk," he said. "Otherwise she'll have to throw you out, and that would bother her something awful. She's been like a mother to us, you know?"

"Go to hell!" I said, and I left the house. Ron forgave my

outburst, however. He said it was typical of me. That was typical of him, I said. Anyway, the next morning he spoke to Mom. She would let me stay, he said, because he'd given his word I'd behave myself. But his word was not quite enough for Mom. Whenever I walked past her, my eyes lowered in shame, she would fix me with a wary and ominous gaze that hinted at dire consequences for any future transgressions.

Once the initial excitement of my arrival in McCook and the start of my career had worn off, I discovered it was a dull life. The mornings and afternoons were free and seemingly endless. Only the hours from 6 to 11 P.M., when the games were played, held any excitement. Those games were our only reality. Our lives were lived within their nine innings and were greatly affected by what took place during them. The rest was nothing but dead time somehow to be filled. There was a pool hall that opened at noon and a bar that served those over 21. There were the two movie theaters, both of which opened at 7 P.M. and closed at midnight. After a night game we could rush to see the final minutes of the same movie two weeks running. So we had only ourselves to alleviate the boredom. Most of the players drifted into cliques and shared the boredom as if its weight would lessen in proportion to the number of shoulders bearing it. For instance the Spanish-speaking players from Cuba, Puerto Rico and the Dominican Republic stayed to themselves on the outskirts of town where they lived. There were never more than a few of them in McCook at any one time. And it was seldom more than a game or two before they were released, so I don't remember their names (except Elrod's, of course). I saw them at the armory and at Cibola and, occasionally, at a restaurant in town where they sat together and spoke in rapid Spanish, which they'd abandon only to order "Ham'n egg, over easy, orange juice," a meal that served for breakfast, lunch and dinner.

The older American players—Ken Cullum, Joe Shields, Bill Stevens and others—shared a large house in the residential section, while the families of Chuck Carlin and Frank Saia lived close by. Often the two married players visited their single teammates, as they were united by the common bonds of age and maturity (all were over 21 and had graduated from college) that the rest of us lacked. These men were not so single-minded about their baseball careers and so, unlike most of us, did not live or die with each base hit or strikeout. Instead they approached the game, outwardly at least, with a cool and mocking cynicism that confused the younger players and served only to reassure us they would never make the major leagues with such attitudes. They even doubted themselves, and were not reluctant to speak disparagingly of their talents, or lack of them. They preferred to regard baseball as simply an extension of their college life that would lead to a more meaningful career. I'm sure they secretly harbored the same fantasies as we did— of someday making "the bigs" and becoming "a star"—but if they did they considered it bad form to admit to such romanticism. They looked with annoyance on our open and unabashed enthusiasm toward baseball, our only topic of conversation. They had other interests. They discussed politics and literature and existential philosophy. And when they discussed women (not girls) their conversation was foreign to the rest of us, who treated girls as simply "clean" or "dirty." They spoke on a different level than we did; they were more analytical, more introspective, and were, in short, adults. This bond was so strong as to eventually unite Bill Stevens, a black, and Chuck Carlin, who had once thought of him as a clubhouse boy. Before the season was over, Mrs. Carlin would have Bill Stevens to dinner many times.

These older players seldom ventured into town, preferring

to spend their mornings and afternoons sleeping off the effects of large quantities of beer they'd consumed the night before. In my mind there was always an aura of mystery surrounding their lives in McCook, and I was fascinated by them. I'd heard, for instance, that Stevens was dating a white girl who worked at the telephone company—although only his roommates had seen them together. I'd heard also about night-long parties and the strange girls entering and leaving their house at all hours of the day and night, and about garbage cans filled with nothing but empty bottles. There was a rumor, too, that after Ken Cullum drank 20 or so bottles of Falstaff, he'd go outside on particularly hot nights and fall asleep on the lawn waking in the morning to find himself covered with dew and still wearing only his white boxer shorts emblazoned with red cupids.

Word also got around that Lois Steinecke, our manager's 21-year-old daughter, had come to McCook to visit her father and promptly fallen in love with Cullum. I remember seeing her once after I'd heard that rumor and wondering just what Cullum saw in such a plain-faced girl. Of course, I never noticed her spectacular body at the time, nor was I aware of her impressive I.Q. and disposition so gentle as to draw anyone. They carried on their romance throughout his minor league career, and often Lois would appear in Boise, Idaho, or Eau Claire, Wisconsin, or Davenport, Iowa, just to be with Ken for a short time. Never during those years did she make the slightest demand on him. Finally, sensing he would not marry her, she left for South America one day, where she taught English to Indian children.

One night, walking home from the armory, I passed the town's bar. Through its dusty window I could make out the figures of Cullum, Stevens, Shields and Carlin. The bar was dimly lighted, but their faces were illuminated in an eerie way

87

by the flickering colored lights of the pinball machine around which they stood. They held bottles of beer, and every so often one of them would raise a bottle to his lips, tip his head back and take a long swallow. They took turns playing the pinball machine. As the silver balls ricocheted underneath the glass top, they laughed and pointed at the lights jumping on the scoreboard. At one point Cullum walked over to the bar and returned shortly with four more bottles, which he passed out to his teammates. I watched for a while, not daring to go inside and suffer the humiliation of being denied service because I was under 21. Besides, I had not yet acquired a taste for beer, or for pinball machines either for that matter, although I longed for the camaraderie they seemed to be sharing.

A few nights later I got up the nerve to walk over to their house after a game. They were all sitting around in their underwear talking and swearing, and drinking beer, in that effortless natural way. They offered me a beer, too, and I sat down with them. I didn't say much at first, but after a few sips I began to talk loudly and slur my words. I was not drunk, really, just showing off, and it wasn't until I saw the disgusted look on Stevens' face that I realized I had done the wrong thing. But I was undaunted, and a few days later made another attempt to befriend them. I saw Cullum and Shields standing in front of a drugstore talking with two pretty girls. I walked over to them and said in my most blasé tone, "Hi, who're the cunts?"

The girls turned to me with looks more startled than shocked. For a split second they could not believe what they'd just heard. When it finally did register, they were at a loss to respond. Cullum and Shields ignored me. They moved closer together so that their backs formed a barrier between me and the girls. They continued talking to the girls as if nothing had happened, as if *I* had not happened, and when the girls turned

88

back to them I went away.

I lacked something, I decided after that experience. But what? I gave up trying to befriend the older players. Still, I did not spend much time with my roommate either. Despite Ron's intercession with Mom, I had grown more and more estranged from him over the weeks. We had little in common. I was restless and preferred to spend my free time downtown. He would rather stay home with Mom or else walk over to the house where most of the younger players lived—Bruce Brubaker, Dennis Overby, Ray Orlikowski, Phil Niekro, Dave Breshnahan and others. I went there once but found little to interest me. They spent most of their time writing long letters to their moms or girl friends, from whom they were forever receiving cookies or snapshots. The latter were treated with great reverence no matter how unpretty the girl might be. Each player was faithful to his snapshot during his stay in McCook. ("It's been 32 days since I last saw her.")

To display the seriousness of his intentions toward his girl friend, Dennis Overby went so far as to bring her to McCook for a few days. I saw them together once. They were holding hands while walking up and down Main Street one hot sunny afternoon. They looked serious, did not speak much and paused frequently to look into store windows. They lingered especially long in front of the jewelry store and its display of engagement rings. She was a thin, ordinary-looking girl with a complexion as pale as his own. She pointed to a ring. He nodded once. That night, a Saturday, Dennis struck out 17 batters, and the following morning he and his girl friend were at eleven o'clock mass. They went to Holy Communion, too, before she flew back to Fond du Lac, Wisconsin.

I had a girl friend "back home" also. She is now my wife, and has been these past 12 years. She says my letters from

McCook were rare, never more than a few lines scrawled in large script across one side of a piece of notepaper. She kept one.

Dearest Carol,

I miss you so much. I love you an awful lot. I can't wait to see you again. How are you? Fine I hope. I pitched yesterday but was wild. My arm didn't feel real good. But I still throw harder than anyone on the club. And I'm learning lots about pitching and lots of other things, too.

Love and Kisses XXXX
Pat

p.s. Please don't
worry about my arm!

And I was faithful to her, at least for a while. But unlike the celibacy of my younger teammates (which earned them one another's respect), mine was due more to circumstance than inclination.

On those rare occasions when players like Overby, Niekro and Hunt ventured downtown it was usually in groups of five or six, either to watch the last half-hour of a movie at the Fox Theater, where they sat in the balcony and tossed popcorn at the seats below, or to eat at Modrell's Cafe. Modrell's served the best food in town and had the prettiest waitresses. There were three of them, all blonde and in their late teens. The players flirted with them in an antiseptic, brotherly way, and the girls responded like sisters. They gave the players advice about their girl friends and commiserated with them over their careers. They all promised to keep in touch when the season was over. And they did, too. They wrote letters every month at first. Then every few months or so. Then only an occasional card at Christmas or Easter. Then nothing.

90

The cashier at Modrell's was a beefy woman with a booming voice. The waitresses called her "Mom," which was only natural since she was their mother. She, too, treated the players affectionately (some of them, anyway), and it was only a matter of time before I walked into Modrell's one day to hear Ron Hunt call her "Mom."

One afternoon I returned to our house to find Ron standing on the front lawn with one arm around a middle-aged man in a business suit and the other around a middle-aged woman with a corsage pinned to her dress. Our landlady was peering at all three of them through a Brownie camera. After she snapped their picture, Ron introduced the man to me as "My dad," and the woman as "My mom." I got over my initial confusion quickly and realized that this was his real mom, his mother, the woman who'd given birth to him. Somehow the knowledge that such a person existed, that like the rest of us he had a "real" mother, not just surrogates, restored a portion of sanity to the world. However, a few weeks later I returned home to find the same scene being played out once again. Ron, smiling, his arms around a man and a woman. Only they were different. Not the same as the last two. Mom snapped their picture. Ron called me over. "I want you to meet my dad," he said. "And this is my mom."

Later I learned his parents had been divorced and had remarried, so that Ron had two sets of moms and dads, not counting all the others he could pick up here and there throughout his career.

By mid-July I no longer ate at Modrell's. (Actually, I had made a less than antiseptic pass at one of the waitresses and had been soundly rebuffed. Ron was very upset with me. I hadn't followed the rules, it seemed.) Instead, each morning I walked to the bottom of Main Street and then right for a few blocks to the M-and-E Diner. The M-and-E had only one waitress, a silent, 28-year-old Indian girl with a pockmarked face and lumpy white scars on her dark arms. She kept a knife in her teased hair. Only its handle showed, and at first I thought it was simply an odd-shaped barrette. But one day a cowboy patted her behind and the next instant the knife was quivering in the tabletop inches from his hand. Unlike Modrell's, which catered to businessmen during the day and families at night, the M-and-E served mostly truck drivers (it was on U.S. 6) and drifters and rodeo cowboys from the Red Willow County Fair. Every so often Ken Cullum would eat there, too. He would come in at about 3 P.M., his eyes red from a night of drinking, and order a breakfast of eggs and sausage and pancakes and a quart of orange juice. He always ate at the M-and-E after such a night, he said, so Steinecke wouldn't find out about it. I discovered what he meant one night when Steinecke came up to me before a game and, grinning, said, "So, you wanna get in the pants of that waitress at Modrell's, eh, kid?"

After breakfast I walked back to the Keystone and sat on the bench out front and read the newspapers. I read *The Sporting News* first, beginning on the last page which was nothing but tiny columns of statistics on every minor leaguer. I checked these for all the pitchers in the Braves' farm system and then turned to the front page to learn about Whitey Ford and Warren Spahn. I always had a paperback book with me, too, although I seldom read one. I'd just lay it on the bench beside me hoping that one of the college-educated players might come along and see it. "What's that you're reading?" he would ask, and I would shrug and say, "Nothing much," and hold up my new copy of *The Greatest Story Ever Told*. But the only person who ever noticed my book was Lois Steinecke. She stood in front of me one day and pointed to the book. "What are you reading?" she said, and the moment she said it I was struck dumb, saw instantly what a fool I was, my little ruse! She picked up the book and looked at its cover painting of a finely-featured man with long blond hair, blond beard and sorrowful eyes. She looked at it for a long second and I knew she was going to laugh, was going to humiliate me, but all she did was nod her head seriously and say, "It's a good book." Then she looked at me. "I like to read a lot, too."

When I finished with the newspapers I spent the rest of the morning walking around town, looking into store windows, occasionally going inside a store, wandering up and down its aisles without the sightest intention of buying anything until a salesman would step in front of me. "Can I help you, sir?" I would panic, snatch the closest thing, buy it and escape. One morning, the third in a row of 100 degree heat, I grabbed a woolen sweater and thrust it at the salesman. He looked at it and then at me. "It's cold back home," I said, as if "back home" was the North Pole.

I also spent a lot of time drinking coffee in drugstores. I often hit two or three drugstores in one morning. I liked to sit at the long formica counters, drinking my coffee and watching the waitresses. They were husky farm girls with thick bodies that strained against their nylon uniforms as they reached and stooped and knelt. The sound of those moving bodies, their nylon slips and stockings rustling, never failed to excite me. I was fascinated by the off-hand way they glided through their routine—tapping huge stainless-steel urns, balancing cups and saucers halfway up each arm, cleaning a counter with one swipe of a damp cloth and pocketing their tips in the same motion —and, upon seeing a familiar face enter the store, had coffee on the counter before that person even reached it. I fantasized that one day I would walk through the door and, before I had mounted my stool, before I had swung my leg over it, there would be a cup of coffee waiting for me, too. I stayed in those drugstores for hours, nursing my coffee and waiting for mid-morning when businessmen and farmers and housewives and secretaries would pour in for their coffee breaks and the counter would grow crowded and noisy around me. I liked the feeling of being in the midst of such a crowd, in the midst of people moving through familiar lives, meeting familiar faces, while my life, at the time, was so unfamiliar to me and all the faces in it were those of strangers. Sitting at the counter, eavesdropping, I shared in their lives. But I never once abandoned my anonymity, never once turned to my left or right and reached into one of those lives. I just took comfort from being near them, and poured more and more milk into my coffee until it was nothing but milk. I preferred my anonymity. It gave me freedom and a certain distance from those lives, which, if entered, I might discover to be oppressively familiar to their possessors in a way I did not care to see. They could never escape them as I could, by simply standing up and walking outside into the daylight of my own unknown and myriad possibilities.

At noon I walked up U.S. Highway 6 and waited outside the poolroom until its proprietor, Shorty, came by to open up. He was a neat little man with wavy red hair and a handlebar mustache. He wore fancy cowboy shirts with snap buttons and new dungarees that were always pressed to a knifelike crease. He rolled up the cuffs of these until they were 12 inches wide and exposed his pointed cowboy boots branded with elaborate scrollwork.

The poolroom was as small and neat as its proprietor. The walls were paneled in light pine and stacked with dozens of new cuesticks. The Brunswick pool and snooker tables were of dark wood polished to a mirrorlike finish, their green felt tops bright and unscratched. After Shorty had cleaned his spotless room

94

—swept the floor, waxed the wood tables, brushed the chalk dust from the green felt—he took his accustomed position behind the counter, where he could survey the room through narrowed eyes, and began to wax his moustache. This he'd wax for hours on end, pausing only to dispense bottles of beer and cellophane packages of beef jerky or bags of Red Man chewing tobacco to his infrequent customers. There was a brass spitoon in front of the counter, and any man who failed to hit it was promptly ushered out the door. Shorty also kept two guns behind his counter—a 12-gauge shotgun as well as a .38-caliber pistol—and both were loaded. When he found out I was a baseball player he asked me to get him a bat, a 38-ounce Louisville slugger, and when I did he kept that behind the counter, too. Possibly this is why I never saw more than three or four men in his pool room at any one time. Most of the town's cowboys and farmers preferred to shoot pool at the bar next door, whose proprietor was not so fastidious as Shorty.

The first few times I came into his establishment Shorty watched me carefully for signs of slovenliness. Finding none, he took a liking to me. He taught me how to hold a cuestick and the basic rules of nine-ball, eight-ball and rotation, and then left me alone to shoot pool most of the afternoon. I loved the game. It was simple and orderly and not difficult to master. During my years in professional baseball I spent lots of time shooting pool. The game was an excellent refuge from the frustrations of my career. And when I left baseball in 1962, having no trade, no education and no ambition, the first thing I turned to was the cuestick. It supported my wife and me for two years. It also helped assuage the demands of my ego, which, without baseball, was shrinking daily. Pool was still a refuge, only by then from other frustrations.

At Shorty's one afternoon I met a teammate, Julius French. He was a year older than I and supposedly a great troublemaker. Most of the players on our team avoided him. He had an air of self-destructiveness about him that threatened to carry down those in his wake. A few days before I arrived in McCook, the players were invited to a party at the home of one of the girls who worked at the telephone company. Soon that girl was huddled in the corner with Julius, rapidly succumbing to his courtly southern manners (he could light a woman's cigarette as if it were an inherited gesture) and his exquisite good looks. He had fine, almost delicate features, deeply-colored lips and a mole on his cheek. His blue eyes were always half-lidded and when he spoke to women his lashes fluttered. They were fluttering then, as he spoke to this girl at her party. Her fiancé noticed and protested to Julius. Julius invited him into the bathroom to discuss the matter privately. The door closed. When it reopened Julius's right hand was wrapped in a towel and the fiancé was unconscious in the bathtub.

As we shot pool that afternoon. I asked Julius about the incident. He showed me his hand. Its knuckles were hardened scabs. He was used to fighting, he said. He had been a Golden Gloves boxer in Georgia before his career had been terminated one night. He was in a bar with his girl when a sailor made an obscene remark to her. Julius knocked him down. The sailor got up and rushed Julius with a chain. The next few minutes were a blank. Julius could only remember five men pulling him off the unconscious body of the sailor. He had continued to beat the sailor, it seemed, long after the sailor had collapsed. Eventually the sailor died. Julius said he had never gone to prison for that killing but he had had to leave Georgia, and playing minor league baseball in McCook, Nebraska, was a more tempting offer than the possibility of playing for the Georgia State Penitentiary.

Julius signed a contingent bonus contract with the Braves. He was promised $10,000 if he remained on the McCook

96

roster for 40 days. If he was released within 40 days he would get nothing. Julius had already passed 21 days in McCook, and, though he was as talented as most of our pitchers, had done little more than pitch batting practice before each game. He threw with a vengeance. The hitters groaned when he took the mound. They complained to Steinecke. They feared for their lives, they said. Steinecke only laughed. "It'll do the fuckers good," he said "If they can hit that red-ass they can hit anybody." Steinecke loved to sit in the dugout and watch Julius throw. Whenever one of our players did hit the ball solidly off Julius, Steinecke would get excited and start elbowing whoever was next to him. "Watch this! Watch this!" he would say. Invariably, Julius would fire the next pitch at the offending batter's head, and the batter would sprawl in the dust. "Heh! Heh! Heh! That's a nasty little fucker out there!" Steinecke would cackle to no one in particular. "Yes siree, Podner, that's a nasty fucker!"

Why did I become friendly with Julius French of all people? I often wonder. Obviously, neither of us quite fit in anywhere on the team, and so perhaps naturally we seemed to fit in with each other. Yet that's a shaky foundation on which to build a friendship consisting primarily of sullen silences. At best, we shared a common moodiness, a dissatisfaction, but with what we did not know. We met every afternoon at Shorty's to play pool. Our games began jovially enough, but always turned sour. We released our private frustrations in those games. The day's loser stalked out of Shorty's determined never again to speak to the winner. Those resolutions lasted a few hours, sometimes even a day, but never longer. We were both parted and reunited by our murky dissatisfactions and the grudging admittance that we needed someone with whom to share them. Yet, even as we befriended one another we held something in reserve. We *were* strangers! Our situation had thrown us together for the moment (we never saw each other after McCook) and to act as if we'd become intimate friends on such short notice would be false. We sensed this in McCook, and so we shared our tenouous friendship just at odd times and at a certain level.

Julius and I watched our home games from the bullpen in the left field corner. We sat on the picnic bench and chewed tobacco. We stretched our legs out in front of us, dug the heels of our spikes into the ground and pushed back slightly so that the bench tottered on two legs and we rested against the wire fence that separated us from the Mexican and Indian fans behind us. We held this pose for innings, hats pulled down over our eyes, hands folded on stomachs, stirring ourselves only to spit tobacco juice high into the air, part our legs quickly and close them again before we lost our precarious balance. The bullpen was in the shadows and so far from home plate that we could see the ball in the catcher's glove a split second before we heard its "crack." We watched the games with but faint interest. They were being played by someone else and so influenced their careers, not ours. We rarely found ourselves a part of those games, and then only by accident.

One night a base hit skipped over the foul line and hooked under our bench. We were so surprised at this intrusion into our solitude that we didn't move until we heard the cursing and pounding feet of the opposing team's left fielder. We dove off the bench just before he grabbed it and flung it into the air. He picked up the ball and fired it to third base. Immediately, his shoulders sagged. He muttered to himself as he walked back to his position. Julius dusted himself off with mock solemnity, "Goddamn, fella, show some manners!" Without looking back, the left fielder gave us the finger. The fans behind us laughed as we righted our bench and resumed our pose.

Such intrusions were rare, however, and often the closest we

98

came to the action was when Phil Niekro sprinted to the bullpen to warm up before going in to save yet another game. Most of the time we just sat there, chewing our tobacco (getting slightly drunk on it) and cursing Overby's luck. To help pass the time there were always a few young boys rattling our fence. They pleaded with us to show them our gloves. Like prisoners, they reached their hands through the wire mesh to try on the gloves. They pounded their fists into the gloves and shouted, "Fire it to me, Babe!" And when we turned our backs they tried to pull the gloves through the fence, but they were too big and the openings too small. They lost interest in the gloves and asked us to give them a baseball. Often we did, but only in return for a hot dog or hamburger, which we ate behind our upraised gloves so that Steinecke would not see us from his spot in the third base coach's box. Every so often we asked the boys if they had an older sister. They always did and she was always good-looking. They ran off toward the home plate stands and returned minutes later towing a 14-year-old girl wearing glasses. While their sister, or whoever she was, giggled and blushed, the boys began shouting for their baseball—"You promised! You promised!"—and we tossed it over the fence just so they would go away before Steinecke heard the commotion and looked down at us.

When not pitching (which for Julius was frustratingly frequent) we preferred to sit in the bullpen rather than the dugout. In the dugout, alongside our teammates who were playing those games, we would be expected to show an enthusiasm and interest in their outcome that we did not feel. It's difficult to sustain such enthusiasm when not in games (even when your team is winning regularly, as ours was), and perhaps even more so considering the number of games we played in two months. We played six night games a week and one afternoon doubleheader, usually on Sunday. Rarely was a game rained out, and even then only after we had sat much of the night in the dugout and watched the field turn into a swamp before the umpires finally rendered their decision. The game would then be rescheduled as part of a twi-night doubleheader the following day. We had no open days, even for travel, because none of the Nebraska State League's six towns was farther than a three-hour bus ride. Our road trips were one-night stands. We arrived in time for batting practice, played that night's game, ate supper at midnight and were back in McCook by 4 A.M.

Because we never stayed overnight, I have retained no sense of those other towns. I remember only that to reach Hastings and Holdrege and Kearney and North Platte and Grand Island we had to pass through miles of flat land that smelled of sweet alfalfa, and occasionally through a quick town like Funk or Indianola or Wellfleet or Juniata or Arapahoe that was simply a few stores, a railroad crossing, a huge grain silo and a population sign that read less than 1000 people.

I remember specifically only one afternoon. We had stopped to eat at a roadside cafe outside Holdrege when it began to rain. The drops splattered against the restaurant's plate glass window. While eating I became conscious of a pinging sound and looked up to see hailstones. They grew larger and larger before my eyes until they were the size of a paperback book. They were flat, jagged chunks of ice that looked as if they were being torn from an iceberg and hurled against the window by some savage and unseen god. The sound was deafening. The ice struck with a "clang" and the window rippled like a tissue-thin sheet of aluminum. Everyone in the cafe—players, patrons, waitresses—left their seats and huddled against the far wall away from the window. We stared in disbelief and waited for it to shatter. But the hail stopped as suddenly as it had begun, and seconds later the sun was shining. We hung back a few minutes more and then, like stone age savages, ventured out-

100

side. The hot sun had now melted most of the hailstones to the size of rock salt. We searched for the large pieces but could find none. We even began to doubt our senses until one of the waitresses pointed to some parked cars, their windshields shattered and bodies pockmarked.

The sun stayed out for the rest of the afternoon, and that night we played a doubleheader against the White Sox. I don't remember how those games turned out. In fact, I don't remember much about any of the games we played on the road (or at home, either, for that matter) except those I pitched in, which affected my career.

I remember in detail, for instance, a game at Grand Island in mid-July. I defeated the Athletics 1–0, for my first victory in professional baseball. My mound opponent was Jose Santiago, a tall, lean Puerto Rican with stiletto sideburns. Santiago would one day become a successful pitcher for the Boston Red Sox. However, that night in 1959 I was the better pitcher by a slight margin. I threw harder. We matched serves for eight innings. Then Ron Hunt scored from third base on a fly ball to shallow center field, diving headfirst past the lunging catcher. I hugged him when he entered the dugout. I ended the game by striking out the last batter on three pitches. In nine innings I had struck out 11 batters, walked 3 and given up 2 singles. It was the kind of performance that would hound me throughout my career. I would produce such games about once every four starts. After them, my manager would say, "It shows you can do it." But those games had a will of their own. I could never summon them on command, and, in fact, the harder I tried to duplicate them the more they eluded me. In my next three starts I would fail to last beyond the fourth inning. Then, when I was about to despair of ever duplicating such a game, everything would return in a whoosh—speed, curve, control, savvy, luck—and I would pitch a game of both blinding and maddening brilliance.

I was standing in the lobby of the Fox Theater waiting for Julius to buy the popcorn. We had rushed over after the ball game to catch the last 30 minutes of an Elvis Presley movie. It was a Saturday night and the theater was packed. From inside I could hear the teenage girls screaming at Elvis. A girl walked by me. I thought she smiled. She started up the stairs that led to the balcony.

"Heh, wait up!" She stopped halfway up the stairs and turned around. She had long brown hair that flipped up at the ends. She was wearing a white blouse and very tight black shorts. The blouse was tucked into her shorts in such a way that her smallish breasts strained against it. She wore a wide belt that made her waist look unbelievably small for such a big girl. She must have been about five feet, seven inches tall. Her face was pretty. I remember a broad, white forehead.

"Where you goin'?" I said.

"To the balcony."

"Want some company?" I smiled but my heart was pounding.

"Sure. Come on." I followed her up the stairs.

"My name is Sally." She looked back at me and smiled. "It isn't really. It's Sarah. That's a biblical name, you know. I hate it. Everybody calls me Sally."

"Sure," I said. "My name is Pat."

"I know."

The balcony was crowded and noisy. Hunt, Overby, Niekro and a few others were sitting in the first row. They were slouched low in their seats and their feet dangled over the railing that kept people from falling into the orchestra. When they saw me with a girl they turned around and stared. I made believe I didn't see them. Sally led me up the steeply inclining balcony until we were only a few rows under the bright, conical light coming from the projection room. She turned into a row and sat down. I sat beside her. The light from the projection room fanned out over our heads, grew wider and fainter as it approached the screen far below us. Suspended in the light were particles of dust. I put my arm around the back of her seat and she moved close to me. We stayed that way for a long moment, both of us staring at the screen. I let my hand drop onto her shoulder and she pressed her head against mine. I could feel her soft hair against my cheek. I breathed its sweet fragrance and closed my eyes and kissed her. She opened her mouth and breathed in deeply. I began to tumble slowly through space, spinning and falling faster and faster until I feared I would pass out. I opened my eyes and saw overhead a whirling prism of color. I focused hard on the prism and it began to spin more slowly, and finally it stopped. I saw it was only the cut-glass chandelier. We parted. I took a deep breath and became conscious again of the darkened theater and the conical light and the people around us. Down below, I caught a glimpse of Ron Hunt turning back toward the screen. My head filled quickly now, with thoughts of my unbelievable luck.

Sally and I kissed throughout the movie. Each kiss was less dizzying than the last. We pressed our lips together so tightly that our teeth cut into them. We tried to press our bodies together, too, but the armrest between us bruised our ribs. Still we strained and pressed and began to sweat. Her blouse was wet and it stuck to her back. When the movie ended and the lights came on, I saw that her hair was damp and thick strands of it were matted to her forehead. Her lips were red beyond the lip line and looked swollen. My lips were sore. I left her in the lobby after we had made plans to meet at the band shell in the small park across from the Fox after tomorrow night's game. She did not seem surprised to find out I was a ballplayer. Julius was waiting for me outside the theater. "You look like shit," he said and began to laugh. He was not the least bit upset over my having deserted him for Sally. "Those are the rules," he said. "I would have done the same thing." We both laughed and he offered to keep me company while I waited for Sally the following night. "I don't exactly have any pressing appointments of my own," he said.

After the ball game, Julius and I bought a fifth of gin and a quart of lemonade and walked over to the band shell to wait for Sally. It was 11 P.M. and the park was dark and deserted. We sat inside the shell, and after we had drunk most of the gin and lemonade we began to sing to an imaginary audience. We walked to the edge of the stage and took profuse bows. Julius accepted roses with his usual grace. When Sally finally drove up in her '50 DeSoto, we were both deliriously drunk and I was beginning to feel sick. I introduced Julius to her as "a fine Southern gentleman" as we both grinned like idiots and swayed beside her car. She did not get out of the car at first. She looked at each of us, a flicker of doubt passing over her eyes, and then smiled. She shook her head in mock disgust the way women do. I moaned. "I don't feel so hot," I said. She made me get into the back seat and then she got out of the car and into the back with me. She told Julius to drive. We headed down Main Street and turned right onto U.S. 6 toward her home. She lived with her parents and three brothers on a farm on the outskirts of McCook. I lay my head in her lap and closed my eyes. Everything began to spin wildly, and when Julius turned off the highway onto the bumpy dirt road that led to her house, I vomited. "Jeezes!" said Julius and jammed on the breaks. I opened the door and rolled out of the car into a field. I threw up again. Sally wiped herself off, and then she and Julius got out of the car and picked me up. They both supported me

104

while I continued vomiting. When I stopped, they put me back in the car, which had a horrible stench, and we drove the rest of the way to her house.

It was after midnight and everyone was asleep. Sally told us to be quiet and not to turn on any lights. They deposited me on the couch in the living room and, while Julius watched television without sound, Sally cleaned me up by its faint light. She washed my face with a wet cloth and then rinsed it out in cold water and folded it across my forehead. She took off my shirt and brought me one of her brother's t-shirts. I heard her washing mine in the kitchen sink and then I passed out. I woke to the sounds of whispered shouts. Sally's 21-year-old brother was standing in the living room and she was pleading with him. I could make out only their shadows. She grew adamant. "I don't care," she said. "I won't throw him out the way he is." Her brother's shadow moved toward me. Julius suddenly appeared and grabbed him by the shirt. He grabbed Julius's shirt. Sally pleaded with them to stop. They held tight to one another, neither one moving. I raised my head and moaned. Sally began to cry. I saw the shadow of her brother's head turn toward her and then back to me, and then his hands flew up into the air in disgust and he left the room. It was almost four in the morning when we got back to town. Sally dropped Julius off first, then drove me to Mom's house. "Are you all right?" she said. Nodding, I stumbled out of the car into the house.

I did not see Sally for the next few days, nor did I ever expect to see her again.

I started my third professional game a week later, the first game since my two-hitter in Grand Island and my first ever at Cibola Stadium. The McCook Gazette carried an article about me. It described me as one of the brightest of the McCook Braves' pitching prospects and mentioned I was a bonus baby. I was very nervous before the game and was determined to impress the 1000 fans with at least a repeat of my performance against Grand Island. I walked the first three men I faced and then struck out a batter. The fans cheered. I saw myself striking out the side with all those runners stranded on base. I walked the next man and the next, and when Steinecke came out to the mound and I saw Niekro walking toward me from the bullpen, I made no attempt to dispute Steinecke's decision. On the contrary, I breathed a sigh of relief. When the inning was over Steinecke told me I could return to the armory and take a shower. "You're through for the night," he said. I stepped out of the dugout and walked through the fence into the parking lot. Sally was waiting for me.

"I read about you in the paper," she said. "I wanted to see you pitch."

"You didn't see much," I said.

"Oh, it's only one game. There'll be others." She laughed as if embarrassed. "I even dressed up for the occasion." She was wearing a white blouse with a scooped-out neck and short, puffy sleeves. It was tucked into a long, full skirt. She wore white socks and loafers.

"Are you going back to the armory now?" I nodded. "Come on, I'll give you a ride."

We drove the short distance in silence. I was so disconsolate over my pitching that I forgot to apologize to her for my performance of a week ago. She seemed to have forgotten it, or at least to have forgiven me. She parked in front of the armory. "I'll wait for you," she said. I went inside, showered and dressed, and returned to the car. She drove aimlessly through McCook. I stared out the window at the darkened streets and thought of home. I scarcely listened as she spoke about herself. She had just turned 18, she said. She had been graduated in the top quarter of her high school class. "Which wasn't much," she added with a laugh, "since there weren't

50 kids in my senior class. Still, I thought I might go on to college. I wanted to go to college. Are you going?"

"What?"

"Are you going to go to college?"

"Yeh, in the fall."

"I wanted to go a lot," she said. "But my mother took sick and someone had to take care of her and do the chores. I don't mind it much, really. I kind of like it, even. But someday I want to get away. I'd like to work in Denver or even go to school there. McCook is okay but it's so small. You don't know how small it is until you get older. Every year it gets smaller." She laughed. "That sounds stupid, doesn't it? Is Fairfield a small town?"

"Kinda," I said. "But it's close to New York City so it doesn't matter much."

"I'd love to go to New York City," she said, and then she was quiet for a long time. I looked across at her. She sat erect in her seat. From the waist up she was rigid and leaning forward to see over the huge steering wheel of the ponderous old DeSoto. Her chin—I remember now—was slightly squarish and, at that moment, it was thrust forward as if she were trying to peer over the top of bifocals. With her eyes still on the road she said gaily, "Come on, don't be so glum. Cheer up! We could go to the drive-in, if you want."

"Sure, let's go."

She turned the car onto U.S. 6 and drove past Shorty's and the M-and-E Diner and the A-and-W Root Beer stand, which was filled with cars and carhops in black shorts rushing back and forth with their orders. When we reached the Drive-In Theater at the edge of town, she drove past its entrance.

"Heh, you passed it," I said.

"Uh-uh. We'll go in the exit. We won't have to pay." She drove behind the theater's towering screen, which leaned forward, away from the road and toward the cars that were facing it on the other side. Sally flicked off the headlights and turned into the exit. We were on a bumpy dirt road that first led past the screen and then past row after row of parked cars. Sally drove even more carefully now, her back very rigid.

"Do you do this all the time?" I asked.

"Lots. There's a place!" She turned right into one of the rows and passed behind three or four cars before coming to an open space. She backed the car up and then tugged on the steering wheel with great effort and guided the car forward in little spurts. She turned off the engine and reached out the window for the sound box. Hooking it over her half-opened window, she clicked it on. "See, I told you," she said, turning toward me. "Nobody ever catches us."

I don't remember what the movie was—gigantic images on an overwhelming screen—because the moment Sally turned toward me we began to kiss as we had in the Fox Theater. There was no arm rest between us now, and we pressed our bodies together as tightly as we could. Our tongues touched. I put my hand on her breast. She did not move away. After awhile I said, "Let's go sit in the back seat."

Breathing heavily, she pulled away and sat up. "No," she said.

"Why not?"

"I don't know. Let's stay here. Please!" She tried to kiss me. I pulled away.

"All right," I said. "We'll watch the movie."

We sat apart in silence and stared at the screen. Finally she said, "I'll be right back." She got out of the car and I saw her darkened form moving between cars toward the small shack that served as refreshment stand and rest rooms. I breathed a sigh of relief. What if she'd said yes! But she hadn't. My heart stopped pounding. By the time she returned to the car I was

108

no longer scared. I was relaxed even, and unbelievably confident. When she sat down I began to kiss her again and she responded. She responded feverishly, more feverishly than I, in fact. My mind was clear. With confidence, I renewed my protestations.

"Let's go in the back."

"No, please!" She did not stop kissing me.

"Come on!" I said when I could.

"We shouldn't."

"Yes!"

"All right." She opened the door and got out of the car. I was alone in the front seat. I looked at her standing there, and for a split second I wondered what she was doing. Then I opened my door and got out, too. We both slammed our doors at the same instant and the sound of those slamming doors still echoes in my mind. I felt the eyes of every person in that drive-in on me. My God! They all knew! I grabbed the handle of the rear door and pulled. It was locked. Sally was sitting in the back seat waiting for me. I grinned through the window and pointed at the lock. She pulled it up. I opened the door and got in beside her. I shut the door carefully so as not to make a sound. The door did not fully close. She reached across me, opened it again and slammed it hard. That sound wilted the last remnants of any passion I'd had. It seemed to renew Sally's, however, and she began to kiss me with even more fervor. We kissed wildly as she lay back in the seat, pulling me down on top of her. The car's upholstery smelled stale and faintly sour. I propped my elbows on the seat so not to crush her with my full weight. The seat was not long enough. When I tried to stretch my legs out my shoes banged against the door window. I thought for a moment and then pulled them up under my stomach, so that now, like a crouching cat, I looked ready to spring.

"Your knees," she rasped. "They're in my stomach."

"Oh, I'm sorry." But what to do with them? Should I open the window and stick my feet out?

"Bend your legs backward," she suggested. "Behind you." When I did, my legs folding like a jacknife behind me, I felt much more comfortable. We began to kiss again, and within seconds were as passionate as before.

"Aaaggghhh!"

"What happened?" she cried.

"My leg! Charley horse!" I began to shake my left leg violently, and my shoe banged against the door window until I thought it would shatter. Gradually the muscles in my calf relaxed and the cramp subsided. I folded my legs behind me again and, as we resumed our kissing, felt only a slight soreness. Would it affect my follow-through?

We had been kissing a long time before I finally reached my hand under her skirt. It froze.

"I took them off in the ladies room," she said, and so, after more fumbling with my pants, we made love. A euphemism, perhaps. Maybe she made love. I never thought of it at the time, though over the years such a possibility has, with distressing frequency, crossed my mind.

It was over quickly. When I was finished, I stopped. She looked up at me with wide, mad eyes that momentarily frightened me. "What's the *matter?*" her voice was like glass.

"Nothing," I said and sat up. I zipped up my pants. She lay there on the seat, breathing heavily, then less heavily, and at last, with a deep breath, she pulled herself up beside me. We sat in silence. I remembered something I'd read once. I tried to recall what it was.

"Did anything move?" I asked.

The following morning, sitting on the bench in front of the Keystone Hotel, I was assailed by unbearable guilt. Surely God

110

would strike my arm dead! At the very least He would give me a disease as my mother had warned me. I would go insane. My flesh would rot as my black soul already had begun to. I waited for lightening to pin my charred and shriveled corpse to the wall. Nothing happened. It occurred to me that I had also betrayed my girl back home, but that guilt was assuaged quickly by knowing she would never find out. I cursed Sally. It was her fault. How could she let me do such a thing? She'd seemed okay at first. But now—after she'd let me do *that*. . . . No girl had ever let me do *that* before! I resolved never to see her again.

She was waiting for me in the parking lot after that night's game. I told her.

"But why?" she said.

"It wouldn't be fair. I have a girl friend back home."

"I know," she said. "But I won't let myself think about it."

"I don't want to hurt her," I said, and, immediately I began to feel much better.

"Oh! I understand."

A few days later I was scheduled to start my second game at Cibola. It was a chance to redeem myself in the eyes of the McCook fans. I sat in the dugout after my warm-ups and waited for the game to begin. Steinecke was at home plate with the umpires and the opposing team's manager. Bill Marnie sat beside me.

"I hear you've been messing with that Sally broad."

"I might be," I said.

"Don't waste your time. She's flakey." He tapped his head with his finger.

"What do you mean?"

"You should know. She won't let anyone touch her. She thinks she's a goddamn princess or somethin'."

"Oh, you think so?" I said, and I gave him my best cat-that-swallowed-the-canary smile.

He grinned back. "I know so."

I didn't pitch much better than I had the game before. I lasted a few innings, at least, before I was tagged for two hits and began firing the ball like a madman. Finally Steinecke came out to the mound. "What a fucking exhibition!" he snapped. "Go take a shower!"

"Fuck you, too!" I stormed off the mound.

"That'll cost you," he yelled after me.

I kept walking past the dugout, through the fence, into the parking lot and beyond to the road that led to the armory. I was furious, and only after I'd walked a few minutes in the darkness did I realize what a long way I had to go. I could see the low, flat silhouette of the armory far in the distance. I passed a few houses, my spikes clicking on the sidewalk, and then the paving ended and I was on the dirt shoulder beside the road with only the crickets for company.

The houses were behind me now and I was walking between the road and a darkened field. My rage became despair as I walked, and finally self-pity. Not until I was half-way to the armory did I realize that someone was following me. I looked back and saw overhead the lights of Cibola. On the road below I saw the headlights of a car. It was about 100 yards behind me and barely moving. As I began to walk faster I heard the car drawing closer. Its headlights caught and illuminated me and then they were shining ahead of me.

"Hello," she said.

"Hi." I continued to walk, and Sally drove slowly beside me.

"How've you been?"

"Okay, and you?"

"Okay." She laughed a little, and I looked at her for an

112

instant. She was steering with one hand and leaning across the seat, facing me. Every few seconds she would glance quickly at the road and then back to me. "Can I give you a lift?"

"That's all right. I'd rather walk."

"It's a long walk."

"I don't care!" She must have taken her foot off the gas just then because the next instant I was bathed in the car's headlights. They grew fainter and fainter as I walked. I did not look back until I reached the armory. When I did the car was stopped by the side of the road, its lights still on.

That night I woke from my sleep with a thought. Why me?

Before the next night's game, I waited until Steinecke was alone in the dugout before I apologized.

"It'll still cost ya," he said, without taking his eyes off the playing field where our team was having batting practice.

"I know. I deserve it." Then I said in a rush that surprised even me, "But I don't deserve to be starting games the way I'm pitching. I know you're just starting me because I got a bonus and all."

"That's my problem."

"But I don't feel right. It's not fair. Guys like Julius aren't even getting a chance and I am."

He leaned forward and spit tobacco juice onto the wooden planks of the dugout floor. "Well, Podner, I might just agree with you there. Yessir, I might." Then he looked at me and grinned—a fat, bald, lecherous old man. "But did it ever occur to you I might not have a fucking choice in the matter?"

"Oh!" I nodded.

"So until I get different orders you will start every five days whether you deserve it or not." He watched batting practice for a few seconds, then said, "How's it feel, Podner?"

113

"What?"

"That first thought."

But I'd had another, I wanted to tell him.


I was fascinated by Bill Steinecke from the first moment I met him. I introduced myself to him and said, "You must be my coach."

"Coach, my ass," he said. "That bastard who put flowers in your hair in high school was your coach. I am your manager. Your skipper. Skip. Steinecke. Steiny. Bill, Anything, but your fucking coach." And he walked away from me.

He was right, of course. He was not like any coach I'd ever had. My high school coach led us in prayer before each game. We knelt on the ground in a circle, lowered our heads, put our hands in the center of that circle and prayed to St. Jude for victory. Steiny did not lead us in prayer. He led us in other ways. One night, sitting on the top step of the dugout, he was berating the homeplate umpire. All the while a woman fan screamed epithets at him. Steiny ignored her for a time. She cast aspersions on his manhood.

"Can't cut the mustard anymore, you old fart!"

He shouted back at her, "Not with an old piece of meat like you."

At the end of the inning he returned to the dugout bench, out of the woman's vision. He was cackling to himself. Julius, Overby, Brubaker and I thought he was mad. "That old whore!" He shook his head, as if in admiration. "Used to be one helluva lay in her day. Yessiree. But so did we all, I guess. Well, she got the change and now she's just a nasty old bitch. Don't wanna do much of anything anymore. Ha! 'Cept let you do all the work." He looked across at us, at our pink and puzzled faces, as if discovering our presence for the first time. "I don't suppose any of you know what I'm talkin' about? No,

114

I expect not. You think it's just push-push and good-bye, huh? Well, Podners, it's time you got educated. With a woman you gotta do things. Make them happy, too." And then, while we listened with rapt attention—and the opposing team loaded the bases—Bill gave us our first course in sex education. His course was very thorough, touching all the bases: physical (various positions, unusual acts), anatomical (a description of the female body); medicinal (prevention of disease), and psychological ("Make them happy, too.") It was very graphic and, at appropriate moments, punctuated by darting little gestures of his tongue, while his eyes, no bigger than Le Suer peas, gleamed.

Throughout most of each game Bill sat on the top step of the dugout, from where he could easily torment the umpires. He began the moment they walked past him toward home plate. "Hello, girls," he would say in a falsetto voice. They would look at him—skinny, pink-faced youths like ourselves—and smile weakly. Bill said it was his job to torment them. "Keeps the bastards on their toes, know what I mean?" But secretly, I think he took pleasure in it, and, in fact, viewed each game as a dramatic production that would be incomplete until he found an excuse for his entrance. When he did, when some poor 22-year-old umpire called Barry Morgan out on a close play at the plate, Bill would stand, hitch up his pants, mutter "Show time" and step out of the dugout. The McCook fans clapped and roared their approval as he waddled with agonizing slowness toward the plate. The umpire would take off his mask, his shoulders sagging, and stand there for what seemed like an eternity while Bill, a crusty old rhino, took his sweet time amid the fan's growing cheers.

"Now, Bill! Don't get hot! You know . . ."

But it was no use. The umpire's logic and even his person were superfluous to Bill's performance. The umpire was needed only as a playwright sometimes needs a butler—"Madame, the Archduke." Once Bill had made his entrance, the umpire, like the butler, might just as well have vanished. Since he didn't, Bill used him as a foil.

Bill's monologue began rationally enough, with him explaining in pantomine (elaborate gestures of the arms) and using the simplest logic (which even such a dunce as this umpire could understand) how Barry Morgan had successfully evaded the catcher's tag. Eventually, of course, Bill would have to become indignant when the umpire did not accept his account of the play. Bill's eyes bulged in disbelief. His face bloated. He cursed the umpire's ancestory, expressing some doubt, at first, that he had any, but then deciding it was surely of the foulest kind—horse thieves and highwaymen and ladies of the night. His rage spent, Bill turned his back to the umpire, banished him to the wings and, with outspread arms, addressed the audience behind the homeplate screen. They cheered his every word and gesture. The umpire, relieved that his ordeal was past, stooped over to dust off the plate. He bent low to the ground, his tail to the wind. So flustered was he that he forgot to face the home-plate fans (as he had so recently been taught in umpire's school) and, instead, was facing the centerfield fence. Bill turned instinctively back to his victim and pointed to his upraised rump. The fans laughed uproariously. Bill shook his head in disgust, and with just a bit of pity, and then left the stage.

One night in Grand Island, the fans behind home plate interrupted his monologue with a shower of popcorn, beer, boxes, cups and hot dog remnants. Bill did not flinch, but turned toward our dugout and exited with the greatest dignity. Debris rained down upon him. Once inside, his eyes glistened with pleasure. "Gave them fuckers their money's worth, didn't I?" After that game, as we walked across the parking lot to our

116

dressing room, the Grand Island fans tried to run us down with their cars and trucks.

Needless to say, I worshiped Bill Steinecke. I spent hours learning how to chew tobacco without getting sick. I cursed the umpires, called Julius "Podner," would do anything Bill asked. But he asked nothing. He demanded nothing, explained nothing (other than sex). He assumed all. When I figured out the real reason for his starting me every five days, he did not congratulate me on my perception as I'd expected. I should have had it sooner. An adult would have. He was the first adult ever to treat me as an equal. Whether I was or not seemed no concern of his. That was my problem. What he assumed at the time was often vague to me. I struggled to discover what it was, wondered if that was not his intent.

"Is your arm sore?"

"No."

"Can you throw about 10 minutes of batting practice?"

"Sure, Skip."

No matter how much I grimaced on that mound, clutched my aching arm, indicated to him that I was pitching in pain, for him, for his admiration (and pity, too), he ignored me. After 10 minutes he sent in another pitcher. He did not ask how my arm was. He assumed it was fine. So the next time he asked me such a question, I answered truthfully. Still I got nothing for it.

"Did you do your running today?"

"No. Should I?"

"It's up to you."

Perhaps I am giving Bill more credit than he deserves, that in retrospect I am imparting to his indifference intents and reasons he never had. Possibly, as I've always felt of W. C. Fields, he really did hate dogs and little children and wondered to his dying day, why the laughter? Whichever is true, the effect on me then and now remains the same.

I pitched well for the rest of the season. I won my next game 4–3 (at Cibola, finally) and, even though I lost the one after that in Kearney, I pitched a beautiful game. I was leading 1–0 in the bottom of the ninth inning. A walk and an error put runners on second and third with two outs. I induced the next batter to loft a routine fly ball to Ken Cullum in center field. I started off the mound, but saw Cullum circling the ball oddly. He staggered, and the ball dropped at his feet. He picked it up and threw it over Ron Hunt's head at third base, and both runners scored. When Cullum reached the dugout, his face had a pixie smile and I knew he was drunk.

My mound opponent that night in Kearney was a chunky righthander named Jim Bouton. He was only one of a number of players in the Nebraska State League who would achieve fame in the majors—and, in Bouton's case, beyond. Bill Hands, once a 20-game winner with the Chicago Cubs, was, in 1959, a seldom-used pitcher for the Hastings Giants. Duke Simms, who helped the Detroit Tigers reach the 1972 American League play-offs, was a second-string catcher with the North Platte Indians. José Santiago pitched for the Grand Island A's and Al Weiss played second base for the Holdrege White Six. These future major leaguers were far from the most talented players in the NSL in 1959, however. In fact, Bouton was the fifth fastest pitcher on the Kearney Yankee team. He was surpassed by Hub King, Ralph Scorca, Jack DePalo and Jim Lasko. They all looked as if they had brighter futures than Bouton, but none ever reached the major leagues. Al Weiss, a .200 hitter in 1959, played in the majors for over 10 years, while Woody Huyke, who led the NSL in home runs and RBIs and

118

batted over .300, never reached the majors and, in fact, at 35, is presently a second-string catcher with the Sherbrook Pirates in the Double-A Eastern League.

At the time, the most talented player in the NSL was a tall, handsome, light-skinned black named Jim Hicks. He could do everything well—run, hit with power, throw, field—and do it all with uncommon grace. He once played basketball for the Harlem Globetrotters and looked as if he could master any sport within minutes. He led the league in almost every hitting department during the first month of the season. Then one night some pitcher threw a fastball at his head and Hicks ducked a little too soon. Word spread through the league. Everyone took a shot at him. His average dipped below .400. I remember sitting in the dugout one night and watching as he rapped out three hits against our best pitcher. When he came to bat in the ninth inning of the hopelessly lost game, Steinecke brought in Julius to pitch to him. When Hicks stepped into the batter's box, Steinecke yelled, "Give him a little pierce arrow, Podner." Julius's first pitch caught Hicks on the ankle. He limped toward first base, could not make it (he'd already stolen two bases against our catcher) and was taken out of the game. "That'll slow the bastard down a little," said Bill. Hicks finished the year with a batting average below .300.

Despite the presence of such talent on other teams, the McCook Braves had the most talent of all. Bill Marnie pitched so well for us that he was promoted to a Class C league in mid-season, and Paul Chenger was eventually voted MVP. Dennis Overby won the league's strikeout crown with ease, and Phil Niekro was far and away the best relief pitcher. The rest of our team had almost as much ability and, at times, it seemed that Bruce Brubaker and myself alone, of all the bonus players, made only modest contributions to the success of the Braves.

We assumed the league lead in mid-July and by the first week of August had an even firmer grasp on it. We eventually won the NSL title.

Julius French was given his unconditional release in August, a few days before his $10,000 contingent bonus was due. He had pitched sporadically and then only indifferently. He *seemed* to be a major league prospect but, to the Braves, not worth the money they would have to pay to find out for certain. If the decision had been Steinecke's, he would have kept Julius. But Steiny had little say in the matter. Julius did not get a cent from his hypothetical bonus, except for the money he'd been paid as a salary. I learned of his release when I arrived at the armory one afternoon. He'd left McCook without saying good-bye. I was glad. I don't like good-byes, never have. I distrust the emotions that rise from them, which are magnified and distorted by them. This indeed had been the basis for our brief friendship. We both distrusted emotion, saw in its external show hints of false sentiments.

I never heard from Julius again, though I saw his name once —on the roster of a Triple-A team in the Cleveland Indian organization.

Julius French was not the only player to vanish suddenly that August. Dave Breshnahan, our freckle-faced relief pitcher and reader of erotic love letters, disappeared even more mysteriously. One day, after the team cuts had been made, he was gone. None of his roommates—Niekro, Derr, Overby, Orlikowski—would admit to any knowledge of his disappearance, beyond saying that Breshnahan had not been released. It wasn't until 12 years later that Niekro, then a star with the Atlanta Braves, revealed the reasons behind Breshnahan's disappearance. It seems at McCook, the personable redhead had organized games of nickle-and-dime poker with his room-

120

mates. He always won—10, 15, 20 dollars a night. He won every night for a month and none of his roommates grew suspicious—surely, they were the most trusting gamblers in all Christendom. One evening, Breshnahan won three consecutive hands by virtue of his possessing the ace of spades. A strange coincidence, thought Niekro, and he counted the deck of cards before dealing the next hand. The ace of spades was missing. Niekro asked everyone to stand up and look for it. They found it under Breshnahan's left thigh. Niekro's roommates wanted to banish Breshnahan from their house forthwith, but Niekro pleaded Breshnahan's case. "It was too late at night for him to find a place to sleep," said Phil. His roommates grudgingly let the culprit stay the night, after they had herded him, the black sheep, into his bedroom and locked the door.

"Later that night in bed," said Niekro, "I remembered that Davey kept a gun under his pillow. He was always showing it to us and bragging about his marksmanship. I couldn't sleep at all. I kept waiting for him to come blasting into my bedroom before wiping out the rest of the household. But he didn't. The next morning he packed his things and left McCook. We all made a vow not to tell anyone what had happened."

Without Julius during those final weeks, I was left to my own devices—drugstores and pool and the bench in front of the Keystone. I saw my teammates only during the games and occasionally, by accident, downtown. Ron Hunt and I seldom spoke anymore. We passed each other with faint nods as we entered or left Mom's house. Our final break had come over my brief friendship with Sally. "I thought you had a girl friend back home?" he said. "So what?" I said. But I was shamed by his faithfulness to his girl. She was more than that, he said, she was his fiancée. He missed *her* a lot, he said. She must have missed him a lot, too, because one day she surprised him with a visit to McCook. That first evening as the engaged couple drove through town a car forced them off the road. The car was driven by one of the blond waitresses at Modrells, who, it seemed, had been sharing Ron's affections these many weeks. The thought of the following scene, how it must have played out, more than sustained me during the final weeks of the season.

Walking home from the armory one night, I was given a ride by a 21-year-old Mexican named Anthony. I never learned his last name. He was short and fat with black shiny hair and a tan complexion. He spoke with a lisp. He knew little about baseball, seemed to have no interest in it. Yet he contented himself with picking me up after each game and commiserating with me over my pitching as we drove the town's streets until early in the morning. We drank beer, which he bought, and he taught me certain Spanish words that I should never use in mixed company, he warned. We laughed. He was unlike any friend I'd ever had. We had little in common. He was much more intelligent than I and, I realize now, possessed an adult sensitivity. He was repulsed by my crude talk (in imitation of Steinecke), and yet he often tried to imitate it, to curse and swear, it seemed, for my benefit alone. But the effort pained him. I liked him well enough, as one likes someone who does them small favors, but I never thought about him, never once wondered why he shared his beer and time with such a dull, single-minded youth as myself. The depths of his loneliness escaped me then. We often drove the streets in long silences (we had nothing really to say to one another), during which I would gaze blankly out the window and think of home or my pitching. When I woke from these reveries and turned toward him, saw him sitting behind the wheel, his small feet barely reaching the pedals, I sometimes caught him looking at me. He

122

would then turn immediately back to the road and, flustered, make one of his infrequent coarse comments, at which I would laugh and be distracted from what I had just seen.

It was because of Anthony that Sally and I were reunited two days before I left McCook. I had mentioned her name to him a few times, hinted crudely at our intimacy, and he said he knew her. Then, one night when he picked me up at the armory, she was sitting in the front seat beside him. It surprised me—how glad I was to see her. I wondered why. She was very nervous when I got in beside her. "I hope you don't mind," she said. "I wanted to say good-bye." I put my arm around her and she put her head on my shoulder and smiled. Anthony drove us through the darkest of the city streets and, while he did, we kissed—the three of us sitting in the front seat, Sally between us, Anthony drinking beer while he drove. At one point, as I was kissing Sally, I looked across and saw him staring intently at the road ahead. Sweat glistened on his forehead, which shone white as we passed under a street lamp. His eyes never left the road. The can of beer was resting on the seat between his legs. He picked it up, took a long swallow and, still without taking his eyes from the road, replaced it.

We would end the season with a game in Kearney, and from there I would fly to Omaha and then home. Before I left with the team I called Sally.

"Meet me in Kearney," I said. "We can stay the night there."

She said she couldn't. Her mother was too sick for her to leave even for a day. Then she was silent for a long moment.

"I think I'm in trouble," she said finally.

"What?"

"It's been two weeks," she said. "You know . . . since I should have gotten it . . ."

I was stunned, unwilling to believe her. "Are you sure?"

123

"Pretty sure."

My only thought was to escape. To get off that telephone, onto the team bus and as far away from her as possible. Then it would all vanish like the bad dream it was. I knew, now, what she had wanted from me. She wanted to use me to escape McCook. She wanted my bonus. She wanted to ruin my career. My future. My life.

"That's impossible," I said. "It can't be."

She didn't answer right away, and then she said, "Maybe you're right."

I finished that first season with a 3–3 record and a 3.54 earned run average. I gave up 41 hits in 56 innings. I walked 55 batters and struck out 56. I obtained these statistics from a back copy of *The Sporting News*. I'd forgotten them. I'd forgotten much about those games, which, at the time, were so important to me. Small fragments, like the hailstones in Holdrege, they have melted in the warm waters of my memory. There are some fragments, however, that have not melted but have surfaced, hard and cold and sharp, from my subconscious. They seldom concern those games ("my only reality"), but deal instead with all that "dead time" I passed in McCook. These float about, knocking against one another in a disturbing way, until two at length fit together to form a larger piece and, repeating that process, a still larger one, until they have taken on a shape I now can recognize.

I called Sally a month ago. It had been almost 14 years since our last conversation. I'd gotten the telephone number from a relative of hers who still lives in McCook, and then, for days, I stared at it on the desk in my attic room. Downstairs, my wife of 12 years was moving through her day, making breakfast for our five children, cleaning the house, preparing lunch, while I sat transfixed by that accusing number. Finally, I dialed it. A woman answered. I asked for Sally by her maiden name.

"This is she," she said, adding that now she was Mrs.—and I did not catch the last name. I told her who I was, and then blurted out that she would not remember me probably, that it was stupid of me to call, after all these years, I'd had a whim, and so . . .

"Yes, I remember," she said. "How are you?"

We talked for a while. I was nervous, laughed a lot, spoke quickly in a loud voice. She seemed strangely calm, assured even, as if she had been waiting for this second call all those years.

She told me she had married shortly after I left McCook. Her husband sold farm equipment. They moved from one small town in Nebraska to another and were now living in a town even smaller than McCook. "I'll never escape small towns, I guess," and she laughed. I wondered what she looked like now, at 31. I tried to remember but saw only a broad white forehead.

"Do you remember Anthony?" I asked. "The Mexican fella? What was his last name?"

"Oh, yes," she said. "He was a nice person. I never knew his last name, either. He wasn't part of our group, really. I knew him only in that casual way everyone in a small town knows everyone else. But, yes, he was such a nice person."

I reminded her of the night I had gotten drunk, the first time I had ever been drunk, and how she had taken care of me and I had never thanked her. I remembered, too, the night in the drive-in, but said nothing about it. "It's so embarrassing to remember such things," I said. "To remember what a fool I was. Why did you bother?"

"You weren't so bad," she said. "We were all foolish at that age, weren't we? I don't remember it being as bad as you do. In fact, I miss those days. It's hard sometimes living in such a small town as we do now. I won't ever get used to it. I reminisce a lot. It passes the time. Sometimes I wish I could go back to those days. They were exciting—for me, at least."

"They were horrible days for me," I said. "I don't remember much of anything nice about them. That's why I called. You were one of the few people in McCook I remember fondly."

"Really! I'm glad." Then she asked how many children I had. She knew I was married, of course. Our generation always married.

"I have five. And you?"

"Three."

"That's great." There was nothing else to say. There was an awkward silence during which I tried to think of some way to say good-bye. Her suddenly flat voice intruded upon my thoughts.

"We have a daughter," she said. She paused a moment, as if, for a second time, waiting for me to respond. I said nothing, wondered curiously why she did not mention her other children. "Our daughter will be 13 years old soon."

# ...4

I AWOKE to the first light of day and the chill from the mist that had moved in from the swamp during the night and bound the camp, like a mummy, in its gray and gauzy embrace. The mist hovered low to the ground. From my window in one of the wooden barracks, I could see over the low-lying mist to the line of trees that marked the beginning of the swamp 100 yards away. The mist wove between the trunks of the trees, which seemed, now, to be growing directly up from it. They were mostly tall pines and weeping cottonwoods with thin, tentacle-like limbs that drooped earthward and disappeared in the mist. The cottonwoods were draped with a filmy gray moss that hung from their limbs like cobwebs from an eerie corpse. Through the spaces betwen the tree trunks appeared shafts of sunlight that fanned out across the open space separating the swamp from the camp. The shafts faded and dissolved in the mist before they reached the ground. Soon the heat from that sunlight would loosen the bonds of the mist and it would evaporate, and the camp would begin to stir. But now, at six o'clock in the morning, nothing stirred, and the only signs of life came from the swamp beyond the trees, where I could hear the caws of strange birds and the slap of alligators' tails as they woke from the mud in which they had slept.

The Milwaukee Braves' minor league spring training camp was located at the edge of the Okefenokee Swamp on the outskirts of Waycross, Georgia, a town of about 20,000 people in the southeastern corner of the state. The camp was one-half mile square and completely surrounded by swamp. It contained nine wooden buildings, five baseball diamonds and a cylindrical brick rotunda that stood in the midst of the diamonds. The rotunda, which resembled a giant rook chess piece, was 15 feet in diameter and two stories high. Its roof was flat, and around its perimeter were numerous deck chairs. These chairs faced out over the diamonds below. And each diamond fanned out from the rotunda like petals of a flower. The home plates were closest to the rotunda (each about 20 yards from it), and all but one of the outfield fences marked the beginning of the swamp.

The rotunda was the tallest building in camp, and from its top one could see everywhere in the camp. Several hundred yards north was a large wooden building that served as both the dressing room and trainer's room for the camp's 250 to 300 players. A thin tar road ran alongside of that building and eventually snaked through the swamp to the highway that led to Waycross, 10 miles away. Across the road from the dressing room was an open space dotted with a few pine trees, where players who had brought their cars could park them. Next to this parking lot was a second large wooden structure that served as the recreation room for the players and headquarters for all the scouts, coaches, managers and front-office personnel.

Fifty yards or so farther north were the six Army-type barracks where everyone slept. All the barracks looked identical: long, narrow, wooden buildings that resembled old covered bridges. Each barrack was parallel to the next with about ten yards between them, so that from above they looked like six Roman numeral ones side by side. All six were perpendicular to the main office building. The coaches, scouts, managers and front-office people slept in the first barrack; the white American players slept in the next three; the Spanish-speaking players in the fifth; and the black players in the sixth barrack closest to the swamp. North of the barracks by about 20 yards was the small boxy cafeteria. Behind it the swamp began. The cafeteria had a tightly hinged screen door, as did all the buildings in camp, and each long day was punctuated by a thousand slaps of those screens springing back.

I'd begun my first spring training in 1960 with the Milwaukee Braves' most prestigious minor league team, the Louisville Colonels of the Triple-A American Association. The Colonels trained at a small, neat park across the street from the more elaborate stadium used by the Braves in Bradenton, Florida. At the time, Bradenton was a small resort town on the Gulf Coast, which, like St. Petersburg to the north, was inhabited by many an old Yankee who had retired in the sun. The town's streets were washed each morning, and its buildings seemed all white or pink stucco. It was a quiet town of carefully fabricated but somnambulant activity—shuffleboard tournaments and softball games in which the aging competitors never wore shirts and whose skin was brown and slack like familiar leather. Bradenton came to life only in the spring with the arrival of the Milwaukee Braves (the Colonels were only incidental) and their host of sportswriters, broadcasters and such minor celebrities as Joe Garagiola. The town bulged with this spring-training crowd (white loafers and pale skins), and the town's citizens sat on the benches that lined the sidewalks (always the same bench, *their* bench) and pointed out to one another the players and celebrities as they walked by.

I had my own hotel room, for which the Colonels paid $25

129

a day in-season (out-of-season it was half that). The pink stucco hotel was surrounded by palm trees, the first I'd ever seen, and tropical plants with gigantic leaves that looked artificial. I was given $15 a day for meals and other expenses, and I spent most of that on Banlon jerseys of every possible hue and a pair of lemon-colored slacks I was too embarrassed to wear.

During those early weeks of spring training the Colonels comprised young prospects like myself and older veterans who'd played their last three years at Louisville and had abandoned all hope of ever making that short walk across the street. Among the veterans was Ed Charles, a black third baseman in his late twenties. Charles, surprisingly enough, would one day reach the major leagues and star for the New York Mets in the 1969 World Series. He seemed incredibly old to me then (1960). He had a few wiry strands of gray hair, which I assumed revealed him to be much older than he admitted. (My father once told me that the only way you can tell the true age of a black man is by his hair.) Charles shared the hotel room next to mine. His roommate, a veteran infielder with a thick body, an unintelligible southern drawl and a face like a bloodhound, was Jack Litrell. Litrell, who was white, had played briefly in the majors and now at 31 was beginning his fourth straight year in the minors, from where he would never escape. They were an odd couple. They never slept. As I lay in my bed I could hear the two men talking, drinking, swapping hunting stories through the night. Always at about 3 A.M. Charles, sitting on the edge of his bed, would raise his favorite shotgun, take quick aim at a vanishing covey of quail and blast them out of the air, while Litrell, imitating his favorite hound dog—Ole Blue— howled.

I stayed with the Colonels until the Braves made their first roster cuts. Those players then walked across the street to the Colonels' camp, and all rookies like myself were promptly

130

shipped by train to Waycross, Georgia.* At the time I had pitched only two undistinguished innings (one earned run, three walks) in an intra-squad game but still believed the Braves had glimpsed something in my performance at McCook, which, although it had escaped even me, had convinced them I should play at Louisville in 1960. What I did not know then, but learned later, was that it was the policy of most major league organizations to give their young prospects a taste of life at the top (or, in my case, almost the top) during at least one spring training, so that upon seeing such minor league camps as Waycross they would be inspired to a level of play that would guarantee their never returning to Waycross.

Furthermore, professional baseball clubs; unlike most employers, believed that young prospects should be started at the top of their profession each spring and be allowed to sink to the true level of their ability. Seldom did a player finish the season with as prestigious a team as he had started with. It was not uncommon, in fact, for a player to begin spring training with a major league team and, by dint of inefficiency, work his way down until he finished the season with a Class D team. Each drop was mildly traumatic for such players and often produced a confusion and panic that affected their performance in a way that guaranteed a concomitant drop. Often an organization knew precisely at what level a prospect would play the season but kept this knowledge from him, so that his anxiety mounted unnecessarily as he sunk daily in the system.

• • •

*Every time a major league team made a roster cut, whether in the spring or during the season, the repercussions were felt throughout the minor league system. Each minor league team would then cut its roster. Players at Louisville would go to Austin (AA), and those at Austin to Jacksonville (A), and so on all the way down to Davenport (D). Players cut from Davenport went home.

I lay shivering beneath the cold sheets of my cot in the third barracks at Waycross. All around me, other players slept and snored fitfully. The cots, spaced only a few feet apart, were lined up perpendicular to both walls so that from my cot I was looking directly at the feet of the player on the opposite side of the room. The room was long and narrow, with about 20 cots against each wall. In the middle of the room was a picnic table with benches on either side, and an old electric heater that was turned on each morning by the first player to wake from the chill. At one end was a screen door leading outside to the cafeteria; at the other end were two partitions on either side of a narrow hallway. Immediately behind these were a few sinks, a long stained urinal and three open-stalled toilets. The stalls were littered with pages from *The Sporting News* and *Playboy* centerfolds. Further down the hall were four small private rooms. Each room was occupied by a veteran player— one who had returned to Waycross for two or more years without having been invited to the major league camp at Bradenton. Such players were accorded many small privileges, and having their own room was one of them.

In 1960 I was in my first spring training, and the thought that someday I might receive such preferential treatment filled me with pleasurable anticipation. When I finally did return to Waycross for the second straight year, I too was given my own cubicle. And, like those veterans I had envied, I too hooked up my elaborate stereo system and saw in the eyes of the younger players who slept in the open end of the barracks the look of envy as they passed *my* room. But by then I took no pleasure from that room, the meager compensation for my stalled and fading career. I soon hated it, saw it for what it was—a cell, the "Cancer Ward" in which I'd been quarantined so as not

132

to contaminate those younger players with my incurable failure.

I got out of bed and turned on the electric heater. From the center of the room I could see down the hallway where two players, wearing only shorts, were studying the bulletin board hanging from the wall. Every morning before daylight one of the scouts would pin to that board several sheets of colored paper. On each sheet was typed the name of one of the camp's minor league managers—Al Monchak, Red Murf, Joe Brown, Billy Smith, Travis Jackson, Bill Steinecke—and below it, in two neat columns, the players assigned to him for the day's games. The players shifted from manager to manager during the course of spring training. The manager under whose name you appeared on the last day of spring training would be the manager with whom you'd begin the season. At Waycross there was no mention of the teams those managers would lead during the season, but everyone knew that Monchak managed Austin of the Double-A Texas League and Murf managed Jacksonville of the Class A Sally League and Brown managed Cedar Rapids of the Class B Three-I League and Smith managed Boise of the Class C Pioneer League and Jackson managed Davenport of the Class D Midwest League and this year Bill Steinecke would manage Eau Claire of the Class C Northern League. Small tragedies were played out in the minds of players as they scanned the board for their names. Each day their fortunes rose and fell like those of small firms on a stock exchange whose entire future could be read in the morning's quotation. .

The players whose careers were shakiest always woke first. They went immediately to the bulletin board and looked for that pink sheet at the top of which was typed the following: "Will the players listed below please report to Mr. Cecil's office

133

before nine o'clock this morning." Richard Cecil, a husky blond man in his late twenties, was the Braves' executive whose task it was each morning to hand out unconditional releases. It was an unpleasant job over which he had no control. The future of those players had been decided the night before by a vote of all the scouts, coaches and managers in camp, and Dick Cecil was merely the functionary who, the following morning, would slide a piece of paper across his desk and ask the released player to please sign his name thus formally terminating his association with the Milwaukee Braves baseball club. Some refused, as if they could retain their career by simply refusing to sign the document that ended it. Some signed in stunned silence; others cried, begged, pleaded for another chance; and still others departed like the father of Dylan Thomas, cursing, raging, and, in a final act of defiance, crumpling their release and flinging it back into Dick Cecil's face. But that was just bravado, theater for the satisfaction of their pride. Their true feelings had already been revealed at the moment when they read their names on that bulletin board at six o'clock in the morning. They moved then like sleepwalkers back to their cots and sat on them for long moments. Next they looked around the room to see if anyone was watching. I was always awake by then, but when they glanced my way I pretended sleep, and, through one half-closed eye, observed their ritual.

They slid their suitcases out from underneath their cot and filled them quickly with their belongings, the small space around their cot suddenly bare and soon to be filled by the belongings of some new player in camp. They moved in quick silence so as not to wake any of the others, who would then be witness to their humiliation. Finished, they got dressed, glanced about the room and left. They let the screen door close with great care. And then, without saying good-bye to anyone,

134

often without even picking up their official release from Dick Cecil, they drove home.

Once home they faced interminable interrogation. What had happened? They explained. The manager, a sore arm, no batting practice. Some lied: They'd quit. After a week or so the questions withered, expired, and they began to forget. They picked up the branches of their common lives—took a job in a gas station, became engaged to their steady girl, forgot boyish dreams. Then one day about a month after they had returned, they received a registered letter. The envelope was adorned with a savage Indian. They fingered their unconditional release, stared at it, their day ruined, possibly the week, forced now to abandon the false spring of their new lives and begin again.

With time they would discover that their experience had marked them off from their contemporaries, who, no matter how talented, had never gone to spring training, never, even for a week, been a professional athlete. It was as if they'd been privy to a vision, had been blessed with a divine grace that would always remain a mystery to the unblessed. They learned to play to this grace, to build myths around their experience, which, to them, had been no big thing at the time. They had seen no mysteries. But they never let on. They even took pleasure in the manner in which their town's sports-wise people now referred to them. "He was the boy who went away." Vague, yet oddly precise. The boy who went away. That was all anyone knew. He'd gone away and then come back, and whatever had occurred in between, only he knew. It elevated him. He floated on a cloud now, above his contemporaries whose talents would forever be suspect because they had not gone away. Of those contemporaries, people said, "He was good. The best around. But who knows for sure. He never went away." Implied was a flaw in their talent, which, unseen by

135

familiar eyes, had been all too glaring to the scouts who had rejected them. Of course, some of those contemporaries had rejected the scouts, had declined offers to go away. They had preferred to end their careers in high school or college rather than gamble for a far riskier but more gratifying success. So they simply stopped playing the game, hoarded their small winnings and saw them devalued with the years. When they eventually realized their mistake, the enormity of it (for an athlete anyway), it was too late. For in trying to preserve their small successes untainted by failure, they had tainted not only those successes, not only others' memories of their talent, but also their very own character. They lacked courage. Everyone had seen it. They had been so afraid of losing that they had lost more than any of those athletes who had gone away and been released and had come back home. Now they knew the nature of that divine grace they would never possess.

Those who had gone away had learned, many for the first time, how to lose. And what they'd lost was the first, the purest and the most precious dream they would ever have. They'd lost perpetual youth, innocence, the dream of playing a little boys' game for the rest of their lives. In their minds no dream would ever equal that, and so no future loss would ever affect them in the way that first one had. When they returned home, then, it was with an indifference to loss and with the grace to shrug off defeat in a way those who never challenged that dream could never do.

But such thoughts, fears really, of being given an unconditional release were not of my world in 1960. Those things, like accidents, happened only to others: those without talent, without youth, without bonuses or with irreparable injuries that made them pale images of their former selves. Still, I checked the bulletin board every morning. All of us did—all, that is, except those 18-year-old kids who had been given a one-way

136

bus ticket to Waycross (they would pay their own way home), where they signed a blank contract which, they were promised, would be filled out at the end of the spring, "after you've showed your stuff," the scouts said.

They all looked alike. They all arrived with a pair of spikes with plaid laces and a baggy gray sweatshirt with the name of their high school stenciled across the front. They gravitated to their kind and were indistinguishable one from another, so that all the coaches and managers and scouts called them "Red" or "Lefty" or "Stud," and when they did, more than one head turned in response. Few of them ever made a club, and their contracts, which were just kept in a drawer in Dick Cecil's office, were never filled out. At the end of each spring Cecil would take these contracts from the drawer, pull out 1 or 2 from 60, and after stacking the rest in a neat pile thick as a telephone book, rip them in half and drop them in his wastebasket.

Most of those boys never expected to make a team in the first place. That wasn't why they'd come. Their trip to Waycross was a spring vacation in the sun. They treated it as such, walking shirtless about camp so as to get a good tan. In general they treated their experience without the fear and reverence the rest of us did. They broke camp rules, drank beer in their barracks, played practical jokes on one another and were so loud and obnoxious that they were a nuisance to all of us serious athletes. Secretly I envied their indifference, the freedom it gave them.

Breakfast was served from 7 to 8 A.M. I ate early. As I walked toward the cafeteria my ankles were brushed by the tall grass still cool and wet from the mist that had blanketed the camp but now, at seven o'clock, had already dissolved in the warm sunlight, whose heat would soon be oppressive. To my right,

137

far down the road that cut through the swamp, I could see black women moving singly and in pairs toward the camp. They walked on the side of the road close to the swamp. Their faces from a distance, looked like black plums. They looked incredibly black in shapeless white cotton dresses that reached almost to their ankles. They carried their lunches in brown bags and walked erectly so as not to topple the large bundles— brightly colored kerchieves filled with laundry—balanced on top of their heads. Throughout the day those women moved about the camp. They swept floors, made beds, scrubbed toilets, dispensed food, hovered, dark shadows around our illuminated lives.

The cafeteria was a small, square room with picnic tables and benches on either side of an aisle that led to an open kitchen. It was almost deserted this early in the morning. A few managers sat at one bench nursing mugs of coffee. Farm boys in their youth, they would never shake the habit of early rising. I nodded solemnly as I passed. Who knew me? At another bench sat some of the camp's Spanish-speaking players. (That's how players from Central and South America are always referred to in professional baseball circles.) Like the managers, they were used to rising with the sun. In their native lands many of them spent all the daylight hours cutting sugarcane and would be there still, in the hot fields, if one day a scout in a shimmering aqua suit had not offered them $125 a month to play baseball in the States. Life at Waycross was idyllic for them. They ate two and three helpings of each meal. I remember watching one morning in fascination as Rico Carty, a massive black figure from a Communist mural of the thirties, heaped food on his tin tray, deposited it on a table and returned to the kitchen for three glasses of Kool-Aid. He lined up the three glasses in front of his tray—grape, lime, orange—and, satisfied, began to eat. He never drank from those glasses, but with each forkful of

138

food, looked up and smiled at their beauty.

Black women ladled out food from huge rectangular aluminum pans. The food was plentiful but, except for a strong hint of aluminum, tasteless. Hot and cold cereal. Limp pancakes. Toast piled in a heap so that the heat from the top slices turned the lower slices soggy. Sausage patties made of God knows what. Bacon that had been cooked the night before and reheated in the morning. And eggs. I always asked for my eggs sunnyside up and happily endured the extra wait as they were cooked to order. The scrambled eggs had already been cooked, and they lay, watery, in one of the pans. My father had always warned me against scrambled eggs in strange restaurants. They would be powdered, he said. But with what? There was also a rumor in camp that the scrambled eggs had been liberally sprinkled with saltpeter. To channel our ardor solely toward a love of the game, I suppose.

Someone must have decided that too many players were avoiding the scrambled eggs, must have glimpsed too many bulging crotches, because one morning when we tried to leave the cafeteria we were stopped at the door by a scout who ordered us to the cafeteria's back room. Inside, a fat man sat on a stool, his legs spread apart. He had a pencil-thin flashlight in his hand. He motioned me to him. His face was level with my belt. "Drop 'em," he said. He examined me with his flashlight, found no signs of venereal disease (which I was sure I had acquired in McCook) and sent me out the back door. "Next!" I heard him call.

Outside I breathed a sigh of relief. From all the barracks I saw groups of players approaching the cafeteria. I wanted to warn them, but I said nothing. I walked toward the recreation building and saw Lois Steinecke. She was one of the few women who ever visited the camp, the others being wives of Milwaukee executives such as Roland Hemmond, the assistant

139

farm director. Lois often came for breakfast and then strolled aimlessly about camp. In the afternoon she drifted over to the diamonds (the recipient of a hundred lustful glances), watched an inning of the game on diamond one, a few innings on diamond two, stopped to chat with a manager, who rose, grinning, and offered his chair in the shade of the rotunda.

Walking toward me now, Lois looked beautiful. (McCook was six months ago.) Well tanned, she wore a large, floppy-brimmed hat, dark glasses and a silk dress. The dress was orange with white polka dots. It was cut low in front and revealed her ample bosom, which, at that moment, aroused me. She wore no stockings. Her brown legs were lean and faintly muscled. My heart pounded as she drew near, and then, flashing before my eyes, was the doctor. "Drop 'em!" Lois knew! She had seen me come out the back door! She stopped in front of me, smiled. "Hi, Pat!" I mumbled something without pausing to look at her and walked on. A few seconds later I heard the slap of a screen door, and when I glanced back she was gone. Were we destined only to meet at such moments, the albatross of shame hanging from my ego? Would we never pass at a moment when, in complete control and despite the difference in our ages (18 and 22), I could toss off some witty remark at which she would laugh, laying her hand on my forearm?

Morning workouts began at 8:30. I passed the time between breakfast and then in the main building where most of the players congregated. This building had one large open room (the players' recreation room) and a number of private offices. No matter how early I arrived, someone was always playing a fierce game of Ping-Pong. We were united, if at all, it seems, by a compulsion to compete and win. A fiercely contested victory in Ping-Pong was compensation, no matter how slight, for a miserable performance on the diamond the day before.

140

Some players sat in the tattered and faded armchairs and read letters from home, others wrote letters, talked, did nothing. There was a television set in one corner of the room. Twelve card-table chairs faced it. A few minutes before eight each morning, the players would scramble for one of those chairs. Those who were unsuccessful stood behind the chairs, and then we all waited expectantly until at precisely at eight o'clock, Debbie Drake, wearing black tights, appeared on the screen. Our eyes were red and half-lidded with sleep, our bones ached from the previous day's workout, our stomachs were filled with too many scrambled eggs, and yet nothing could dissuade us from watching Debbie Drake twist and stretch her supple body at eight o'clock in the morning. Occasionally, during a particularly interesting maneuver—Debbie flings her arms wide, thrusts out her chest and exhorts the nation's housewives to "breath deeply" (would my wife ever breath *that* deeply, I wondered?)—there would come from our number a universal sigh.

Only the veteran players bypassed Debbie Drake. They had already stood in front of that television set for more years than they cared to remember. They preferred, instead, to play contemplative games of bridge at a small card table at the other end of the room. They assumed the same chairs each morning —Archie White in the big easy chair near the window, Dave Eilers in the other stuffed chair, Mike Fandozzi in the small deck chair facing the TV, Bobby Stoiko in a folding chair across from Fandozzi. They wore backless slippers and white socks, pajama bottoms and flannel shirts. They smoked pipes mostly, occasionally cigars. They were in their late twenties and early thirties, married, with children. They no longer expected an invitation to Bradenton but contented themselves with their springs in Waycross and summers at Jacksonville or Cedar Rapids. They were organization men who often served as coaches, too, and who waited patiently for an offer from the Braves to manage someday (Fandozzi would be my manager at Palatka in 1961), or to scout or to cash in on their seniority in some other way. Outside in the parking lot it was easy to spot their cars. They drove station wagons already packed to the rafters with utensils and boxes of goods they would need once their wives and children joined them at Cedar Rapids. They often talked of gas mileage, the advantages of a new Corvair, and looked with disdain on the young bonus players who went to the parking lot early each morning to wipe the morning mist and the sap from the pine trees off their new convertibles.

The locker room across the road from the parking lot was built in the shape of a capital I. The black and Spanish-speaking players dressed at one end of the I, the white players at the other end. The trainer's room was the stem in between. The floor and walls of the dressing room were concrete. The floor was littered with chunks of red clay dislodged from hundreds of pairs of spikes. The walls perspired. The entire room was dark and cold and damp, and it smelled of sweat and mildew from the hundreds of sweatshirts and uniforms hanging up to dry in narrow stalls. They never dried. And when you put them on each morning they were cold and seemed even damper than when you'd taken them off. The uniforms were not hand-me-downs from the Braves, just cheap, gray practice uniforms that never fit. The shirts billowed like sails and the pants like harem pants. Each player was given a number to sew on the back of his shirt. The numbers ran as high as the number of players in camp. There was something quite humbling about dressing into a shirt with 299 on its back.

As many as 200 players might be dressing in that locker room at any given time each morning. The room was so crowded, with jocks and sweatshirts hanging in peoples' eyes, and players jostling one another as they tried to lace up their spikes, that

142

inevitably tempers flared. Seldom did a morning pass without a loud argument or an occasional punch. One morning Rico Carty of the Dominican Republic argued vehemently with a Cuban second baseman as to the relative merits of Juan Perón and Fidel Castro. Carty, a six-foot, 200-pound former boxer, resolved the argument by flattening the 5–6, 150-pound Cuban with a single punch.

Unlike Whitey Ford, we had no leather armchairs in which to relax while reading the *Wall Street Journal*. We had only tensions and mustiness, and so we dressed quickly and went outside where we could draw a deep breath and the hot sun could begin to dry our wet uniforms.

We assembled at our respective diamonds at 8:30 A.M. The roll call was taken by the managers and then the morning workouts began. Only the injured players in camp did not take part in these. They were given red arm bands and sent, the walking wounded, to Diamond Five, where they amused themselves in some way throughout the morning. The rest of us went through light calisthenics, then began infield and outfield drills—the pitchers covering first base and fielding bunts—and finally, batting practice. All four major diamonds were awhirl with activity—ground balls, double plays, whistles, shouts, the crack of the bat—all orchestrated in a surprisingly efficient manner considering the number of players involved. A pitcher delivers the ball. The batter swings and lofts a fly to center field. A coach to the batter's right hits a ground ball to the shortstop; a coach to the batter's left hits a ground ball to the second baseman. As the ground balls intersect, the center-fielder catches the lofted fly and tosses the ball to the player backing up the pitcher behind the mound. The two infielders gobble up their grounders and lob the balls in parabolas that crisscross somewhere over the pitcher's head back to their coaches. The pitcher has already begun his windup, and the

143

process repeats itself endlessly for the rest of the morning.

The players not directly involved in such activity spent their time in one of the batting cages next to the locker room or on one of the warm-up mounds in front of the cages. The batting cages looked like those in a zoo except their bars were strands of rope woven into a net. When a batter hit a ball into the net the ball fell harmlessly to the ground. The balls were delivered by a mechanical pitching machine called "Iron Mike." His arm never tired, never suffered pulled muscles, always delivered up a ball with a clank every 10 seconds. Facing Mike a batter needed to get himself in a certain rhythmic groove, because if he didn't, he found fastballs buzzing past him while he was preoccupied with his stance.

Standing outside the cage and always available for advice was the camp's batting instructor, Johnny Mize. He had been a huge and powerful homerun hitter for the New York Giants in his playing days, but now, in his late forties, he was simply a substantial man running to fat. His face was blazing red and so swollen that his tiny eyes were barely visible. He could be seen always in the same pose, half-sitting, half-standing on an upright bat. It was the kind of pose one sees on the fairways of the Augusta Golf Club during Masters Week: old men in caps sitting on their portable golf seats before folding them up and venturing on to the next hole. Whenever a player asked Mize for advice he grumbled a few sullen words and fell silent. He did not rise from his bat until the bell was rung for lunch.

The camp's pitching coach was Walter "Boom-Boom" Beck. Like Mize, he too was a big man, but he was more gentle than sullen. He was given his nickname "Boom-Boom" because of the frequency with which batters used to "boom" line drives off his serves. During his major league career (from 1928 to 1945) Boom-Boom posted such records as 12–20, 2–6, 7–14 and 1–9. His earned run average varied from 9.88 to 7.42 to

4.75. Whenever he talked about pitching it was always to extol the virtues of Walter Johnson, Rube Waddell, Chief Bender and Christy Mathewson. He wandered about camp smiling at everyone. He'd stop to chat as you worked on one of the warm-up mounds. He'd toss off a few bits of advice and then, always in reverential tones, impart to you the secret of Mathewson's success. "The fadeaway," he'd say. "He mastered the fadeaway." Then with a nod and a wink, he'd drift off to another mound.

He never saw you begin practicing that fadeaway, never saw you bouncing balls in the dirt, becoming frustrated at your attempt to master such an esoteric pitch (a change-of-speed screwball) when, as yet, you could not control a simple fastball. But he meant no harm. He was just passing a pleasant spring. He wore a Braves' uniform and never throught for a moment that young pitchers like myself took him seriously. He did not take himself seriously! Everyone knew *that!* One day when I called him Mr. Beck, he grinned, threw a beefy arm around my shoulder and said, "Call me Boom-Boom, son" He *liked* his nickname! But I did take him seriously. In those days I took all adults seriously, had this unshakable belief they were always right, always had one's best interests at heart. When they appeared foolish to my eyes, I questioned my sight.

One spring when it was all slipping away, I sought out Boom-Boom. Be with you in a minute son. I began throwing from a mound. It was noon. The diamonds shadowless. The sun so hot and white it bleached the sky. The grass pale yellow, the red clay pink. Sweat burned my cheeks. I threw and waited. Panic rose. Finally, Boom-Boom appeared. Smiling. He put his hand on my shoulder. What's the matter, son? My hot pleas melted that smile like wax. He pulled his hand away as if burned. Stepped back. Then his smile re-formed. Relax, son.

145

He gave me advice. I tried to master it, failed, tried again, failed, began my motion a third time, caught Boom-Boom's eyes wandering to the next mound. The ball bounced in the dirt. I screamed out. *"Jesus Fucking Christ!"* Flung my glove high into the air. We both looked up, faces shadowed by a dark speck suspended in the blazing sky. It came down on top of the batting cage. Boom-Boom stared at it. He blinked. Then he looked around, saw, on every diamond, umpires, players, managers, scouts, all stilled in mid-motion, heads turned toward us. Boom-Boom looked at me, aflame, and raised his hands, palms out, in front of his eyes. Don't you worry, son, you'll get the hang of it. He began backing away. You keep practicing, I'll get back to you in a bit.

At noon we ate lunch outside in the shade of the dressing room. Milk, consommé in paper cups, a Hershey bar, an apple and an orange. Then back to the diamonds for the afternoon's games. We played a game every afternoon for the first three weeks, and after that we played one in the morning, too. By the end of the spring we would play about 40 games. The various teams in camp mostly played against one another— Austin against Jacksonville, Cedar Rapids against Boise, Davenport against Wellsville. Occasionally another major league organization would bring one of its better minor league teams to Waycross to play either Austin or Jacksonville.

One day a farm team of the Minnesota Twins came to camp. Its star, a 19-year-old Cuban refugee named Tony Oliva, had already fashioned a legendary reputation in the minors as a "pure hitter." Players drifted away from their diamonds and wandered over to Diamond One to watch Oliva hit against the best pitchers in camp. He went 7 for 9 in a doubleheader, hitting nothing but line drives. These left the infield seven feet off the ground and continued rising so fast that they were over

146

the heads of our outfielders before they could turn around. After each line drive (hit to every field), the players watching from behind the homeplate screen shook their heads in disbelief. Oliva batted with a knock-kneed stance. As he waited for the pitch, his weight rested on his front foot, the one closest to the pitcher. He lunged at the ball. It was all wrong, argued the players watching. You're supposed to keep your weight on the back foot. Someone grabbed a bat, assumed a stance behind the screen and demonstrated. Others argued. Ted Williams says. . . . That's Williams, interrupted another. Meanwhile, Oliva, unnoticed, steps into the batter's box and lines the first pitch six inches over the cap of our pitcher, who dives to the ground.

All the games were played before a sparse but potent audience of managers, coaches, scouts and executives. Many of them sat in deck chairs behind the homeplate screens of each diamond. But the most influential of them—Monchak and Murf; Birdie Tebbetts, a vice-president; John Mullins, the farm director; Roland Hemmond, the assistant farm director —sat or stood on top of the rotunda that commanded a view of all five diamonds. I remember my first impression of Waycross was that there were so many players in camp, I would never be noticed. But when I saw that rotunda and the men on top of it, their arms pointing out some action on Diamond Three, I realized that not only would I be noticed but my every move would be watched.

Over the winter a strange thing had happened to me. I had grown 1 1/2 inches taller and 15 pounds heavier. I thought nothing of it until the first time I threw a fastball in spring training. Not only had my pitch gained speed with that added weight, but it had also acquired a lightness that caused it to rise perceptibly no matter where I threw it. The faster a ball cuts through the air, it seems, the less force gravity exerts on it, and

147

so the ball becomes lighter and rises. I was fascinated by this new toy, which eluded batters like an exhaling balloon. They sighted its course, waist high, and swung. And when they looked back and saw the ball in the catcher's glove at a level with their eyes, they shook their heads. There was a drawback to this added speed and movement of my pitch, however. Whenever I threw a waist-high fastball, it often rose out of the strike zone before crossing the plate. I found myself with even less control than I'd had in McCook. Still, in spring training 1960 I had great success, for most batters were so anxious to impress managers they swung at pitches they would ordinarily let go by during the season.

From my first day at Waycross I had been assigned to Boise, Idaho, of the Class C Pioneer League. After a few weeks it became so apparent I would pitch at Boise that I no longer bothered to check the bulletin board in the morning, where my name always appeared third from the top on that sheet of paper headed by Billy Smith. At first I was disturbed at being assigned to such a "lowly" club, but eventually I learned that Boise was a showcase for all the best young pitchers in the system.

The Braves packed Boise with such talented hitters and fielders (many of whom could have held their own at Cedar Rapids or Jacksonville) that it was virtually impossible for the team's young and inexperienced pitchers not to have a winning record by season's end. In fact, it was not uncommon for a pitcher to have a winning record and a 4.76 ERA. If a pitcher can't win at Boise, the saying went in camp, he can't win anywhere. The Braves believed it was important for young pitchers to gain confidence in their ability to win games (even if that confidence was artificially stimulated), because once a pitcher thought himself a winner, he became a winner. This was certainly true of me at the time. I'd always had confidence in my natural talent, my ability to throw a baseball harder than most, but I had yet to discover whether or not I was a winner. To have talent and to be a winner are not necessarily synonymous in professional baseball any more than to have intelligence and to be a success are necessarily synonymous in business. Success in baseball requires the synthesis of a great number of virtues, many of which have nothing to do with sheer talent. Self-discipline, single-mindedness, perseverance, ambition—these were all virtues I was positive I possessed in 1960, but which I've discovered over the years I did not.

The manager of Boise was a Southerner in his mid-thirties who had played a number of years in the minors without ever having reached the major leagues. Billy Smith had been a first baseman and even at Boise he occasionally played that position. He stood five feet, eight inches tall and weighed about 155 pounds. He had a frail, young boy's build, blue eyes and extremely fine, short, sandy hair. His skin turned pink in the sun. He had one of those Audie Murphy faces that must have been exquisitely pretty as a child and burdensomely adorable as a teenager but which even in his thirties made him look years younger than he was. At least from a distance. Up close one noticed a slackening of the skin under his eyes and chin, a slight atrophy that lent him the curious air of an aging cherub.

He chewed tobacco. He seldom spoke, possibly because his thick drawl was high-pitched and became whiney when he grew excited. In general he was a taciturn man with a reputation for hardness that his looks might have denied him in adolescence but which he had managed to cultivate in his thirties. All of Billy's players, 10 to 15 years younger than he, admired his toughness. When an opposing pitcher knocked down one of his players, Billy Smith was the first man out of the dugout to challenge that pitcher. He protected his men.

149

After a particularly satisfying victory or dispiriting loss, he often went drinking with his players. When I heard such stories, I instinctively recalled that night in McCook—my teammates drinking beer in a darkened bar—and the thought that I would be a part of such camaraderie this season so thrilled me I couldn't wait to get to Boise and pitch for Billy Smith. I would have, too, if not for an incident that appeared trivial when it happened but which, I see now, damaged my career in a way that I could never repair.

Billy told us that spring that he was not bound to take "certain bonus babies" then on his roster to Boise. He would damned well have the final say over the players he took, he said, or he'd tell the front office where to go. And the players he took would not necessarily be the most talented, nor the biggest bonus babies, but those who'd proved to him they had the right attitude. Billy never bothered to define precisely what that attitude was, beyond dropping hints by praising certain players, like Tony Cloninger, and disparaging others, like Mike Marinko.

Cloninger, a $100,000 bonus pitcher from North Carolina, worked harder than any player in camp. When told to run 10 wind sprints, he ran 20. He seemed always to be sweating, always to be working painfully hard at tasks that were either senseless or so much easier than he made them. At first I thought this was simply his desire to prove that despite his bonus he did not expect a free ride through the system, as many bonus players did. Eventually I realized that Tony was proud of his ability to do things the hard way, proud of his refusal to quit even when *he* knew his efforts were senseless.

In 1960 Tony pitched for Austin but one day he would become a 20-game winner for the Atlanta Braves. When his fastball disappeared a few years later, he refused to accept the fact. He simply threw harder—that is, with greater effort. I remember seeing him pitch against the Montreal Expos in 1969. His career was all but over then. He lasted three innings. After he was relieved he walked to the right field bullpen and began firing fastballs to his bullpen catcher. He threw for five innings, as if punishing himself would redeem his career. At 29, he was the same pitcher he'd been at 19.

I talked to him after the game. He told me he needed just a few more wins to achieve his hundredth major league victory. Nothing would stop him from reaching that goal, he said, not even the sore arm he now suffered. He just pitched with it, he said, and didn't tell his manager, because if he did his manager might drop him from the starting rotation.

Mike Marinko, a left-hander from Bridgeport, Connecticut, had signed with the Braves when he was 18 years old. At that time, he stood six feet tall and weighed 155 pounds. In 1960, in his early twenties, he stood six feet, four inches tall and weighed over 200 pounds. During those years he had become the hardest throwing pitcher in the organization and one of the hardest throwers in baseball. Still, he was odd. Everyone in camp knew that. He had unusually long, thin arms that so embarrassed him he wore a sports coat in the hottest weather. He would walk about camp in Bermuda shorts, a t-shirt and a plaid wool jacket. He was indifferent to his career. He ran wind sprints only when he felt like it. One day at Waycross he hooked up in a pitcher's dual with Juan Pizaro, at the time the brightest prospect in the Braves' system. For six innings Marinko was so much more dazzling than Pizaro that scouts and managers and players came from all over camp to watch him pitch. The crowd behind home plate grew inning after inning, and in the wake of Marinko's speed, Pizaro was forgotten. In the sixth inning Marinko told his manager he didn't want to pitch anymore. The manager asked why. "No reason," said Mike, "I'm just bored." "That's not good enough," said

151

the manager. "Okay," said Mike, "I have a sore arm." And he walked away. Mike walked over to another diamond, where he got someone to hit him fly balls in center field, and while that small crowd behind the screen of Diamond One watched, he fired ball after ball into home plate. Eventually Pizaro went on to stardom in the major leagues, while Mike Marinko became the star outfielder for a slow-pitch softball team in Bridgeport.

I was so determined to impress Billy Smith with the rightness of my attitude (as if it was a three-button suit with narrow lapels one just slipped on) that I affected an earnestness the remembrance of which embarrasses me to this day. There was no task too menial or unpleasant (carrying the bats to and from the diamond) for which I did not volunteer. And when I suffered a minor yet painful sore arm, I told no one. I knew it wasn't serious, was just a spring training sore arm that would heal with a few day's rest, and so, when Billy asked for a batting practice pitcher one day, I couldn't resist offering myself. My arm was so sore my pitches barely reached the plate. The batters, thrown off their timing by my lobs, swung so far ahead as to hit them foul or miss them entirely. They complained to my catcher, Joe Torre. He fired the ball back to me and said, "Put something on the damn ball!"

"Mind your own business," I replied. I lobbed another pitch, and the batter swung and missed. He said something to Torre. Joe stepped in front of the plate. He held the ball up in front of his eyes and said, "If you can't put anything on this," and then he fired it back to me, "get the hell off the mound." He turned around and I threw the ball at the back of his head. I missed and the ball bounced off the screen. Joe flung down his glove and his mask and started toward me. We'd certainly have come to blows if Billy Smith had not come between us. With a hand against each of our chests, he told us to cool off, forget it. I remember being surprised by the look on Billy's face as he separated us. His eyes were wide and there was a tremor in his voice.

I was glad Billy stopped us. I had no desire to fight Joe Torre, who at 19 already had the looks and attitude of a 30-year-old veteran. Joe was fat then, over 220 pounds, and his unbelievably dark skin and black brows were frightening. He looked like a fierce Bedouin tribesman whose distrust for everything could be read in the shifting whites of his eyes. Like myself, he, too, was earnest that spring. Joe's earnestness was genuine, however, not recently picked off the rack like mine. He was unwavering in his dedication to baseball. He tolerated no lapses of desire or effort from either himself or his teammates. Billy Smith called him a "hard-nosed sunuvabitch." It was a term of endearment. Joe viewed my feeble lobs during batting practice as "unprofessional." He was right. I should have either confessed a sore arm and not pitched, or else ignored the pain and thrown at good speed. My weak compromise hurt my teammates.

Yet this was Torre's first spring training, too. He had acquired his professionalism from his brother Frank, then a star with Milwaukee; from his desire to prove he expected no favors from the Braves because of Frank or his own $30,000 bonus; from his Roman Catholic, Italian working-class upbringing in Brooklyn; and from his own nature. At 19 Joe was simply a mature and serious youth. He seldom smiled. He took everything seriously—his baseball, his family, his religion, his brother's career and even the *Playboy* bunny he would one day marry. It was an odd marriage, I thought, and I was not surprised when it did not last.

After their divorce, Joe's ex-wife made the New York *Daily News* one morning. It seems that two policemen had knocked on the door to her apartment to investigate a complaint of loud

153

noise. She'd answered the door, smiling, wearing only her *Playboy* fame, and invited the officers to join the party. I was out of baseball when I read the story and Joe was a major league star. I could not believe that the Joe Torre I knew at 19 could marry such a girl. A few years later I met a Catholic priest who was a friend of the Torres. I asked about Joe, and spoke of the marriage. "It was a real tragedy for Joe and his whole family," the priest said. "They were a close family, very devout. They'd warned him about her." Then the priest said that Joe was putting his life back together again. "He's going steady with a good girl now," the priest said. "A good girl," he repeated, and the faint image of a broad white forehead flashed before my eyes and was gone. Who was she?

I did not see Joe Torre for years, nor did I think much about our argument or his difficulties until one night I was watching *The Cardinal* on television. I recalled Joe immediately as Tom Tryon began earnestly plodding toward his Cardinal's red hat, his sanctity trampling all the less saintly in its path. And when the future Cardinal began to anguish over his illicit love affair with Romy Schneider I thought suddenly of Joe's ex-wife and Sally, too, and even poor Romy, all three buried under the weight of *our* oppressive and private grief.

The night of our dispute in Waycross, I lay on my cot thinking that Billy Smith would admire me for standing up to Joe. At that moment the scouts and managers and executives were assembling to pick tomorrow's teams. I could almost hear Billy's high voice as he picked me: "That's my kinda player. Won't take shit from no one." But the following morning when I passed the bulletin board my name was under that of Travis Jackson, manager of Davenport of the Class D Midwest League. Later that afternoon, I discovered that what Billy Smith had actually said the night before was, "I won't have no

154

red-ass guinea on my club." Surely he meant Torre, I thought. But *his* name was still under Billy's, while mine remained under Travis's for the rest of the spring. Why? How had Billy decided that *I* was the red-ass guinea?

In future years, the reputation I was fitted for that first spring (as one who does not get along) was stitched more tightly with similar incidents (my outburst with Boom-Boom) until I could no longer slip it on or off at will, but, like that assassinated archduke, was trapped inside. . . . Or was I? Was it just an ill-fitting suit, I began to wonder? Or was it not a skin I'd grown and nourished on my own? The Joe Torre incident had not burdened me with an undeserved reputation. It had exposed something in me to myself and others. So, I began to think, it was *me* all this time? I realized I had never gotten along. I remembered sitting, at 12, on a schoolmate's porch and listening to the sound of happy voices inside. I knocked. Once. Twice. Called out my name. The voices stilled. I put my ear against that door and heard a common "sssshhhh."

I discovered that spring that I didn't fit in and never had. My efforts were doomed to failure because of some strange lack or excess in me I have yet to define. After that, I stayed apart. Why burden others, I rationalized? It was a pose at first—the abused and misunderstood sulking off alone—but it has now grown into a way of life I enjoy. More than that. I derive an erotic pleasure from being alone, particularly in crowded places. Unknown, I sit in a bar or diner and eavesdrop on the lives of others. That girl! The one who looks like Lois! The way she smiles and lays her hand on her boyfriend's arm! I feel her touch. Am satisfied. Those men debating Tom Seaver's talent! I listen, then resolve their debate with my precise and irrefutable logic. I may sit there late into the night, never speaking, never leaving some darkened corner, as I fantasize and wait anxiously for the morning when I can sit at the desk in my attic room and begin, again, to express what I feel about that girl, those men, myself, and in so doing lend to myself a sensitivity on paper I lack in reality.

# ...5

$A$T Davenport I assumed an attitude. The aloof veteran. It was a pose. A "veteran" is one who has played at least two years in professional baseball. I had played only two months at McCook. Still, that was two months more than most of my teammates, who, before the 1960 season began, had yet to play in a professional game. Ordinarily such rookies would have been sent to McCook, but because the Nebraska State League had folded after the 1959 season, they were now distributed like so many lottery tickets between Wellsville and Davenport. Most of them went to Davenport.* Only one of them—Rico Carty—ever paid off. The rest were modestly talented players who might climb as high as Austin or maybe Louisville before they finally left baseball. None compared in talent to my teammates at McCook—Hunt, Chenger, Overby, Niekro—and only first baseman George Kopacz and I had received more that a $20,000 bonus. Besides money and talent, however, these boys lacked professional experience. At McCook my teammates had lacked this experience, too, but it didn't really matter since we competed against rookies like ourselves. Most teams in the Midwest League, however, were stocked with

• • •

*Most of the veteran minor leaguers went to Wellsville in 1960. Wellsville won the New York–Penn League title and Bruce Brubaker, a former teammate at McCook, won 15 games.

veterans.* And it seems that many a parent organization with a team there also had a team in the Class-D Appalachian League, which, like the NSL, was a rookie league. These teams sent their rookies to the Appalachian League and their minor league veterans to the Midwest League.† Although many rookies are potentially more talented than veterans, (how talented can a player be who returns to a Class-D league three years running?) in the lower minors it is often experience more than talent that tells. It was this lack of experience that doomed the Quad Cities Braves to last place in the Midwest League from early in the season.

Nor was I truly aloof. I remained so more by a fierce act of will than desire. Often it took all the will power I could summon to refuse my teammates' offers to join them for a pizza after a game. I preferred to eat alone, I lied. Soon they no longer bothered to ask. I seldom spoke to them in the locker room or during games or even on the long bus rides to other towns. When we stayed overnight in one of those towns I took a single room whenever one was available. The Lone Ranger rides alone, my teammates said, and laughed. It's ironic for me to see this now (I have the knack, it seems, of catching the drift of a conversation only after it has switched to another topic), but my teammates actually looked up to me when the season began. They respected my talent, my bonus and my brief

• • •

*There were eight teams in the Midwest League: Pirates (Decatur, Illinois), Giants (Quincy, Illinois), Tigers (Dubuque, Illinois), Dodgers (Kokomo, Indiana), Red Sox (Waterloo, Iowa), Cardinals (Keokuk, Iowa), White Sox (Clinton, Iowa) and the Braves. Actually, the Davenport Braves were officially known as the Quad Cities Braves since they represented the four towns of Davenport, Iowa, and Moline, East Moline and Rock Island, Illinois, all on the banks of the Mississippi River.

†The player–manager of the Kokomo Dodgers was a 34-year-old catcher in his twelfth year of professional baseball.

professional experience, and it was only after I belabored them with my studied aloofness that this admiration dissolved and was replaced by wariness. Billy Smith had been right after all.

I had assumed my little pose because I thought myself far superior to my teammates in talent (I was); because I was embarrassed and disheartened at returning to a D league while most of my McCook teammates had gone on to higher classifications; and because I had decided that spring that I would no longer try to fit. It was a delusion to think I could. When I tried I left myself open. Indecent exposure, I call it now. And I'm seldom caught anymore. Seldom, but not never.

Davenport, Iowa, was a large, gray, industrial city not unlike Bridgeport, Connecticut, where I was born and raised. Maybe this explains why I don't recall much except that it was built along the banks of the Mississippi River, had a population of about 90,000 and consisted mostly (in my memory, at least) of tall, soot-stained, concrete buildings—banks, offices and department stores. I lived downtown in a bedroom on the second floor of an old two-family house. From there I had to walk through much of the city and then across some railroad tracks before coming to the stadium where we played our games. Often I had to stop and wait at those tracks while a trainman guided a solitary boxcar past me. The tracks were littered with dilapidated and unattached boxcars, all of which seemed no longer in use, except by that trainman, who moved them only when he saw me approaching.

The stadium was on the banks of the Mississippi. Its entrance was a few yards beyond the tracks and its outfield fence only a few feet from the river. Across the river was Rock Island, Illinois, famous since the Civil War for its U.S. Army arsenal and large contingent of federal troops. The presence of those troops over the years had given birth to a strip of gaudy night-

159

clubs close to the river. North of Rock Island were the Illinois cities of Moline and East Moline, which, with Rock Island and Davenport, formed the Quad Cities.

Unlike Cibola, Davenport Stadium really was a stadium— a scaled-down replica of a major league park. It was sufficiently lighted at night by a ring of metal towers that resembled oil riggings. It seated almost 13,000 people, no more than 500 of whom ever appeared at any one game.* It had permanent concrete stands in left field and right field and behind home plate. There were no stands behind the outfield fence (a 10-foot high, wooden wall painted with various advertisements) because of its proximity to the river. The seats along the foul lines were bench type, while those behind the plate were individual chairs exactly like those in major league parks. The homeplate seats went back 30 rows and were protected from foul balls by an overhead screen that, like an awning, inclined parallel to those seats all the way to the thirtieth row. An overhanging roof protected the homeplate seats from the elements. During afternoon games it cast a shadow over the homeplate area.

The stadium was enclosed. Playing inside it, one had the sense of playing inside a vast, roofless warehouse rather than on an open baseball field like Cibola. Because of the high walls and even higher concrete stands, and the frequent absence of fans (whose bodies would have deadened sound), it became an echo

• • •

*Unlike the citizens of McCook, Davenport residents had a choice of more cosmopolitan entertainments than that of a last-place Class-D League baseball team. Furthermore, they had grown accustomed to the superior play of a successful Class-B, Three-I League team that had played in Davenport only a few years before. The hapless Quad Cities Braves of 1960 were a less than adequate substitute. Whereas the McCook Braves had averaged 700 fans per game, 1/10 of the town's population, the Quad Cities Braves averaged 500 fans per game, 1/400 of the total Quad Cities population of 200,000.

chamber. Whenever a bat made contact with a ball, one heard not one, not two, but a series of loud-then-diminishing cracks that ricocheted over the players' heads like invisible pinballs.

I remember the first time I saw the stadium. It was a cold, windy night in May. I stood in front of the entrance and watched as my taxi bounced over the railroad tracks and disappeared into the darkness. The stadium loomed black and deserted. I pushed open its wooden gate and stepped inside. Before me was the concrete runway and wall that curved halfway around the park like the rim of a wheel. The runway was underneath and behind the homeplate stands. Overhead, I could see what must have been the top rows of those stands. I turned left and began walking along the runway. My footsteps echoed. The runway was almost totally dark. It smelled of stale beer and urine. It was littered with crushed beer cups and popcorn boxes and crumpled hot dog wrappers. A poster was taped to the wall. A third of it had been ripped away but I could still make out parts of an elephant and a clown and the dates of a circus. A few yards farther along, a narrow tunnel branched off from the runway like a wheel spoke. I turned into the tunnel and was momentarily blown off balance by a gust of wind coming from the other end. A huge bird rose up, flapped its wings in my face and flattened itself against the wall. An old newspaper. The wind died and the newspaper floated to the floor. The tunnel rose before me at a slight incline and at the other end I could see a square patch of black sky. I began walking toward it.

When I stepped out of the tunnel I found myself halfway up the stands behind home plate. The park spread out dark and empty around me. A wind blew in from beyond the outfield wall, from the wide, flat, black expanse of the Mississippi. The river was flecked with gold and red and white, the colors shimmering on the black water, rising and dipping gently on the

161

swell. It was only when I looked beyond the river, to the banks of Rock Island, that I saw, a mile away, the beckoning lights of the nightclubs.

His wife and daughter called him "The Major." He did not look like a military man, not even a retired one. He was very fat, almost elephantine. He wore the same white, short-sleeved shirt day after day until it was no longer white but gray with age. He wore the shirt open at the neck, exposing a yellowed t-shirt. His black flannel pants were baggy and shiny, and backless slippers slapped the floor as he padded about the house. He had a military man's gruff, booming voice, although its purpose seemed not so much to command as to be heard in a world that was hard of hearing. His wife and daughter were like him, only softer, quieter, more timid. His daughter was 19. She had an hourglass figure that would soon lose its contours but was then not unappealing. Her face was plain and white and puffy, and she wore thick glasses through which she peered with tiny eyes.

The Major and his family owned the house in which I slept. They lived on the first floor and rented out the second-floor bedrooms to four transients and myself. The transients were silent men of indeterminable age. Drifters, they looked like either very lean and muscular old men or very haggard young men. They kept odd hours, sleeping through the daylight, leaving the house at night (we passed on the stairway with lowered heads) returning, lurching up the stairs at 4 A.M. I remember seeing one of them in a shabby bar one night. He was a small man with an enflamed face and slicked-back yellow hair. He wore levis and a plaid shirt, the sleeves rolled past his biceps to expose taut muscles outlined by bulging veins. He was hunched over the bar staring into a shot glass. A woman in her forties, no longer pretty, stood behind him and massaged his back with the palms of her hands. Her palms made small circles as if his back were a window she was polishing. Every so often she would press her body against his back and whisper in his ear. He seemed oblivious to her ministrations and then, without warning, his right fist shot over his left shoulder and the woman lay on the floor. He did not turn around. No one bothered to revive her. Men just stepped over her on their way in and out of the bar. I left immediately and did not return until a week later. He was sitting at the bar again, staring into his shot glass, while that same woman, her left eye blackened and half-closed, stood behind him and massaged his back.

I never spoke to that man either in the bar or on the stairway of the Major's house. Nor did I ever speak to any of the other tenants, or say more than a few words to the Major, and those few only when he addressed me first. He always spoke to me when he saw me. He waited for me. He sat in the living room off the front hallway waiting for me to come through the door. When he heard me he always called out in a voice that shook the house, "Is that you, Pat? Pat, is that you?"

"Yes, Major." I would move to the living room's entranceway. The room was dark, except for the light from the television set. A big, winged armchair faced the set. I could see only the Major's huge belly and the bottom half of his legs and occasionally, when he raised a beer can to his lips, a hand, too.

"Join me, Pat," he would say, never looking out from behind the armchair's wings. "Come watch the ball game with me."

I never joined him, never accepted his offer of a beer, just mumbled how tired I was and went upstairs to bed. Soon he stopped asking, although he never stopped speaking to me. His wife, however, never tired of saying in a hushed pantomime so he would not hear, "Go join the Major, Pat! Don't be bashful! He'd love to have a beer with you!"

*     *     *

The Major came to all the games I pitched in Davenport. From the mound I could see him sitting directly behind the homeplate screen, with his wife and daughter on either side of him. He cheered my every strike. And when I didn't throw strikes, when I started walking batter after batter and our few fans began booing and yelling for Travis Jackson to put someone else in, I would hear a voice that drowned out every boo: "DON'T LISTEN TO THEM, PAT! YOU'RE DOING FINE! FINE, SON! JUST RELAX A LITTLE, THAT'S ALL!"

"The Major's right," his wife would yell. "You're doing fine, Pat!" Only their daughter never said a word. She just sat there, wearing white gloves, the gloves folded in her lap, her back rigid. And when I was finally taken out of the game, and had showered and dressed, I would always find the Major and his family waiting for me outside the dressing room. I usually declined his offer of a ride home. I preferred to walk through the darkened city by myself. "Of course," he would say. Occasionally, though, I accepted. Once home, the Major would toss me the keys. "Go for a ride," he would say. "Take Marge, if you'd like some company." I sensed even then he was not pushing his plain and timid daughter on me. He knew I had a girl friend back home and he took great pleasure in our long-distance romance. Several times as I entered the house he would shuffle out of the living room, smiling, a letter in his hand. Once, when she telephoned from Connecticut and I wasn't in, he accepted the long-distance charges and spoke with her. She told him she was worried because I hadn't written for weeks. He reassured her. "Don't worry," he said. "He'll write. He's a fine boy." He's a fine boy . . . he's a fine boy . . . ?

No. I'm sure he never intended a romance between his daughter and me. It was just that he knew Marge was a shy girl and that I was lonely and so he saw no reason why he shouldn't

164

nudge us together, just for the moment, to lighten our common solitude. Often we drove back to the stadium late at night. It would be deserted by then. We'd park and walk along the river wall. There was always a strong wind by the river. The black tide lapped below. The lights from the nightclubs across the river shimmered off the water and illuminated our faces with an eerie greenish-yellow tint. We had little to say. We stopped and kissed now and then. Passionless kisses. She seemed not to know how. She clutched me as if *I* could save her from drowning. She pressed her lips tightly together, closed her eyes, and did not move a muscle until we parted. Sometimes as we walked I held her hand. She kept her white gloves on even in the hottest weather. She took them off only once, and then I felt her hand, rough and scaly as if it had been burned severely. But because of the darkness I never knew for sure. I could see only that both hands were unbelievably pink, like a baby's, in marked contrast to her white face.

During one of those walks I asked what branch of service her father had been in.

"None," she said. "He's a retired major in the Salvation Army."

I can't remember what the Major looked like. His face, I mean. I only remember his substantial size, his shabbiness and his voice. That was all I saw then. A frozen frame from a black-and-white film. I never saw his textures, his real dimensions, his movements. Of course, I see them now. I remember the Major fondly—*now*. Then, he was just a fat man I tried to avoid.

It's almost noon as I write this. Through my attic window I look out on a sunny June day. I shall stop soon, go downstairs, do errands for my wife. I may browse at the bookstore or spend an hour at the beach admiring firm young bodies. At night I'll go to a movie or sit in a bar for a few hours, then return home to read myself to sleep. And as I go about my ordinary day, I'll wonder, now, what people are passing, unseen, through my life, only to be remembered years later with a warmth I never felt at their moment of passing.

I started the fifth game of the season at Davenport Stadium. It was an insult, I thought, all those rookies starting ahead of me. I struck out six batters in four innings and was working on a shutout as I took the mound to begin the fifth inning. I was throwing beautifully, without effort, and was anxious to get this game over with, to pitch my shutout and get on to the next one. I knew a string of such games would propel me out of the Midwest League shortly. I walked a batter. Where would the Braves send me? I walked another batter. Cedar Rapids? I could pitch in the Three-I League. Wasn't Overby there, and with a sore arm? And Hunt. I should be, too. I saw Travis Jackson walking toward me from the dugout. I heard the fans booing, "You shoulda yanked him sooner," someone yelled. The bases were loaded. Travis patted me on the behind, gave my relief pitcher a few words of encouragement and led me, a docile lamb, back to the dugout.

My relief pitcher, Dave Breshnahan, whose reappearance at Waycross this spring was as mysterious as his disappearance from McCook last summer, gave up a double that cleared the bases. I was charged with three runs, although I would not be charged with our eventual loss.

The next night Travis told me that all I needed to become a major league pitcher was confidence in my ability to throw strikes. I would get that confidence by doing a lot of pitching, he said. He sent me to the bullpen. A few days later I pitched an inning of relief in Clinton. The game was hopelessly lost when I entered it. I walked a few batters, hit one or two, and struck out three. A week later I pitched three innings of relief

166

in Keokuk. I gave up a run on a few walks, a hit, and then I struck out eight of nine batters. After eight innings of pitching I had yet to gain a decision. I had given up four hits, five earned runs, 13 bases on balls, and had struck out 17 batters. Cedar Rapids, 70 miles northwest of Davenport, might as well have been in a foreign country.

Toward the end of the second week I started a game against the Tigers in Decatur. The game was rained out before the sixth inning could begin. I was credited with a 4–1 victory, after which Travis patted me on the rump and said, "It shows you can do it." He smiled his toothless smile.

Travis was a funny-looking old man. He had no teeth, except, as he used to say, "store-bought ones." He had lumpy, chipmunk jowls that were never clean shaven. His legs were skinny and bowed, and he walked like a cartoon cowboy, listing left then right. He seldom said much to his players, most of whom were 40 years younger than he. And even when he did speak it was only to mutter some cliché he'd absorbed after 40 years in the game.

A native of Waldo, Arkansas, Travis Calvin Stonewall Jackson, had become a major league shortstop with the New York Giants in 1922. He was 19 years old. He played in the majors for 15 years, was an All-Star shortstop and then retired with a .291 lifetime batting average. He managed for a number of years in the minors and then left baseball. He returned in 1960 to manage the Quad Cities Braves. He was 58 at the time. There was talk that "Ole Travis" had took sick when he was out of baseball—a euphemism for heavy drinking, although I never once saw Travis even sip a beer during the season—and that he had returned to the game to recapture his health. To get clean. He immersed himself in the game—but only in a physical way, as if the game, like the waters of Lourdes, could cure him simply by his physical immersion in it. Before each

167

game he hit fly balls to the outfielders and ground balls to the infielders and, occasionally, he pitched batting practice. One hot afternoon he collapsed on the mound. Players rushed to the mound and tried to pick up old Travis, crumpled like a ragdoll in the dirt. "Don't touch me!" he said. "Leave me alone! If I'm gonna go, I wanna go here."

Yet, as a manager, Travis seemed only to be going through the motions. He was bored once the games began since they were, then, no longer a vehicle for his rehabilitation. He watched them all from the dark, narrow passageway at the mouth of the dugout. He could see only the pitcher, the right side of the infield and the rightfielder. He sat on a folding chair, legs crossed, elbow on knee, chin cupped in palm, a cigarette dangling from his lips. We could not see him from our seats in the dugout, but occasionally we heard his shrill voice: "Atta boy, Chuck! Atta boy!" His comments were few, never more than a brief exhortation. Mostly, he sat in silence. We knew he was still there from the smoke that curled out of the passageway and hovered in the dugout like an unraveling ball of twine. The smoke hung there, inning after inning, and only when it disappeared, usually around the seventh, did we know Travis had finally fallen asleep.

A week after my first victory Travis gave me another start. Although I lost the game 4–3 (on a three-run home run in the ninth) I pitched well enough for Travis (or the front office) to decide to start me every five days. As in McCook, I pitched well every four starts. One night I pitched a one-hit shutout against the Kokomo Dodgers and four starts later I won a game 2–1, striking out 14 batters. Even my losses were well-pitched: 1–0, five hits, 12 strikeouts; 2–1, three hits, 11 strikeouts; 3–2, four hits, 14 strikeouts. That year I threw a baseball with more speed than I would ever have again.

One night I stepped out of the dugout to start a game

against the Clinton White Sox and overheard my fellow pitchers talking about the Sox's awesome hitter, Jim Hicks. You've gotta give him breaking stuff, they agreed. He kills fastballs. I looked over my shoulder and said, "He kills *your* fastballs, maybe, but the sunuvabitch won't kill *my* fastball." That night I struck out Jim Hicks three times. I threw him nothing but fastballs down the middle of the plate. He swung through them all, with such force that he fell to one knee. He righted himself with his bat. There were times during that game when I knew I could fool him with a curveball—I had a sharp if erratic curveball that year—but I never threw him one. I just threw fastball after fastball, and he kept swinging as hard as he could, falling to one knee each time. The sight of him on one knee was what I pitched for. I loved such moments even more than a satisfying career. I know that now. I had neither the patience nor the vision to develop a strip of moments into a successful season much less a satisfying career. My career was no aesthetically well-made movie—rising action, climax, denouement. It was a box strewn with unnumbered slides. A box of pure and frozen moments through which I have been sorting, picking up a moment here, a moment there, holding them to the light, seeing previously undefined details, numbering that moment, then putting it with all the others in some order which, I hope, will eventually produce a scenario of my career. But this process goes against my grain. I still prefer moments. Moments are fathomable in a way my career, my life, any life can never be. Sitting here, I can see Jim Hicks, fallen to one knee. He glares at me through time and space before he begins to right himself, like an old man, with his bat.

Despite striking out Jim Hicks three times and the other Clinton players six times for a total of nine strikeouts in six innings, I lost the game, 2–1. Errors, walks, the memory fades. I only remember Hicks on one knee and, afterward, Hicks stopping me in the runway of the stadium. Smiling, he says, "Man, there oughtta be a law against you! Know what I mean? Make it eee-legal to throw a baseball that hard!"

I float on his words. "But don't you worry," he adds. "Jim Hicks gonna get you yet."

"You keep trying, Jim." And we both laugh.*

I was seldom able to sustain such moments for nine innings. I would pitch four, five, six innings of beautiful baseball and then would lose it all. Not all, really. I never lost the speed. But the control vanished without a trace. Travis used to tell me that if I could get through the sixth inning without losing my control, I'd probably finish the game. I thought he meant I suffered a lapse of concentration about then because I was retiring batters so effortlessly. And he might have meant that, too. But I think he really meant that after the sixth inning he would be asleep and I could pitch for eternity as long as nothing woke him. Only the fiercest boos and epithets from our fans could make him stir.

I had the knack of causing such noise, however. One night I pitched a no-hitter for six innings and then opened the seventh by walking four batters in succession. My shortstop yelled, "Throw strikes!" I glared at him. Boos ricocheted overhead like rifle shots. Travis leaped off his chair and bounded out of the dugout as if he'd been jabbed with a hot poker. He was still fuzzy with sleep when he reached the mound and

• • •

*Hicks had played in the Nebraska State League in 1959. He was six feet, four inches tall, weighed 210 pounds and was one of the most graceful, powerful and talented athletes I have ever seen. He had once played basketball with the Harlem Globetrotters and eventually would become a big-league outfielder, although he would never achieve the kind of success in the majors that his physical talent prophesied. Another Clinton player I struck out easily that night was Tom McCraw, presently an 11-year veteran with the California Angels.

170

encountered a madman.* "Sunuvabitch . . . motherless bastard
. . ." Travis tried to calm me down, to sooth me with soft words
while he slipped the ball out of my hand before I noticed my
relief pitcher walking in from the bullpen.

"Get the fuck outta here!" I yelled at Travis.

"Now, son . . ."

"And take him with you!" Travis sighed, shrugged, threw his
arm around my relief pitcher and led him to the dugout. The
fans booed my relief pitcher with gusto. Someone yelled "It's
about time you took him out!"

After awhile Travis rarely started me at home. He wanted
to be spared the boos, not to mention my rages in front of our
fans. He waited for the road trips, which, unlike those in the
Nebraska State League, lasted six or seven days. He started me
in Dubuque, Decatur, Waterloo, Quincy and Keokuk. In those
towns the fans applauded my wildness. They shouted, "Keep
the bum in there, he's not done yet," whenever Travis trotted
out to the mound. As in Davenport, Travis always found me
boiling, cursing, kicking dirt. "You're not taking me outta this
game, you old bastard!" Travis just smiled his toothless smile
and laid his hand on my shoulder. "Don't you worry, son. You
can pitch as long as you like. They love you in Keokuk."

But those inexplicable bouts of wildness were maddening.
They were unlike any I'd ever known. True, I had never been
a "control" pitcher and never expected to be one, because a
fastball pitcher like myself always issues more bases on balls
than one who relies on softer stuff. Batters swing at and miss
superior fastballs more often than they do sliders, curveballs or
knuckleballs. The latter are easier to hit, although harder to hit

• • •

*By mid-season I was no longer the docile creature Travis had led from the mound
in May. The disparity between my physical talent and lack of success had begun to
frustrate me.

solidly. Frequently they produce quick outs (on a single pitch), while superior fastballs most often produce mighty misses that require another pitch, which, if missed, demands still another. Fastball pitchers generally throw more pitches per game than do breaking ball pitchers, therefore they have more opportunity to walk batters. (With a 3-and-1 count on a batter, a pitcher *wants* his next pitch to be hit, preferably to a fielder. If a 3-and-1 pitch is missed, the pitcher has gained little and still may walk the batter.) Furthermore, because fastball pitchers throw more pitches per game, they tend to tire sooner, which causes them to lose control.

I knew also that a pitcher acquires "control" when he masters his delivery. Every part of that delivery (pump, kick, stride, release, follow-through) helps determine at what point a ball will or will not cross the plate. To throw a perfect strike, a pitcher has only to synchronize all those parts. To throw a ball to a specific spot (low and over the outside corner of the plate), a pitcher has only to alter parts or all of his delivery. The knowledge of which parts to alter and how to do so is easily acquired (a longer stride produces a lower pitch). The physical mastering of that knowledge, however, is painstakingly difficult. For some pitchers it takes years of practice. Others never master it. I felt that if I worked hard enough over the next few years I could eventually reduce my ratio of bases on balls to three every nine innings. In the past I had issued four, five and sometimes six per game. Those walks were spaced out—one every other inning or so—over nine innings. There were reasons for them. Like most young pitchers I had first been wild due to inexperience. In high school I had been wild because I was trying to throw the ball harder than was natural in order to impress the scouts, just as in McCook I tried to impress my manager and teammates. But at Davenport I threw with so much more speed than my rookie teammates that I did not have to strain beyond my natural limits to impress them. Still, I had yet to master my delivery, which I had altered slightly since high school (I now threw more directly overhand), nor had I mastered the newfound speed and movement of my fastball, which I had grown into over the winter of 1959–60.

I expected to walk those four, five and six batters per game. That was logical. But what actually happened wasn't. I would not walk a batter for five innings, six innings, eight innings, and then nothing but walks rained down on me. Four, five, *six in a row.* No matter how I altered my delivery (shorter stride after a low pitch, longer stride after a high pitch), nothing stopped those walks. I could not even stop them by throwing strikes. One night, with the bases loaded and two outs, I threw a perfect 3-and-2 fastball. The ball passed over the heart of the plate at a level with the batter's waist. He dropped his bat and took a step toward his dugout. Then, realizing that the umpire had not called "Strike three!" he bolted toward first base. The runner on third trotted home, and as he did his path crossed that of Travis Jackson, who was walking to the mound. It was all happening so quickly, all these perfunctory movements without any argument from my catcher or Travis, that I began to doubt I had seen what I had just seen. I was so stunned that I allowed Travis to relieve me without a protest.

As we crossed the thirdbase line on the way to our dugout, the homeplate umpire took off his mask and stepped toward me. He shook his head and said, "Sorry I missed that last one, Pat." Something must have snapped in me then because I don't remember what happened next. I remember only what the players told me the following day—that I had lunged at the umpire and would have got him, too, if old Travis hadn't tackled me and then the rest of my teammates hadn't rushed over to half-drag, half-carry me into the dugout, where I continued to shout obscenities at the poor umpire.

On those rare occasions when I survived my wild streaks and remained in the game, I threw nothing but strikes from then on. It was truly maddening. No matter how late I walked the streets of Keokuk or Quincy, no matter how many times I replayed those disastrous periods in my mind, I could never understand them. Something was missing. A reason. The wildness just appeared, did its damage and vanished.

By mid-season I had won three games, lost seven and was working on a 4.50 ERA. I was issuing about eight walks per game while striking out 11. I had not lost any games because I was hit unmercifully by the opposition. In fact, I was surrendering only about four hits every nine innings. And when a young pitcher allows less than nine hits per game this is considered a sign of strong potential.

I lost some of those games for reasons other than my own wildness. Often when I managed to survive a wild streak—escaping an inning with only one or two runs scored—my teammates either failed to score any runs or made costly fielding errors. (I lost eight games by the margin of one or two runs that year.)

I remember one game in particular. I was winning 1–0 in the ninth inning with two outs and runners on second and third (a walk and an error). I induced the batter to hit a ground ball to my shortstop, who scooped it up and tossed it to first base. George Kopacz stretched toward the ball and it disappeared in his glove. The umpire's right hand shot into the air, and as it did the ball dropped out of Kopacz's glove. The umpire quickly reversed his call. Kopacz, still in his stretch, did nothing. He looked down at the ball in an odd way. It was not a look of disbelief or despair, but of nescience. It was as if his mind had been suddenly wiped clean of all traces of baseball, and he was unable to grasp, at that moment, precisely what that white sphere meant. As he struggled to refocus on its meaning, the runner who had been at second base crossed home plate with the winning run.

In the dugout I went berserk. George sat on the bench and stared out over the rightfield fence. I stood in front of him, screaming, demanding an explanation, challenging him to a fight, trying to provoke some response—any response—but he said nothing. He sat there and stared off into space as if trying to grasp some very elemental point that the rest of us understood but that continued to elude him.

At times George Kopacz would forget how to function. He wasn't stupid (actually, he was quite bright) but was easily distracted (by faint whispers? the unexpected?) from the simplest of acts—acts the rest of us performed instinctively but that required from George his total concentration. Every movement seemed a conscious and fragile effort. He never walked or stood or simply played first base until he decided on the proper arrangement of his feet or hands, the proper tilt of his head or facial expression (always choosing the vacant gaze of a model, actually staring inward at the self). His poses struck a precarious balance—fine crystal on a taut string. (The dropped baseball so intruded on the classic way he had tapped first base with his right toe as he stretched and caught the ball that his concentration shattered.)

He had a model's good looks. Strong, square jaw, full lips, blue eyes, thick black brows. I remember rooming with him once in Quincy. I woke to find him sitting before a mirror plucking his eyebrows with a tweezer. I stared in disbelief. He seemed unaware of my presence. He turned his head sideways to the mirror and moved it closer to its image. He raised the tweezer and plucked a hair. He had a lean, muscular body always immaculately clothed. His tassled loafers sparkled and his slacks and shirts fit without intrusion of a wrinkle or unwanted fold. His uniform (like ours, a hand-me-down) fit per-

175

fectly (unlike ours). He had taken the uniform to a tailor, put it on, then stood in front of a full-length mirror while the tailor, on his knees, first pinned then later stitched away unsightly folds. George did not slide readily in that uniform. More than once he risked a broken leg at second base by refusing to do so, while Travis, in the runway, screamed, "Why don't the boy slide?" Yet George's vanity was not easy to define. He was shy with girls (he was barely 19) and seldom dated at Davenport. An introvert rather than an extrovert, his face was always clouded by that inward gaze. And what George saw was the only certitude in his fragile world.*

I prowled the streets of Davenport in black despair. I thought of nothing but those interminable wild streaks. Being always alone, I had no peace from my thoughts. They woke with me each morning and shadowed me throughout the day. I couldn't shake them or understand them. Like the strange new streets I walked, they led nowhere. I no longer found comfort in pool halls or drugstores. Nor did I notice familiar faces moving through familiar lives. I saw only the empty cup of my career.

One night I found a bar (the same one where my fellow tenant punched his girl friend) where the bartender served me without question. I ordered a bottle of beer.

"What kind?" he grumbled.

I looked at him and said nothing. "*Schaefer!*" I finally said. I smiled, pleased with myself. "I'll have a bottle of Schaefer beer."

• • •

*Despite his bonus and exceptional talent, George Kopacz never reached the major leagues for any sustained length of time. As a left-handed hitter he had difficulty pulling the ball to the right side of the diamond. He played in the minors 14 years trying to learn how to pull the ball.

"We don't have Schaefer. That's an Eastern beer. How 'bout Falstaff?"

"Sure. If you don't have any Schaefer. Schaefer's the only kind I drink back home." I swung my leg over the bar stool and sat down. For much of the night I bemoaned the absence of Schaefer beer in the Midwest while the bartender nodded perfunctorily and polished his counter. He was a gruff man, neither friendly nor unfriendly. He moved mechanically through his rounds—nodding, polishing, pouring, dropping coasters on the bar and poking at the levers of his register. When he poured beer from a tap he held the glass at a 45-degree angle to keep narrow the beer's width of foam. When he poured whiskey he stuck the bottle's silver spout into the glass, steadily raising it as he poured until the bottle was a foot above the glass and the pouring whiskey was a gently curving stem. With a twist of his wrist, he'd then snap off the flow.

The bartender knew I was a ballplayer, but the knowledge neither impressed nor disturbed him. He must also have known that I was not yet 21, the legal drinking age in Iowa, but that seemed not to disturb him either so long as I behaved myself. Which I did. I never got drunk. After three beers I heard a faint buzz, and after one more my flesh tingled, and after the fifth (my limit) my limbs grew heavy and mildly numb. I liked these new sensations, and I liked that bar, too, with its dark womblike silences. I liked the unspoken bond among its drinkers, who sat hunched forward, elbows on the counter, staring into their glasses. I liked the idea of sharing, for the first time, in this male ritual of drowning one's sorrows. It gave me pleasure—not the sorrows, not the fact that I was adult enough to drown those sorrows, but the knowledge that this solitary act was being shared with others, and in that sharing our common sorrows were diminished. I liked this tacit sharing. It put me under no obligation. It required no talk, no dues, nothing but that I sit there and drink alongside the others.

One night as I approached the bar I saw Rico Carty lumbering toward me. He was frightening—a massive black man stalking the city streets. As he moved, his shoulders tilted left then right like a bully spoiling for a fight. He had unbelievably long arms, and his hands, the size of shovels, almost reached the ground. Today he is one of the few active major leaguers with a lifetime batting average above .300, but that night he was simply a 20-year-old rookie from the Dominican Republic who hit monstrous home runs in batting practice and struck out mightily in games. He was a catcher then. His throwing arm was a bazooka without a sight. Opposing runners stole second base unmolested while Rico fired baseballs to the center field wall. He was so tightly muscled (from work in the fields and his training as a boxer) that he moved in slow motion behind the plate. He let so many balls roll to the screen that our pitchers pleaded with Travis not to have him catch them. Travis demurred. The boy needed work, he said, then added, "He'll be all right soon as he grows a pair of hands on the ends of those arms."

The American players treated Rico like an overgrown child.* Although Rico spoke and understood English well enough, they'd talk to him in pidgin: "Rico strong boy hit ball far way." They laughed at the way he ran—flat-footed, like a clown in flapping oversized shoes. They laughed at his naïveté when a slick clothing salesman sold him 12 woolen sweaters and 12 pairs of flannel slacks in the middle of the summer. Rico was

• • •

*Most American players treat Latins (often the first foreigners they have ever met) in such a condescending way because of their belief that deficiencies in the English language imply other intellectual shortcomings. For certain sensitive Latins this condescension is a constant irritation that leads to a moodiness which only reinforces the Americans' belief that all Latins are overgrown children.

so proud of these new acquisitions (many American players, upon receiving their checks each month, also bought flashy and unneeded clothes) that he assembled one outfit—orange-and-black sweater with a shawl collar and lime slacks—for each week. That same outfit would then be worn all week before it was discarded, never to be seen again.

Rico played to our image of him. Whenever he let yet another passed ball roll back to the screen, he would return to the dugout at the end of the inning and sulk like a child. He sat on the bench—legs spread apart, arms dangling between them—and stared at the floor. Every so often the whites of his eyes would shift left or right to see if we were aware of his sulking. Whenever he struck out, which he did frequently in those days, he returned to the dugout scowling and cursing in Spanish, "Konyo, No-Holla!" and when he saw us grinning at his display of anger he cursed louder, scowled more ominously and finally, began to make menacing gestures. But he never attacked us. He was not really angry. His apparent moods never corresponded to his true feelings. He merely snatched them from the air (laughter, curses) for our edification and then discarded them in a flash. Most of the time he cultivated the booming, back-slapping temperament of a Rotarian. He always greeted me the same way: "Hey there, good-looking big-bonus right-hander who throws smoke!" And then he would tip his head back and laugh uproariously. The laughter contained more than a little contempt, and I think, now, it afforded Rico some measure of satisfaction for the manner in which we treated him.

Rico lived with a few other Latin players in a rooming house in the city. (Most of the players had rented houses on the outskirts of town and gravitated to their kind. Only a few blacks, Latins and myself lived in the city.) One of his roommates was a gaunt, haggard-looking string bean with skin the

179

color of coffee. He claimed he was a 20-year-old Dominican Republic rookie like Rico, but with his graying hair and the slack skin under his eyes he looked more like a 40-year-old veteran. He was reputed to be a homosexual. This rumor was started by one of the other Latin players who walked into his bedroom one afternoon to find him admiring himself in front of a mirror. He was wearing a woman's half-slip and an unpadded bra with each cup stuffed with a can of peas. It was also rumored that this aging rookie was smitten with the charms of one of our fair blond pitchers, who, not mutually attracted, began to forgo his nightly shower in the clubhouse after each game. The latter did not return to the shower until his Dominican paramour was given his unconditional release.

When I saw Rico wandering about that night he looked as lost and pitiful as myself. I felt sorry for him (and more than a little guilty), so I invited him into the bar for a beer. He was the object of curious glances from the bartender and the patrons. (How noble I was!) Rico and I had little to say. After two beers he fell silent as a stone. After the third he folded his arms on the counter, lay his head down and fell asleep. The bartender, polishing glasses, stared at Rico, snoring. The next time I entered that bar the bartender complained about my friend. I apologized for his behavior, assured him it wouldn't happen again, that my friend was just awfully tired . . .

"That's not the point," he said. "My customers don't want no buck nigger in here. Not even awake. You understand?"

"Sure," I said, a little stunned. Then he asked for proof that I was 21 years old, and when I couldn't produce any he said he was sorry but that I'd have to leave.

Except for my silent and infrequent walks along the river bank with Marge, I had sworn off romantic entanglements at Davenport. My fiasco with Sally in McCook had convinced me

180

such adventures were not all they were cracked up to be. Besides, I was sure that God had punished me for my indiscretion with Sally by damning my pitching. My celibacy at Davenport would be rewarded with a string of gems (no-hitters, shutouts, etc.) that would lift me out of the Midwest League and deposit me in the majors. As an afterthought, I decided that I should also be faithful to my girl back home since she would shortly become my fiancée. As always, the abstraction was more appealing than the reality.

After two celibate months in Davenport I had been rewarded with a 3–8 record and a 4.50 ERA. I felt like the suicidal spinster in *The Devil and Miss Jones*, who finds herself condemned to hell without first having tasted the fruits of sin. So I resolved to taste some fruits.

Each morning I dressed impeccably—Banlon jersey, chino slacks, penny loafers—and always about noon, walked downtown. I waited in front of a bank for the city's myriad secretaries to pass by on their way to lunch. I leered at them. No one leered back. I leaned against the bank's foundation and assumed a more seductive pose—arms folded, head cocked jauntily, eyes half-lidded. I smirked. Still no takers. I grew bolder and tracked pretty girls through the streets like some twentieth-century roué, only to be foiled time after time and forced to slink back into the shadows when they were met by boyfriends.

I was drooping sadly at my post one hot afternoon when I sniffed fresh lilacs and looked up to see a curvaceous little blond walking up the street. I gave chase. She had short, wavy hair fluffed up in back like a rabbit's tail. Through a filmy pink blouse I could make out a black bra. I narrowed the gap. Her blouse was tucked into a wide belt, and she wore a long black skirt that reached to her calves and was so tight she could barely walk in it. She had to content herself with tiny steps, like bunny hops, and with each step her tail twitched. Peeking below the hem of her skirt was the faintest hint of tangerine lace.

I tracked her in the hot sun until I was exhausted. She was tireless! She hopped into banks and offices and stores, and while she conducted her business, I waited outside, panting for breath. I was still panting when she hopped out moments later and continued on her way, unwilted. Doggedly, I returned to the scent. Would she never light? Finally she entered a cafeteria. I followed her inside and lost her in the crowd. I sniffed for her scent but smelled only food. I decided to eat. I passed through the cafeteria line, selecting my dishes, and carried my tray to an empty table. No sooner had I sat down than I smelled lilacs. Looking up, I saw my quarry sit down at the same table. I was too surprised to speak. I lowered my head and ate in silence.

She reached over and tapped me on the shoulder. "My, but that looks like a tasty little lunch!" Her voice was filled with wonder. It seemed to emanate from some point above her eyes, from her forehead maybe. She did not stop talking. She called me sir. "And in what institution of employment are you situated, sir, if you don't mind my being so bold as to intrude into your private affairs?"

"What?"

"Work?" she said, with less wonder. "Where do you work?" I told her and she squealed with delight. "Oh, goody!" She began clapping her hands in front of her face; they were stiff, tiny pats, as if she was flattening hamburger meat into patties. "I love athletes!" She lowered her eyes demurely and reached a limp hand across the table. "Allow me to introduce myself. I am Arlita Schwartzfelder." We shook hands over the food and I told her my name. "Wait!" she demanded. "Wait just a minute!" She began rummaging through her bag and eventually produced a black address book and a fountain pen. "Now," she said, as she uncapped the pen. "What was that name again?"

"Jordan. Pat Jordan."

She flipped through the pages which seemed almost completely filled with names, addresses and telephone numbers, mostly of males. Some names had little red stars beside them. When she came to the section lettered "G" she began to write.

"No, it's Jordan. With a 'J'."

"Oh! Why didn't you tell me? I've messed up a clean space!" She flipped forward to the "J" section, which was completely filled except for a bit of room at the bottom. She made me spell my name slowly, then my address and my telephone number, all of which she recorded in a neat little script (i's dotted with a perfect circle) in green ink.

I did not see Arlita again. But as this encounter had considerably cooled my amorous fires, I abandoned my post at the bank and probably would have finished the year in a celibate state if not for the arrival one night at Davenport Stadium of the Kilgore Rangerettes. They are a precision dancing group of about 40 girls, much like the Radio City Music Hall Rockettes except that the Rangerettes usually appear at outdoor athletic functions. They are long-stemmed, pretty girls who wear cowboy boots and hats, and very short skirts. Supposedly, they are all students as tiny Kilgore Junior College in Kilgore, Texas (population 11,000).

When I arrived early for that night's game the Rangerettes were already performing on the field for about 3000 fans, most of whom would leave immediately after the performance, which was considerably more precise than ours ever were. I found our dressing room—a cramped concrete tomb—littered with the girls' belongings. The dented metal lockers resting precariously against the walls were filled with their street clothes, and the wire clothesline strung overhead, from wall to wall, was drapped with their underclothes—bras, slips, panties. I remember thinking it was a shame our Dominican transvestite had been released, because he would have been in ecstasy. I can see him now, trying on this and that little thing, admiring himself in our cracked wall mirror, talking a half-step back, hands on hips, spinning around to face his assembled teammates, who, seated in full uniform and with legs crossed, begin to applaud lightly but with enthusiasm—"Bravo!"

I remember, too, that there was an effluvium of female in that musty locker room that was stronger than any I had ever known and certainly ever expected to find there.

I sat in the dugout with my teammates and watched the Rangerettes perform. Out on the field under the stadium's lights, they looked young and pretty. But when they finished their routine and filed past us into the runway (with only bored glances at our expectant faces), they looked neither pretty nor young. Their smiling faces were a plaster cast of makeup: purple lips, rouged cheeks, false eyelashes with bluish lids, lacquered hair that seemed a solid piece. More than one of those Junior College students had faint laugh lines at the corners of their eyes. The girls went directly to the locker room where they showered, dressed and, later that night, moved on to another town. We had no opportunity to cultivate friendships, which, in retrospect, probably wasn't such a loss since they looked older and decidedly more professional than any of the Quad Cities Braves. Still, they impressed us then. And when we boarded the team bus the following morning for a four-day road stand in Keokuk, Iowa, I could think of nothing but that locker room, their underclothes and those hardened faces, which more than a little excited me.

I turned right off Keokuk's main street and began walking slowly up a side street staring at the houses across the way.

They were mostly large, white or gray Victorian types with a porch, small front lawns and an occasional tree or a few shrubs. It was noon of a blazing day. The sun was a white ball lobbed high in a cloudless sky. The street was deserted and without shade. As I walked and stared, the houses and telephone poles and tar road began to shimmer in the heat and melt before my eyes. I was drenched with perspiration when I saw the house with number 7 on its front door. I lowered my head and walked quickly to the end of the road.

I stopped and drew a breath. I looked back at number 7, a house like all the others. It was gray with white shutters. It had three wooden steps leading to a roofed porch and a screen door. There were two metal chaise lounges and a number of rocking chairs on the porch, more than on any porch along the street. I walked back, my eyes riveted to number 7, and passed it again. After three more passes, I stopped across the street from it. I stared at the house for a long moment. The house grew liquid and dissolved before my eyes. I blinked once, twice, tried to refocus on the house. Now I was growing liquid, would dissolve, too, if I did not finally act.

I walked across the street, up the steps, inside the porch and knocked on the screen door. A shadow appeared far down a narrow corridor and grew larger as it approached. A thin, bent old man in a gray cardigan squinted at me through wire-rimmed spectacles. His hair was gray and short, and he had a stubble of beard around his pointed chin.

"Well!" he said. He was holding a napkin in one hand, dabbing at his lips.

I shook my head. "I'm sorry," I said. "I must have the wrong house."

"Are you looking for my girls?" he asked.

"No, I don't think . . ."

"You want a girl, don't you?"

"Yes." He held the screen door open for me and then led me down the corridor toward another screen door, through which I could see sunlight. Before we reached it he turned right into a small room. "Wait here," he said. "The girls are eating lunch. I'll send one in when they finish."

He left. The room was dark and cool and looked like the waiting room of a doctor's office. Against its walls were a number of straight-backed chairs and two worn couches that faced each other. The couches had flowery slipcovers, and on each armrest was a white lace doily. In the middle of the small room was a large coffee table stacked with magazines—*Life, Look, Saturday Evening Post, Sports Illustrated, Popular Mechanics, Reader's Digest, National Geographic* and others. I sat down on one of the couches and began to flip, unseeing, through a copy of *Life*. From the doorway through which the old man had exited, I could hear the clatter of dishes and knives and forks, and the high-pitched sound of women's voices. I could make out only bits of conversation—a new dress, a day off with the children, the heat, more potatoes.

I leaned forward on the couch and peeked through the doorway into what was the kitchen. It was a blinding white room. Sunlight poured through a window above a white enamel sink. The light glanced off the sink and the white enamel stove beside it, and the white walls, too. Momentarily dazzled by all that whiteness, I could just make out a dark mass in the center of the room. But when my eyes adjusted, I saw the dark mass was a long table and that on each side sat three women between the ages of 20 and 30. They ate and chatted and passed dishes of food back and forth. At one end of the table was the old man, his napkin tucked under his chin, his face low to his plate. At the opposite end sat a plump lady in a faded house dress. Her hair was white and tied in a bun at the base of her neck. Like the old man, who I presumed was

186

her husband, she also wore spectacles. Sitting straight-backed in her chair, she raised an occasional forkful of food high to her lips. And as she chewed she looked back and forth at her chattering girls and smiled. When one of those girls stood up, I ducked my head back from the doorway. I was flipping wildly through the magazine when she entered the waiting room.

"Hi, there!" she said. "I guess you're next."

The girl wore a white blouse with a Peter Pan collar and loose-fitting Bermuda shorts. She was not unpretty, but without makeup she was just an ordinary-looking woman of about 28. Certainly she was not as appealing as those Kilgore Rangerettes.

I followed her upstairs and down a hallway past three tiny rooms. Each room contained a bed—a cot, really—with a pillow at one end and a washcloth and towel folded neatly at the other. There was also a bed lamp that bathed each room in a rose-colored light. And a small sink. She entered the fourth room, saying, "This one's mine." It was identical to the others. Immediately, she began to undress. She moved in that methodical, unselfconscious way women do when undressing alone. "What do you do?" she asked. "I've never seen you before." I told her I was a ballplayer. "We don't service many ballplayers," she said, shrugging out of her bra. "Only visiting teams. The Cardinals wanted us to service their black players, too, but we didn't like the idea. We voted on it—the girls in the house, that is—and we were unanimously against it. When we told the Cardinal's player representative—he was a shortstop, I think—he said his teammates would boycott the house until we changed our vote. But we never did. We stuck to our principles." She dropped her Bermudas and stepped out of them. Then she wiggled out of her panties. They were plain, white, cotton ones. "Since that day we haven't had a single Cardinal player come to the house."

187

She was naked. She had a soft, almost plump, white body. Her breasts were small and sagged slightly. Her belly, a pronounced curve, had thin stretch marks across it. Her thighs were meaty, and the flesh in back rippled where the muscle had begun to break down and turn to fat. It was a mature woman's body that was unattractive to me then, at 19, when I expected all naked women to resemble those taut, tanned, and tinted photographs in *Playboy* magazine. Her pubic hair hypnotized me. It was black. The hair on her head was brown. More puzzled than aroused, I kept staring at her pubic hair.

"Well," she said, "aren't you going to undress?" She was standing in front of the sink, facing me, hands on hips. I looked up to her face, nodded dumbly and began to undress. When I'd finished she said, "Come here."

I went over to her, put my arms around her, closed my eyes and kissed her on the lips. She twisted her head away. "Hey! What's the idea?"

I sprang back. "Jeez, I'm sorry . . . I didn't mean to . . ." I'd misunderstood everything! She was a nurse! A physical therapist! This was a private hospital! Oh, sweet Jesus, let me out of here!

"Is this your first time in a house?" she asked. I nodded. "Oh, okay. But we don't kiss the customers. You understand?"

"Sure! Jeez, I'm sorry, really, I'm very sorry . . ."

"Forget it." She took the washcloth from the cot, turned on the water in the sink and soaped the cloth thoroughly. Then she stuck it between my legs and washed me. "Just a precaution," she said as she scrubbed. "Pa keeps a clean house." When she finished she dried me off with a towel and then examined me with a calculating and withering eye. Satisfied, she finally said, "Well, what'll it be? Straight or half-and-half?"

"Half what?"

"Half-French."

"Oh, yeah! Sure! I'll have a half-French." My God! What had I ordered? Some sexual hors d'oeuvre I'd never tasted and whose ingredients I was ignorant of?

"That'll be 10 dollars." I paid her and she told me to lie down on the cot. I waited for her to lie down beside me, but instead she dropped to her knees beside the cot. *She was going to say her prayers?* Her head was above my waist. She lowered it to me. I watched her in amazement. She kept her eyes open as she worked. All of a sudden she raised her head and stifled a burp with her fingertips. She looked up at me. "Sorry, dear. I shouldn't have eaten those extra potatoes," and then she resumed. I lay my head on the pillow and stared at the ceiling. Was I doomed to fiascoes?

I remember only Keokuk, of all the towns we played in, for the most obvious reason. But I also remember Keokuk because I ate my first fried catfish there (it tasted like chicken), and because our hotel had a sign over its third-floor window that read "Fire Escape" and which opened on a length of knotted rope hanging to the sidewalk, and because Keokuk was a small, sleepy Mississippi River town right out of Mark Twain. The other Midwest League towns were larger than Keokuk—were cities, really—and were indistinguishable. We traveled to them on Trailways buses. Usually we boarded those buses at midnight, after a home game, and then rode for six or seven hours. They were monotonous rides. I tried to sleep but invariably found myself staring out the window at the black scenery, staring for so many hours that eventually I grew blind to it, saw only my own reflection, which I scrutinized with such care that it hypnotized me.

We arrived, stiff and foul-smelling, with the morning sun. Weighted down with our bags, we staggered into the lobby of a third-rate hotel and milled about sleepily while Travis, father to us all, got our room keys. The hotel's early-rising guests stared at us—an odd assortment of youths of every shape and size and color—but we were too tired to stare back. We got our keys from Travis, went to our rooms and fell asleep, fully clothed. Like weekend drunks, we woke late in the afternoon in a strange hotel room, our clothes sticking to our bodies and our mouths sour-tasting. We showered, shaved, brushed our teeth and dressed in the best clothes we had brought on this road trip. (We always wore our best clothes that first day, our next best the second day, and so on, until by the fifth day we had to return to our best clothes, a little soiled now. We'd then wear those clothes for the next two days, so that when we boarded the bus for the ride back to Davenport, we looked as grubby as when we had arrived.) Once we'd cleaned ourselves up we'd go outside to examine the city. It was three o'clock in the afternoon. On the road, our days always began at three o'clock in the afternoon.

The moment we hit the street we went shopping. We bought transistor radios, records, cigarette lighters, shirts, slacks—none of which we needed and all of which were identical to those we could have bought in Davenport. But our purchases, like those of bored housewives, were compulsive. We needed them as proof we had arrived. And later, because our stays were so brief and one city blurred into the next, they served as reminders of where we had been: we had only to put on those slacks with a waistband proclaiming the name of some department store in Kokomo, Indiana. Once we'd made our purchases we could relax and have our meal. It was always breakfast, to the amazement of waitresses. Afterwards, we (my teammates, that is, I walked alone) strolled four-abreast on the sidewalks and gawked at pretty girls. We gawked at the not-so-pretty girls, too, since our intention was never to pick up one of those girls but only by our boisterous swagger to call atten-

190

tion to ourselves. (As if eight youths—three of whom were speaking Spanish—strolling aimlessly about town at four o'clock on a weekday afternoon needed to draw attention to themselves.) But we were professional baseball players and we wanted everyone to know it. But somehow, the way we saw ourselves (the fast new guns in town, Hannibal come over the Alps on a Trailways bus), as objects of worship and envy, was not how we were seen by those townspeople going about their ordinary day. And so, mildly disappointed, we returned to the hotel and waited for our bus ride to the ball park for that night's game. After the game, we would do what we did after *every* night game on the road—eat first, and then spend the hours until our one o'clock curfew in a bar.

Once the initial novelty had worn off and we discovered there was nothing in Kokomo to differentiate it from Waterloo or Decatur, we passed the remaining days close to our hotel. By the third day we seldom left it. We did nothing for hours on end. We waited impatiently for each meal and, finally, the bus that would take us to the game. Throughout the day we sat in the lobby and passed time. We read *The Sporting News*, always turning first to the back pages to check the statistics of other Milwaukee farmhands like ourselves. We made dozens of trips to the hotel coffee shop, talked always to the waitresses no matter how homely, left innumerable half-filled cups of coffee, and then returned to the lobby. We went to the news-stand and bought Dentyne gum, which we distributed to our teammates. We slumped in the lobby's worn easy chairs, jumped up moments later, returned to the newsstand, bought cigars, tossed them to our teammates and sat down again in our chairs. We never read much except *The Sporting News* (occasionally *Sport* magazine, but never *Sports Illustrated*, which was too esoteric and not hard-core-fan like *Sport*), nor did we talk about anything other than baseball, our careers, girls,

191

steaks, beer, or that men's store in Decatur (our next stop) "with the good threads."

By the fifth day we were indistinguishable from the lobby's potted rubber plants. We looked real enough, looked alive, yet day after day we were always the same. We were always in the same pose, the same chair, talking about the same things. We never grew. We didn't have to. As long as we remained "in baseball" we could postpone the unpleasantness of growing. Years later, in the major leagues, we would still be sitting in hotel lobbies on the road, still talking about the same things. From Class D to the majors, life on the road never changed. Only the quality of the things in it changed. Whether in Kokomo or Atlanta, it was always boring, yet it was also elemental and understandable. Our life was simple in a way that life outside of baseball never was, and, so, sitting in those lobbies, we never wanted to leave. We deliberately kept our conversations elemental. We deliberately thwarted growth because we feared it would lead to the realization, not that our little boys' dream was insignificant, but just that it was not significant enough to excuse our wasting all that time. Nothing excused that! So to ward off unwanted doubts we studiously remained, as much as possible, the same person who had first had that dream.

The season ended in Kokomo.* I pitched 6 1/3 innings of excellent relief to win my fifth and final game of the season. I had lost 12 times. My earned run average was 4.67. I had allowed 105 hits in 135 innings, walked 119 and struck out 143. I was consistent all year. Each week when the Midwest League statistics were published, I was at the bottom of the list of starting pitchers with more than 100 innings worked. Those at

• • •

* The Braves finished in last place, where we had been for most of the season.

the top of the list were Bob Sprout, a Decatur southpaw who led the league in strikeouts and once pitched a no-hitter in which he struck out 22 batters; and Tom Haake, a Dubuque right-hander who finished the season with a 19–3 record. Neither of them had a major league career, either.*

After my final victory Travis told me that the Braves wanted to send me to the Florida Instructional League in October. This was a showcase for all the most talented young players in the system, players who needed only a little more experience and coaching before they moved up to the majors. I was one such player, said Travis, despite my horrible statistics. I was thrilled at the news.

"All you need is some confidence and control," he said, for the hundredth time that year. "You've got the stuff."

"I know," I said.

"There's one other thing," he said. "The Braves are worried about you, son. They're worried about your attitude. You don't get along."

"I like being alone," I said.

"That's all right. A lot of guys in this game are loners. But, still, you got to get along with your teammates sometime. You got to fit in someplace or else you'll never make it. You listen to old Travis, now, he's been in this game 40 years."

"I know."

• • •

*Some of the players who did make the majors from the Midwest League that year were (besides Hicks and McCraw) Steve Blass, Wilbur Wood (then a fastball pitcher), Gerry Arrigo, Jim Ray Hart, and, of course, Rico Carty. There were others, I'm sure, but I can't remember their names. All of the players I've mentioned were rookies and none of them (except Hicks) were stars in the Midwest League in 1960.

# ...6

AUTUMN in Bradenton, Florida, is like spring in Connecticut. The nights and mornings and late afternoons are pleasantly cool, and the middays are sunny and warm. Living in Bradenton from September to November 1960, I grew accustomed to its springlike weather. When I returned to Connecticut in late November, I found the days cold and sunless, and the nights freezing. It was winter in Connecticut, and would remain so for months. This fact confused me then and for a long time after, until one day I realized that what I had experienced in Bradenton had been a false spring.

The Florida Winter Instructional League was (and still is) essentially a baseball prep school for the brightest prospects from a number of major league organizations. Among them in 1960 were the Braves, the White Sox in Sarasota, the Kansas City Athletics in Clearwater and the Indians and Twins in St. Petersburg. Players sent to the FWIL, which operated from September to November, were not necessarily the most successful in each system, but rather those with the most potential for success. Each team consisted of 25 players who, it was hoped, would benefit from extensive individual instruction (something minor leaguers never got, I had discovered) and an additional 60-game fall semester, all of which would hasten their graduation into the majors. Each team was a one-room school house of variously educated talent. Under the same roof one found freshmen who had yet to play in a professional game;

194

sophomores, like myself, who had played only in the lowest grades; seniors, who had advanced as high as Triple-A; and even a handful of graduates who had played briefly and tenuously at the top. Despite the disparity of our baseball education, we were united by a natural talent for hitting, fielding and throwing a baseball. Some were closer to fulfilling the promise of that talent than others, but we all had it—the talent, that is. Everyone was paid the same wage: $350 a month.

The caliber of play in the FWIL was comparable to that of a Double-A league. The conditions, however, were big league. We lived in the same towns, used the same stadiums, uniforms, equipment, and had the same weekly schedule as did the senior clubs during their spring training. We played five games a week, had one day of practice only and one day off. The games were played in the afternoon. Mornings were devoted to instruction from the best hitting, fielding and pitching coaches each organization had to offer. Many were from major league rosters, although some also came from their organization's most prestigious minor league teams. The managers of each team were never major league managers. Some had managed recently in Triple-A or Double-A leagues, but more than one had managed recently as low as Class D, too. Unlike big league managers, they were not necessarily all master strategists with a reputation for winning ball games. In fact, there were many who had never won a pennant at any level and had finished in last place more than once during their careers. But their ability to win games was irrelevant to their being sent to the FWIL. They did not deal in wins and losses. They dealt in potential. They were masters at fulfilling it in others.

My manager was Ben Geraghty. He was 45. He had begun his professional career in 1936 as an infielder with the Dodgers, but was sent to the minor leagues that same year. He played briefly in the lower minors until, at the age of 30, he became a minor league manager. In 1960 he had managed the Louisville Colonels to the American Association (AAA) championship. He had been a minor league manager for 16 years and his teams had finished lower than second place only four times. During his nine years in the Braves' system his teams had won six league pennants. In 1957 *The Sporting News* voted him "Minor League Manager of the Year."

Hank Aaron, who once played for him, believed that Ben Geraghty was the greatest manager who ever lived, and certainly the greatest he had ever played for. Aaron gave him much of the credit for his own swift rise to stardom. He remembered Geraghty from his days as the first black player in the history of the Sally League. In 1953 Aaron was a shy 19-year-old second baseman for the Jacksonville Braves, then managed by Geraghty. Whenever the team stopped to eat in cities like Macon or Memphis or Shreveport, Geraghty invited Aaron to join him. Geraghty went always to the best restaurant in the white section of the city, where, invariably, they would be refused service. While Aaron waited nervously outside, Geraghty complained loudly to the management. Aaron could see him gesticulating through the restaurant's window. When Geraghty had spent his rage he left that restaurant and led Aaron to the next best restaurant in the city. The same scene was repeated. They went on to the next best restaurant, and the next and the next, until finally Geraghty located one that would serve an Irishman from Boston and a black youth from Macon. Often they would not discover such a spot until they had crossed that invisible boundary that separated the white and the black communities in such cities and found themselves eating fried chicken in an all-black cafe. Aaron could relax considerably in that cafe, where, he wished forlornly, his manager had let him go in the first place. Geraghty, beside him, never relaxed. He was still gesticulating wildly, still raging at all those restaurants they had been turned away from, and he was not yet conscious of his present surroundings or the curious stares from the black patrons.

When I arrived in Bradenton in the fall of 1960, Ben Geraghty was already a legendary figure in professional baseball. His former players spoke of him in mystical as well as mythical terms, or so it seemed to one who had never met him. They said he was the game's most brilliant strategist. He had the highest winning percentage of any manager in baseball history. He was a master at inducing aging veterans like Ed Charles to surpass their own self-defined limitations, while at the same time and on the same team, he coddled and prodded young prospects into fulfilling their potential. After Ben had soothed aching muscles and psyches, his players performed on the diamond in a way they had never done before, amazing even themselves. Thirty-three-year-old pitchers swore they could reach back for fastballs they had lost four seasons ago, while wild rookies were cutting the outside corner of the plate with a fastball for the first time in their lives. And if you played for Ben Geraghty, they said, and afterwards you could not do these things, then you could not do these things period. For any manager. Whatever you did for Geraghty, it was your potential fulfilled.

Ben Geraghty did not become a legend at the age of 45 because of any magic he worked on the diamond. His players spoke of him with an awe and reverence one associates not with a minor league manager who had enriched their careers, but with a man who had enriched their lives in a way that had nothing to do with baseball. They spoke of him the way football players speak of Vince Lombardi. Yet there was a fundamental difference. The reverence accorded Lombardi was as much a response to his philosophy of sport and life as it was to the man. He was an evangelist of victory ("Winning isn't everything, it's the only thing") in a realm judged only by wins and losses. He preached to his players that their potentials (and his) were fulfilled only by victories. Then he taught them how to win. He fired and softened and hammered their collective wills into a vision all his own. Each victory gave credence to his goal-centered view of life, and thus to the man behind it. Without victories, Lombardi, the loser, would be a fool.

Ben Geraghty was more saint than evangelist. He saw life in terms of means, not ends. He dealt in Lombardi's realm of wins and losses; he appreciated victories and earned more than his share, yet he preached no philosophy of victory. He was devoted first to the means to those victories. Geraghty hammered *his* will into a shape that still accommodated the disparate visions of his players. His first instinct was to help his players fulfill their potential, and after that his own, and lastly to win. Unlike Lombardi, he did not see these possibilities as mutually interlinked like the three Olympic rings. Often they were in conflict, and when they were Geraghty followed his first instinct. His choice was more compulsive than willful. Ultimately it destroyed his own potential as a major league manager, because as long as he was so successful at developing others' talent, he would be more valuable to the Braves' organization in the minor leagues than in the majors. He was a victim of "Catch-22" logic. His players saw this. They saw his loss as their gain, and the witness of his compulsive sacrifice was what led them to speak of him as did Charley Lau, a coach with the Baltimore Orioles in 1969. "Ben Geraghty? Jesus—yes! I knew the poor bastard! May God bless his soul."

The Bradenton ball park was laid out like Davenport Stadium, only it had no concrete runways and it was much smaller and fresher and more open to the sun. Everything in it was made out of wood painted a dark forest green. The exposed bleachers down each foul line were green, and so were the permanent seats behind the homeplate screen and the overhanging roof that shadowed them. The roofed-over dugouts on the field were green, too. Beside each dugout, however, were a few box seats painted a bright orange. These were reserved for major league owners, general managers, farm directors and scouts.

The playing field grass, a lighter green, was thick and spongy as only tropical grass can be. In spots it had become almost yellow from the year-round sun and heavy use. The dirt around home plate, the mound and the base paths were the color of a Temple orange and of such a consistency that it lodged in our spikes in solid clumps and was as difficult to knock off as moist clay. The outfield fence was made of wood, and it, too, was painted solid green, without advertisements. Behind the fence was a line of palm trees leaning this way and that like crossed swords, and some even hanging over the fence so that a fly ball hit into one was a ground-rule double.

The ball park had no lights. All games were played under a bright sun so that every color and texture of the day was discernible without the shadows of artificial light. Thrown and batted balls were no longer hazy, half-spheres but were completely round, white baseballs with red stitches and stains from the clay and grass. Everything in that ball park was sharp and clear, and the sound of a batted ball did not echo overhead like machine-gun fire, but was a solid crack that gradually diminished to silence in the palm trees. It was an unusually quiet place to play baseball. Our only fans were a few old men in sun visors, Bermuda shorts and knee-length stockings. They sat in the exposed bleachers so they could take the sun and doze.

A brilliant play on the field was rewarded with silence. We were never conscious of those fans, never conscious of performing for anyone but ourselves. Nor were we conscious of the

199

sounds of a city, of passing trains, of smoke rising from a factory, because there were no such things. We only saw the grass and the dirt and the ball and ourselves in uniform, and we only heard the smack of leather and the shouts from a shadowed dugout and the shrill whistle of a shortstop as he bent low for the next pitch. It was an ideal place to play baseball. The only thing we had to concentrate on was the game itself, and our performance in it.

Far down the left field line were two warm-up mounds, and beside them a green bench for our relief pitchers. A few yards beyond and behind that bench was a small, square, wooden building painted white. This served as our clubhouse and dressing room. After workouts and games we hung our wet uniforms outside to dry on rusty nails stuck in the side of the clubhouse. From a distance on a breezy day those flapping uniforms looked like oddly-shaped sails on some strange, landbound ship.

Inside, the clubhouse was all freshly cut and unstained pine —except for the floorboards, which had been stained permanently by wet feet from the showers. It was here, on the afternoon I arrived in Bradenton and the players had gone and the floor was still wet and littered with clumps of red clay and used towels, that I first met Ben Geraghty. It was his habit to stay late following practice or game so that he could replay the day's events in his mind in the silence of a deserted room. He was sitting—naked but for a towel wrapped around his waist —on a low stool in front of a locker. His legs were crossed and he was sucking from a can of beer, which he then drained in a long gulp, his head tilted far back, and tossed into a large aluminum pail before reaching down to rip another can from the six-pack beside his stool.

I went over to him, and with great effort he stood up. He was a thin, bent man with a bony chest and slack, grayish skin that hung in a smallish paunch at his belly like the skin of a woman who has had too many babies too soon. I introduced myself and we shook hands. His was soft and cold, the fingers as long and fleshless as pencils, only more delicate, and as I squeezed I could feel their brittle bones. Those fingers were useless to a ballplayer. He did not release my hand right away, but held it in a surprisingly firm clasp while he searched my face. His eyes were blue chips imbedded in dark sockets. The skin underneath the eyes hung in little folds as if pulled down by gravity. He had a long, sharp nose and thin lips that pulled down into his jaw. His face was shaped like a trowel, pointed at the chin. It was red from the sun, and his neck was red, too, in sharp contrast to his body.

He let go of my hand. "You're a good-looking boy," he said in a Boston accent. "A good-looking boy." His praise embarrassed me at first. It seemed unnatural until I realized he did not mean my face or my body but something that included both, and also my talent, yet was really more than the sum of these parts, too. Something in me had rearranged my surface parts in such a way that Ben Geraghty could read them, and in that reading see this deeper thing which I, after 19 years, still could not see.

We talked briefly, and I was surprised at how much he knew about me. Little things, like my closeness to my brother and my being of Italian extraction. Things that seemed to have nothing to do with baseball. After awhile he lost interest in me, or maybe he was just exhausted from his effort at conversation. He directed me to an empty locker and then sat down on his stool and was silent. I went over to the locker and began to store my equipment. When I looked back at Ben he was still sitting, cross-legged, on his stool, holding another can of beer.

I have never forgotten that first and only meeting with him. His sickly body, that drained face, those eyes. They were unbelievably blue and penetrating, and yet they seemed dis-

201

tracted, too, and terror-stricken, so that you could not look into them for very long without feeling that they were looking through and beyond you at some distant vision.

This vision had changed Ben Geraghty's life. Everything of importance before it had diminished to insignificance after it, and from then on his life was defined solely in terms of what he'd seen. No matter where he looked, or at whom, it was always there in the distance, a hard, gemlike image only Ben Geraghty could see. Nor could Ben reject the way that vision had altered the depth of his perceptions. After it, he saw more deeply into things than did the rest of us. His vision set him apart, scarred him. That scar was physically visible only as a thin white line running across his forehead at the base of his hairline. At first glance it looked like a frown line. He had received that scar in the summer of 1946, the year he began his managerial career with a Class B team in Spokane, Washington. Ben was 31. His team, like most lower minor league teams, traveled from town to town by bus. On the night of June 24, after a heavy rain, the team bus was maneuvering down a narrow road cut like a corkscrew into the side of a mountain. Halfway down the mountain the bus driver swerved off the road to avoid an approaching car. The bus traveled for a few seconds on the soft shoulder alongside the road, and then the shoulder began to crumble and fall away and the vehicle plummeted down the side of the mountain. When it came to rest 9 of the 15 players in it were dead, and Ben Geraghty was close to death. His head had smashed through a window, and the top of it was almost completely severed. He was still conscious, though, so he ripped off his shirt and tied it over his head and under his chin to try to stop the bleeding, and then he waited for help to arrive. He never passed out.

He survived that accident and eventually his wounds healed, although he was never again a healthy man. He was easily susceptible to cuts and sprains and colds and fevers, and the slightest effort exhausted him quickly. He was always resting, always catching a breath in the dugout before he walked out to the mound for the second time in an inning to relieve his pitcher. He was susceptible, too, to sudden movements and unexpected noises, which so terrified him that he tried always to anticipate them. After the accident he tried to anticipate everything before it happened, and in so doing he seemed perpetually distracted from what was happening at the moment. The present seemed to hold little interest for him. He'd already seen it, and it was no threat. Only the future was a threat, and so, even as he spoke to you, he was looking through and beyond you into the future. This struggle to intuit threats sharpened and deepened his perceptions to such an extent that in time he was able to see not only threats but many things the rest of us could not see. He saw beyond his players to the things they'd say and do before they said and did them. And in the process he began to know his players better than they knew themselves. This deepened perception was what made Ben Geraghty a great manager and a great man, and he owed it to his accident.

He also owed to that accident an inordinate fear of buses. It caused him such excruciating mental pain to ride in one that he considered giving up his dream of becoming a major league manager. The dream was simply not worth all those team buses he would have to board as long as he managed in the minors. Eventually, though, Ben chose to continue his career, knowing that his decision would force him to confront that fear constantly. On road trips he'd wear his "lucky shirt" and sit in the front seat directly behind the bus driver. Beside him, Ben would have one of his players deposit a case of beer. Throughout the night while his players slept, Ben drained bottle after bottle and, as he did, talked incessantly to the driver. He talked about the weather, at first, and then the land and the city they were driving to, and when he sensed the driver growing bored Ben switched to baseball or football or whatever the driver's favorite sport, and when those topics began to wear thin Ben asked about the driver's wife and children, or his sexual encounters or anything that would hold his interest throughout the night. And as he spoke Ben did not look at the driver's face reflected in the mirror above his seat, nor at the back of his head, but stared instead through the bus window at the illuminated road ahead. Ben searched for signs, and, as he did his shoulders jerked left and right and his foot stabbed the floor. When the bus arrived at its destination, the players would wake to find their manager had consumed all his beer and simply looked more haggard than usual.

But with each year Ben's health deteriorated. He had trouble with his liver because of his drinking, he got an ulcer because of his dread, and finally, in the spring of 1960, his heart began to go. The faster his health deteriorated, the more obsessed Ben became with the idea that he must manage in the major leagues as soon as possible. He had no time, he told the Braves' front office. He had no time. The Braves told him he was a young man, barely into his forties, and that after he had stocked the big team with all those minor leaguers whose talents only he could cultivate, then one day in his fifties he would become their manager. No matter how he tried, Ben could never convince the Milwaukee organization that his life was not spinning out at any natural speed, but that it was more like a 45-rpm record turning at a 78 rpm's.

Even Ben's failing health contributed to his managerial genius. Because he could no longer participate physically in the game (hit fungoes, pitch batting practice) he was forced, like a handicapped person, to cultivate other faculties. Baseball became for him a mental exercise. He memorized its rules and searched for a private advantage. He calculated every conceivable percentage and, yet, was not afraid to go against any of them on a whim. He made a study of the weather of each city and the variances of each ball park, as well as the temperaments, abilities and deficiencies of each umpire and player who ever passed before his sight. He absorbed every shade and nuance of the game until there was no situation to which he, as a manager, could not adjust.

This consumed his waking life. Sitting on the team bus or in a hotel room or bar or dugout, he proposed—out loud—a hundred hypothetical situations that he resolved in a dozen different ways before finding the most satisfactory solution. At times his players thought him mad. In the dugout he might turn to a rookie pitcher and grab his arm, *"Well,* what would you throw him now?" Before the stunned rookie could open his mouth, Ben would snap at him, *"Think first, for Chrissakes! Think!"* And while that rookie thought in tangles, Ben answered his own question and then, forgetting the rookie, sunk back into a corner of the dugout and the privacy of his own mind.

But no matter how Ben resolved his hypotheses, he was no armchair dreamer like Leo Durocher, manipulating Ty Cobbs across a flawless diamond only to discover that in reality he was burdened with mediocre talents who could not fulfill those theories. Ben Geraghty never strayed beyond the limits of players—their strengths and weaknesses.

I avoided my manager at first. I was in awe of him and not a little afraid, too. I was not sure then whether he was a saint or a madman. During our morning batting practice I either shagged fly balls in the outfield or else worked off a warm-up mound in the left field bullpen. Ben always sat in the dugout. From the bullpen I could see only his pant legs crossed in the sunlight. The rest of his body was hidden back in the shadows

205

of the dugout. He sat motionless for hours. He seldom spoke. Every so often he summoned one of his five coaches, who disappeared into the shadows and, seconds later, reappeared with a message. "Jordan, get loose for B.P."

Late in the morning Ben stepped out of the shadows into the sunlight. Instinctively he raised a hand, palm outward, to shade his eyes from the sun. It was a gesture of self-defense. He began walking toward the clubhouse. He passed the bullpen without a word or a glance. I nodded out of fear, but received no response. He disappeared into the clubhouse to rest a bit and drink a few bottles of beer, and then, 20 minutes later, returned to his seat in the dugout, from where he could see everything.

Dixie Walker, our hitting instructor, stood behind the batting cage at home plate. Dixie had been a major league outfielder for 18 years and had compiled a .306 lifetime batting average. His most productive years were spent in Brooklyn in the 1940s, where he was known as "The People's Cherce." Now, in his fifties, he was a tall, soft, slouch-shouldered man with timid eyes. He had a small, high-pitched Southern drawl, and when he spoke spittle formed at the corners of his mouth.

Dixie folded his arms across the back of the batting cage, leaned slightly forward and propped his chin on his arms as if to take a nap. His eyes narrowed as he studied each hitter— Barry Morgan, my teammate at McCook; Ron Liptak, an infielder from Holy Cross College; Joe Torre, soon to be a major league star; Rich Herrscher, a veteran minor leaguer who would play briefly with the New York Mets; Herman Hubbard, a tall, slender, 20-year-old black of uncommon grace and power.

Hubbard played center field like a young Willie Mays. He raced after long drives with his back to home plate and caught them over his shoulder following a last-second, almost indifferent glance. He ran the bases like Mays, too, always rounding first a little too wide as if deliberately giving the opposition an advantage he could erase on his way to second with his lengthening, effortless, ground-consuming, greyhound's stride, his cap flying off in his wake. Hubbard was supposed to play for the Louisville Colonels in 1961 and the Milwaukee Braves in 1962, but he never did. After the 1960 Winter League season was over, he returned to his home in Delaware. One night he took his fiancée out to dinner. It was a cold night in midwinter. When they returned, he parked his car in her garage and, while they talked, he left the motor running. The following morning both of them were dead, asphyxiated by the exhaust fumes.

To the right of the batting cage, a little way up the firstbase line, stood George Myatt, our infield coach. His legs were crossed at the ankle and he was leaning on an upright fungo bat as if it were a walking stick and he a country gentleman in cream-colored knickers. At 46, George "Mercury" Myatt had a thick, muscular, hairy body—the hair swirling down his back —and a voice like a lion's roar, only scratchier, a tubercular lion. George led us in calisthenics in the morning and ran the pitchers in the afternoon. He worked us with that boisterous, grinning, mock-enthusiasm of older men who have retained a good part of their physicality, but at such a great expense and with such conscious effort that, in order to make it worthwhile, they must flaunt their fitness in the face of younger, softer men, like ourselves, who see no sense in cultivating painfully what they have always taken for granted. George had been a part-time infielder in the majors for seven years, and after that he became a coach. He was our thirdbase coach at Bradenton in 1960, as he was with the Milwaukee Braves during the 1960s and the Philadelphia Phillies in the early 1970s. George was famous for the flamboyant way he signaled approaching base runners. At times he would be windmilling one arm like a madman while pointing with his other toward the plate and roaring, *"All the way, Big Stud, all the way!"* At other times George would take a resounding belly flop to the ground— *whoomph*—and, while the dust billowed about him, beat his palms on the ground as if it were a tom-tom and roar, *"Slide, Stud, slide!"* George called everyone "Stud" or "Big Stud" or "Little Stud," because it was easier for him than trying to remember the names of those base runners who flashed by. He became famous for that, too.

George raised the fungo bat to his shoulder and waited for the batting practice pitcher to throw and the batter to swing before he tossed a ball into the air and hit it toward third base. George timed his grounders to follow the swings of each batter so that he would never hit a ball to an infielder in the process of fielding a batter's ball. George hit each grounder with a grunt, followed always by the same exhortation, "Dig it out, Stud, dig it out!" He never seemed to tire or get bored, and, in fact, he built up a certain rhythm—poised like a statue until the batter swung and then tossing the ball into the air and hitting it—that seemed to give him pleasure. He was annoyed when that rhythm was broken by a misplayed ground ball. He would throw his bat to the ground in disgust and, cupping his hands, palms out, between his legs, he would squat. "Get those hands down, Stud! Get 'em down!"

George hit ground balls throughout the morning. He worked around the infield, beginning at third base with Dennis Menke, a $150,000 bonus baby now a veteran with the Houston Astros; and then to Chuck Cottier, a shortstop who glided after grounders in the hole like a skater on ice, but whose weak bat would always keep him a bit player in the majors; and then to Billy Lucas, a black second baseman, who never reached the big leagues as a player but is now the farm director for the Atlanta Braves, the first such black executive in baseball; and finally to Tommy Aaron at first base. Hank's brother. A cruel joke. He was younger than Hank yet looked older. Already in his twenties, he was growing bald. He had Hank's swollen face and droopy lids and stuck-out behind and, viewed from the back, he even had his brother's tight little waist. But in the front that waist terminated in a half-moon belly so that when Tommy walked it was with a seemingly arrogant, high-waisted, stomach-thrusting strut. Tommy was bigger than Hank and looked stronger. He had Hank's quick wrists, too, only every time Tommy swung a bat and hit the ball firmly, the ball hooked foul into the left field stands. When Tommy straightened out that vicious foul it became a routine fly ball to the left fielder. Even then Tommy seemed to realize a joke had been played on him, that as a player he was a parody of his brother, everything the same yet something missing. And so all the while Dixie was assuring him that once he straightened out that vicious foul ball he would join Hank in Milwaukee, Tommy never believed him. He seemed only to be going through the motions of a career, impatient with the charade he must endure as "Hank's brother." I didn't like Tommy then. I could never understand why someone would be in a sullen mood throughout the day when nothing particularly unpleasant had happened to them.

The pitchers shagged fly balls in the outfield. We stood with our legs spread and planted firmly, and our arms folded across our chests. Occasionally we stirred ourselves to retrieve a batted ball and toss it, underhand, to an infielder. We returned to our pose. Bored, we began the pump and kick and follow-through of our pitching motion. We moved in pantomime against the green backdrop of the outfield fence. We practiced our motion over and over, lost in it, trying to perfect some little flaw pointed out to us by our pitching coach Whitlow Wyatt.

Many of the pitchers in that outfield had been teammates

209

of mine at McCook: Brubaker, Niekro, Overby (with a sore arm) and Marnie. They had all played the 1960 season in a higher classification than I, except for Brubaker, who had won 15 games at Wellsville. The other pitchers were Tony Cloninger, who'd played at Austin; Larry Maxie, a hulking farm boy, who had stepped to a Triple-A league in his second full season and would remain there for 14 years, unable to make that final jump to the majors; and Bobby Botz, a soft, white, plump little man who resembled "Spanky" in "Our Gang," and was just as abrasive. Botz was 26 years old and a proven Triple-A pitcher, although his best fastball would not bruise a baby's skin. He compensated for his lack of speed by developing pinpoint control, which was sufficient to bring him to the major leagues for a month in 1962 before he returned permanently to the minors. Botz would learn nothing at Bradenton in 1960, nor did he expect to. He had come only to give his wife a vacation, which, he hoped, would help her forget her recent miscarriage. Bobby never talked about that miscarriage, although he never tired of telling us about his and his wife's sexual encounters, which he detailed so graphically in the clubhouse each morning that it never failed to embarrass me. Bobby took nothing seriously. His humor was acerbic and mostly carnal in nature. He equated the deficiency of his fastball with a deficiency in the length of his penis. He would point to a well-endowed teammate stepping from the shower and say, to our delight and that teammates' blushes, "Jesus, if only I had one like "The Snake" there—what a fastball I'd have!"

Those pitchers not shagging in the outfield during batting practice could be found working off the warm-up mounds near the clubhouse. We threw mostly to the team's catching instructor, 53-year-old George Cyril Methodius "Good Kid" Susce. He caught batting practice for hours and then went to the bullpen and warmed up pitchers. As much as "Good Kid" loved to work, he loved even more to grumble about it, complaining always about the softness of modern ballplayers in contrast to himself and the men he'd played with. "Good Kid" had been a bullpen catcher in the major leagues from 1929 to 1944, although he made periodic returns to the minors. During his career he never got to bat more than 61 times in a major league season, but he did manage to break every finger on each hand so often that now his fingers stuck out in all directions like the short, fat branches of a tree. "Good Kid" had a chest like a block of granite and legs like huge Coke bottles. His face was as gnarled as his hands, and his nose had been broken almost as many times. In addition to his other duties, "Good Kid" was responsible for the baseballs. He counted them in the clubhouse each morning and at the end of each day. He kept them in a leather satchel with a locked zipper, and only "Good Kid" had the key. He tied the key to the shoelace of his left spike. Whenever a player asked for a new baseball, "Good Kid" would interrogate him thoroughly ("Who told you to get a ball? What for?") before finally bending over—a gesture both physically and mentally discomforting—to untie his shoelace. It so upset "Good Kid" to part with a new baseball that whenever he did he followed its progress throughout the day—in a pepper game behind home plate, then a catch along the right-field line—as if each ball had a distinct personality that he wanted to keep track of. "Good Kid" was irritable until the last baseball had been returned to the safety of his satchel. Even then he was not fully placated, for it caused him great pain to see how they'd been abused throughout the day—his stained and scuffed old friends. "Good Kid" took his responsibility as keeper of the balls so seriously (as he did all things) that it never failed to make us smile.

He made Ben Geraghty smile, too. "Good Kid" was devoted to Ben, with whom he had worked for years. His allegiance was so total that there was no errand too menial, no task too unpleasant, that he would not perform for his "Skipper." In the performance of those tasks, "Good Kid" never failed to bring to Ben's perpetually pained face the shadow of a smile. And often, to lighten his day, Ben would deliberately assign "Good Kid" some small task, which he would perform with the utmost seriousness. Ben's smile often confused "Good Kid," for he could see nothing humorous he'd done to warrant it. Still, he must have pleased "the Skipper," and that satisfied him.

While the pitchers threw to "Good Kid" in the bullpen, John Whitlow Wyatt, Milwaukee's pitching coach, stood beside us and whispered soft advice. Whitlow was a handsome, gracious Southerner in his early fifties. He was tall and erect and loose-limbed, and he had the alert blue eyes of a much younger man. His face was soft pink, except for a light stubble of beard, while the rest of his body was the color and texture of worn leather. Whitlow spoke with a measured drawl so creamy that each word blended into the next and whole sentences became sweet parfaits. When he spoke his lips curled back from his teeth the way a horse's do. He seemed to be tasting each word carefully and with pleasure before swallowing it.

I first met Whitlow in the summer of 1959, when I had gone with my brother to County Stadium to work out for the Braves' management. While my brother, Jeff Jones and John Mullins bargained over the size of my bonus in the box seats behind the homeplate screen of a deserted stadium, I was sent with Whitlow to the right field bullpen, where, in Mullins' words, "Whitlow will work with the kid to see if he learns quick." Whitlow stood beside me and watched me throw. I was throwing hurriedly, one pitch after another without a pause, because my mind was not there in the bullpen but back with those who

212

were deciding my future. My motion was stiff and mechanical rather than one fluid piece, and the ball was darting everywhere but over the plate. I began to throw more hurriedly and harder. It was midafternoon and it was hot and I was sweating and tense and angry. And then I was conscious of a voice beside me, a soft and melodious whisper. "Relax, son . . . just a little now . . . thataboy . . . nice 'n easy . . . see how easy it is . . . just let up a shade . . . the ball drops right in there . . . aaaah, that's much better. . . ." Whitlow had moved up very close to me, his face only a few inches from my ear. He had cupped a hand over his mouth and was whispering to me, imparting a precious secret in this empty bullpen. His voice drained the tension from my body. My motion smoothed out and my control sharpened, and it was all so easy that I had forgotten about the others in the box seats and could not even think about them if I had tried, just as when my hand falls asleep during the night and I wake to discover that I can't make a fist no matter how desperately I will it. I could do nothing in that bullpen but throw strike after strike with a fluid and effortless motion.

Later, we walked across the empty diamond toward the seats behind home plate. The stands rising up around us were empty. It was a long walk, and Whitlow talked to me all the way. When we reached second base he threw an arm around my shoulder and told me what a great future I had with the Milwaukee Braves. When we reached the homeplate screen we came upon Mullins and my brother in a heated discussion. Whitlow, smiling at me, said to no one in particular, "This boy sure learns fast." Mullins looked at Wyatt. My brother said, "See, I told you he's coachable. Whitlow could tell that in a minute."

"Listen," said Mullins, "he isn't the one who signs the check." He flung the back of his hand in Whitlow's direction

213

as if to dismiss him. "It isn't *his* money to throw away."

Beside me, Whitlow's smile dissolved. He lifted his hand from my shoulder and moved an imperceptible step away.

When I saw Whitlow again, in the fall of 1960, he greeted me with a big smile and a slap on the back. He was 52 years old then and he exuded a vitality and enthusiasm for life that was infectious. He was one of those rare people who seem to take pleasure in the simplest of acts. There was no part of his baseball life, for instance, that Whitlow seemed not to enjoy. He found his satisfactions in its minutest details, which were hidden at the base of its more stupendous pleasures. I've often seen this quality of Whitlow's in older people whose lives, with age, are no longer filled with stupendous pleasures, and so they develop a more refined sensitivity to life's lesser details and, with greater age, even lesser ones, until finally their satisfaction comes from life itself and every detail in it is a pleasure. Whitlow cultivated this sensitivity at a much earlier age than most because he had learned much earlier than most that his major league career, which for 10 years was filled with records like 0-2, 4-5, 3-5, 2-3 and 0-0, was destined to be lacking in consequential pleasures. If he was to persevere in it, he would have to find small satisfactions beneath the placid surface of a winless season. By the time he became a pitching coach he had learned to find rewards in every detail of his baseball life, in his still *having* a baseball life, the good life, which we overlooked in our hot pursuit of larger satisfactions.

He entered the Bradenton clubhouse each morning with a neatly folded newspaper tucked like a swagger stick under one arm. He wore a straw hat with a madras band, dark glasses, a wine-colored Banlon jersey, cream-colored slacks and black-and-white perforated shoes. As he passed the lockers he dealt out a perfunctory smile and a nod to the players who were in various stages of undress. When he reached his own locker at

214

the far end of the room, he sat down on a stool, crossed his legs and, for the next half-hour, read his newspaper. Always at the same time each morning, he folded his newspaper, laid it on the top shelf of his locker and undressed. Naked, he doused his body with baby powder before dressing, piece by piece, in his uniform. He put on his jockstrap first, then slipped into his uniform shirt, flexed his shoulders until it fell naturally and buttoned it. He picked up a pair of white sanitary stockings and turned them inside out so that the lumpy seam running across the inside top of the toes was on the outside top, where it would not cause a blister once he put on his spikes. He sat down and drew them on, and over them, his colored stirruped stockings. He pulled both stockings tightly to his knee and then, like a woman with her nylons, he gripped one at the ankle with both hands and drew it slowly up his calf until he had smoothed away the wrinkles. He repeated this with the other leg. Next, he slipped on his black spikes, each one polished to a high gloss, and then pulled on his pants and stood up. He notched his belt, took his hat from the shelf and walked over to the mirror near the shower room. He examined himself. He tugged on the peak of his cap until it shaded his eyes just so. Then he fluffed out his shirt at the waist so it billowed evenly over his black belt. Satisfied, he went outside.

While he worked with us off the warm-up mounds, Whitlow reassured us constantly. "Thata boy. It had fine spin. Jus' turn your wrist a bit more. See here. You're gettin' the hang of it, though." He would shake his head once for emphasis. Occasionally, to punctuate a point, he would take the ball from us —"Gimme here"—and begin his own deliberate, leg-kicking-high, arm-reaching-back, effortless motion. He would then deliver a curveball so slow it seemed to be hanging from a clothesline whose wash was being drawn slowly toward home plate. Three-quarters of the way there, the ball fell off the

215

clothesline. Whitlow could no longer throw his curveball very hard, never could in fact, but what spin! God, how we envied it! No matter how hard or sharply our curveballs broke, they never seemed to spin quite right. The threads of the ball did not rotate as fast as they should have, nor were those rotations all in the same groove, so that as our curveballs approached the plate they appeared to be wobbling a bit off-center, like an automobile tire loose on its rim. This caused too much of the white part of the ball to show and the ball looked larger to the batter than it should have, and thus, easier to hit. But Whitlow's curveball had such aesthetically perfect spin—the threads rotating so much faster than did ours, and never varying a fraction—that despite its slowness the ball appeared to be growing progressively smaller and smaller as it approached the batter and then—poof—as if by magic, it disappeared.

Whitlow Wyatt was one of the game's greatest pitching coaches for a number of reasons. He had never been a physically talented pitcher himself, and so he had had to devote more time than most to mastering the smallest details of his craft. As a coach he had the ability to communicate these details so clearly, by word and example, that even the densest rookie could grasp and successfully apply them. Listening to Whitlow's soft advice while you threw was hypnotizing. His soothing drawl was an opiate that dulled then softened resistance, making you helplessly open and receptive to his words. It was as if you were asleep while the recording of a foreign language played over and over, and, upon waking, you discovered you had learned a new language. Only it was not learned, really, not acquired consciously, but rather absorbed as if by osmosis. And it was absorbed so effortlessly that it seemed not so new after all. It became something natural you'd possessed all along, although buried, and which Whitlow had only nudged to the surface. And this new possession—rather, this

216

old possession newly discovered—became in your mind your very own in a way nothing learned can ever be.

As with all opiates, Whitlow's soft words could be dangerous, too. At times his assurances ("You got real fine spin there"), which he delivered primarily to induce confidence, induced euphoria. You believed you had mastered things you hadn't. You tried to perform feats of magic on the mound which you discovered sadly were still beyond your powers. But Whitlow did not consciously try to deceive you. It was just that his enthusiasm for the game was so contagious that it not only infected us, but him, too. After throwing a slow curveball, for instance, he would stand on the mound, hands on hips, and grin. "Well, I'll be! That sumnabuck wasn't half-bad, was it?"

Whitlow's infectious enthusiasm was his most valuable commodity as a pitching coach, and it was greatly prized by the Milwaukee Braves' organization. It inspired young pitchers to emulate him. Whitlow was able to produce this enthusiasm even for the game's most tedious tasks, such as sitting under a hot sun in the bullpen during a game in which we took no part. While the pitchers joked and fidgeted, chewed tobacco and spit, grumbled about the heat and waited for a call to "get loose," Whitlow relaxed. He rolled up his shirt sleeves so that his arms were bare to the shoulder and then draped them over the back of the bench like the wings of a large bird about to take flight. He closed his eyes, laid his head back and smiled into the sun. He remained motionless for long moments, smiling, eyes closed, sometimes dozing, but mostly just talking softly to us about the art of pitching and, on rare occasions, his own career.

"The sun's rays are the best thing for a pitcher's arm," he would say. He spoke to no one in particular. He told us how, in the summer of 1931, he got a sore arm and he thought his career was finished. "I packed my bamboo pole and went home

217

to Georgia, to fish. I fished every day in the cri'k near the house. I sat on the bank for hours trying to understand why all them doctors couldn't heal my sore arm. Pretty soon I got tired thinkin' about it, so I just closed my eyes and fell asleep with the sun's hot rays beatin' down on me."

At this point he opened one eye in a squint and turned his head toward whomever was listening. "And you know, I'll be danged if I didn't pick up a ball one day and all that soreness was gone. Yessir! That's a fact!" He nodded once, closed his eyes again, and resumed his pose. "Mother Nature's the best cure for anythin'." The following afternoon when Whitlow began rolling up his shirt sleeves "to take a few rays," he was not the only one. Whether those rays ever strengthened any of our pitching arms, I can't say. But it makes no difference, anyway. That was not Whitlow's point. It was just his way of telling us that no detail of the game was too trivial, too boring, that it could not be turned to one's advantage. A player who overlooked such details was one who would never fulfill his true potential. Whitlow firmly believed that a player who did not polish his spikes before stepping onto the field before the eyes of the fans was a player who would run five less wind sprints when his pitching coach wasn't looking, "and that's the same man who looks to the bullpen in the seventh inning when the heat's on," said Whitlow.

Whitlow knew about such things because he had made a major league career from 1929 to 1946 with only the most mediocre physical talent by paying great attention to detail. He still remembered every particular of that career, every batter who'd beaten him, every pitch those batters hit, or missed. And he delighted in telling us about such pitches. He told us about the time with the White Sox in 1934, when he came in to relieve with the bases loaded and two outs, and how his manager had come out to the mound and said, "Now, you give

218

this batter your good breakin' stuff, hear? You throw him one of your shit fastballs and it'll cost you money." Whitlow worked that batter to a two-and-two count using mostly his slow curveball, and then, on a whim, he threw a fastball, which the batter stared at in disbelief as it crossed the heart of the plate for strike three. When Whitlow reached the dugout, his manager, true to his word, fined him. "But that fine didn't bother me one bit," said Whitlow. "I learned something that day. I had learned it don't matter what kinda stuff you got, it's how you use it. There ain't no such thing as a 'bad' pitch. Any pitch can be a good one if it's in the right spot at the right time." This lesson was the most valuable of his career, he said, and one which he had never forgotten.

After a span of 10 years in the major leagues, from 1929 to 1939, during which time he won a total of 29 games and lost 43 for three different teams, Whitlow finally found himself with the right team at the right time when World War II broke out. However, he was exempted from military service (for reasons he never clearly defined for us) unlike many other major leaguers who were forced to serve. Subsequently during the war years, the caliber of play in the majors deteriorated greatly. During those years, Whitlow became a star at the age of 34. In 1940 he won 15 games with the Brooklyn Dodgers. It was the first time in his 10-year career he had won more than eight games. In 1941 he won 22 games and one World Series start; the next year he won 19 games; and in 1943 he won 14. But then, when the ballplayers began returning from the war, Whitlow's fortunes collapsed, and by 1945 he was unable to win a single game, while losing seven, for the Philadelphia Phillies. He quit that year and shortly thereafter began his new career as a pitching coach.

Wyatt had not always been the effusive and gracious old Southerner he was in the fall of 1960. In fact, as a pitcher suffering through winless seasons, he had a reputation for throwing at batters' heads at the slightest provocation. Whitlow did not like to be reminded of this former self, and although he delighted in telling us stories about his career, there were some stories he did not like to tell. The DiMaggio incident was one. During the 1941 World Series between the Dodgers and the Yankees, Joe DiMaggio hit a double off one of Whitlow's pitches. While DiMaggio was dusting off his pants at second base, Whitlow took a step toward him and yelled something. DiMaggio charged the mound but was intercepted by three Brooklyn players and the secondbase umpire before he reached Whitlow, who was charging him, too. It would be the only time in a long career that anyone angered Joe DiMaggio enough for him to want to fight. After the game DiMaggio refused to tell anyone what Wyatt had yelled to him. Almost 20 years later, in the Bradenton bullpen one afternoon, I asked Whitlow what he had said to DiMaggio. He just smiled, and without lifting his head from the back of the bench, or turning his face from the sun or even opening his eyes, he said, "It weren't nothing, really. Just the heat of the game, you know. I was a much younger man then, and wilder, too." And then he began telling us that a pitcher should never lose his composure on the mound, and that it had been a good lesson to him, and should be to us, too. And while he was speaking, I glanced over at him, a dignified old man with his eyes closed, smiling into the sun, and I wondered what he had been like then, as a pitcher of so many unsatisfactory seasons. Suddenly, quite by surprise, I found myself wondering what he was really like, now, at that moment, as he was speaking to us in his soft drawl.

As a pitching coach, Whitlow never lost his composure. He had great patience with us, and we admired him for it. He had the most patience with those pitchers who were pitching the best. Whitlow always seemed to be spending time with a pitcher who had just thrown a shutout or won his third consecutive game. Whether that pitcher was successful because Whitlow was spending so much time with him, or vice versa, was not clear. It was clear, however, that it was this patience and enthusiasm and affability and graciousness together with his knowledge of pitching that caused him to be rehired year after year by the same Braves' executives who were firing manager after manager as well as their coaches. Ordinarily, pitching coaches are swept out with their managers, but this was not so in Whitlow's case. He survived the firing of more managers than any pitching coach in history. He survived because he had learned early how to slide.

Finally, in 1969 Whitlow Wyatt was fired by Paul Richards, the new general manager of the Atlanta Braves. "Nobody slides by Richards," said Tony Cloninger, then a pitcher with the Braves. "Not even ole Whitlow." Whitlow was 63 years old then, and he did not even seek another job in baseball. He retired to his sprawling farm in Georgia, which he had purchased early in his career for $20,000 and which was now valued at over $300,000.

Unlike Whitlow, Ben Geraghty never learned how to slide. In the summer of 1963 he died of heart trouble or liver trouble or some such physical ailment. He was 48 years old and was still a minor league manager.

I lived in a small hovel the size of a one-car garage in the shadow of the huge, ultramodern Bradenton Cabana Motor Inn. My hovel was located in the tall weeds directly behind the Cabana, and through its only window I could see the sliding, pane-glass doors and drawn curtains of the Cabana's $40-a-day rooms. I had slept in one of those chilled, antiseptic rooms for three days before discovering this shack, each of whose two rooms rented for $50 a month. The shack was divided down the middle by a plywood partition. Each half contained a cot, a bureau, a card table, two chairs, a small sink, a gas stove, a toilet and a shower stall. The room on the other side of the partition was occupied by a 22-year-old divorcée named Nan. It was Nan who had told me about the vacancy on the night I first met her and her girl friend, Sheila, in the bar across the street, where they both worked as hostesses. The bar was almost deserted when I came in for a drink, and shortly thereafter the two girls sat down on either side of me and struck up a conversation. Sheila was by far the prettier. She was 21, two years older than me, and she had the startled coal-black eyes, white skin and petite-yet-curvy figure of a young Natalie Wood. She wore a crisp pink shirtwaist dress, the skirt fluffed out by crinolines that rustled when she moved. She was an immaculate girl with a sweet-faced beauty one invariably equates with innocence, and I was shocked to learn later from Nan that Sheila was not only divorced but had two small children and was four months pregnant by her boyfriend, who had left a week ago for Los Angeles.

Nan told me the sordid details of Sheila's life with the satisfaction not simply of a woman jealous of another's beauty, but also of one who saw in that beauty one of life's cruelest ironies. Nan knew the coarseness of her life could be read in her face, while Sheila's life, no less coarse, was camouflaged by her exquisite beauty. It was an injustice Nan was only too eager to rectify whenever possible. Nan was not a pretty girl. She had the angular face, protruding cheekbones and jutting jaw of a masculine-looking country-and-western singer. Plus squinting little eyes covered by thick-lensed, horn-rimmed glasses, and a thin mouth curving down into her jaw. Her body resembled a bony teenaged boy, and it was draped in a loose black sweater and even looser black slacks that were narrow at the ankle. A hard, tense-looking girl, she always seemed on the verge of shattering, like crystal, from the sound of her own shrill voice. Naturally, it was Nan who took the greatest interest in me that night, while Sheila scarcely acknowledged my existence.

At night as I lay on my cot, I could hear the rustle of the tall weeds and footsteps crunching along the pebbled path leading to the shack, the sound of Nan's screen door springing open and snapping shut and, inside her room, the mumbling of voices and then silence. I fell asleep only to be awakened in the pre-dawn darkness by that same screen door snapping shut and the sound of a hacking cough and someone spitting and the crash of a discarded bottle and again the crunching footsteps and then silence. I never saw any of the men Nan entertained in her room, but lying there after they had gone, I imagined what they must have been like. Drifters, like those who had boarded at The Major's house, only younger, in their late twenties, men who still "got drunk" rather than "were drunk." They looked with anticipation on new conquests like Nan, and it would be a few more years of drifting before they discovered that, for them, all hotel rooms and bars, and all the women in them, were alike, and then they would lose their anticipation. But still they drifted. Only now, without energy or anticipation, it was merely the winding down of their lives. At one time they had been the force that set their lives in motion, just as some force must first generate the spinning of a child's top. Once they'd generated that motion, however, they ceased to control the spinning, and it would be many years before they realized this.

Nan was like them. She had married in her junior year of high school because she was pregnant, and she divorced her husband after two children because he had left her. She gave up her children for adoption because it was easier than trying to raise them herself, and she worked in a bar because it was

223

less difficult to find such a job than one that demanded a skill. And she slept with strange men because it was pleasant, and even when it was not so pleasant it was still preferable to sleeping alone. One night Nan had a black eye, and in my mind I saw that woman sprawled on the barroom floor in Davenport. This vision terrified me. It was as if I'd seen in Nan, her men, her life, something even more obscene than evil. Evil was forgivable. I was only 19 then and I did not recognize it for what it was, despair, but nonetheless I was determined to avoid it—and Nan, who carried it with her, a contagious disease for which there was no cure.

Early in the morning while I slept, Nan would slip through my screen door, let it snap back just loudly enough to wake me, and then begin tidying up my room. While she swept the floor and threw bottles and cans into the garbage pail, she cast expectant glances at me on the cot. I feigned sleep. Finished, she'd sit at the card table and watch me. After a few minutes she'd get up and leave. One morning she came and sat down on the edge of the cot. She touched my shoulder as if to wake me. I grumbled and, pulling the sheets to my chin, turned toward the wall. She sat there for a long moment, while I lay terrified under the sheets, and then she left.

The next morning I rose at dawn, dressed quickly and left the shack before she had awakened. When I returned that night my room was tidied up as always. I continued waking early for the rest of the week, and finally, one night the room was as I'd left it.

Still, I continued to rise early. I liked stepping outside into a springlike morning where everything was cool and wet and sharply defined by a bright sun that was not yet hot. I liked walking through a still town with its freshly washed streets of old brick and its dark pink stucco buildings that would become pale pink in the afternoon when the sun had bleached out their moisture. I liked stopping for breakfast at a just-opened drugstore and sitting at one end of the counter while uniformed waitresses, drowsy with sleep and wearing sweaters against the morning chill, stood at the other end sipping coffee from paper cups and gossiping before the first wave of customers rolled in.

Most of all, I liked walking to the ball park. I liked *being* at the ball park in a way I never liked being at Cibola or Davenport Stadium. I arrived an hour before my teammates and dressed into my uniform in the deserted clubhouse and went outside and sat on the bench in the bullpen. I looked across the outfield grass, green and silvery with dew, to the rightfield fence, where between two palm trees and just above the the fence lay a deep-orange sun. I rolled up the sleeves of my shirt and draped my arms over the back of the bench, closed my eyes and smiled into the sun—and, for the first time in two years, took satisfaction in my career.

I had arrived in Bradenton as the least successful of all the pitchers. And now, after a month, I led the team with an earned run average of under 2.00 and a 4–1 record (I finished the season with a record of 5 and 2).

For the first week of the season, I did not pitch an inning, but each morning went to the bullpen to work with Whitlow. At first he taught me a change-of-speed off my fastball, and then, gradually, he began to change my motion. At the time I possessed the classic, high-kicking, overhand motion of a right-handed Warren Spahn. It was ideal for a fastball pitcher because it had a great deal of movement, which evolved into a powerful rhythm that propelled every part of my body (arms, shoulders, back, legs) into each pitch. It was also a difficult motion to master. There were so many parts needed to produce that rhythm, and such a delicate balance between those parts, that the slightest variation in any one (too high a kick, too long a stride) would throw the pitch off target. Spahn had mastered

225

this, and so had Whitlow. But it had taken them many years. There were a lot of fastball pitchers who never mastered it. I might be one of them, warned Whitlow. A less stylized, more compact motion would help me throw strikes.

He cut out some of the movement from my delivery, abbreviated other parts (a lower kick), and for the first time in my professional career I was throwing strikes. It was such a pleasure to watch "Good Kid" give me a target on the outside corner of the plate and then be able to throw the ball right to that target that, at first, I wasn't concerned that I was no longer throwing the ball with as much speed as I used to, nor that my new delivery felt unnatural, as if I were merely flipping the ball with my arm and not using the rest of my body. When I did realize what was happening to my speed and delivery, I was still willing to compromise them for control and with it, I hoped, quick success. After two years of failure I did not have the patience or the desire to continue throwing with my natural motion, knowing that ahead of me might lie years of additional frustration before I perfected it, and that there was the distinct possibility I might never perfect it.

The thought of continued and, maybe, permanent failure terrified me. For years I had heard only the sounds of my parents' approval as I pitched to my brother on the sidewalk in front of our house. I had avoided failure so much longer than most (all those years of no-hitters and strikeouts) that its intrusion into my life was at first incomprehensible and then so terrifying that I would do anything to shake it. I was even willing to compromise the only thing in my life I had ever consciously cultivated, and the only thing in myself I had ever valued—my natural talent.

It was an easy corruption, begun first in high school when I had subordinated perfecting that talent to my quest for the largest bonus. That was the first time I had ever consciously

226

used my talent, whose perfection had been my only end, as a means to another end. Now, in Bradenton, when I should have been trying to perfect that talent (to throw a baseball as naturally and as fast as I could, and only then trying to control it), I again subordinated that end to another. I deliberately frustrated the natural limits of my talent in the hope that this would bring me—not success, even—but simply the absence of failure. Such a cowardly satisfaction! And one that ultimately led to a failure so without the satisfaction a nobler failure might have had, that I have yet to come to grips with it . . . to admit that I destroyed my talent, the one thing in me that was special to me. It doesn't matter what that thing was or how trivial it might have been. It only matters that such a thing did exist in me, as it does in us all, and that by refusing to risk perfecting it I was denying what most truly defined me.

I worked with Whitlow every day for almost two weeks, and during that span appeared in three games as a relief pitcher. After eight innings I had yet to yield an earned run. My fourth appearance was a start against the Athletics in Clearwater. Joe Torre was my catcher. He caught a beautiful game. He hunched his masked-and-padded bulk over the inside and outside corners of the plate and stuck up his fat round catcher's mitt. In its center was a perfectly round pocket, stained darker than the rest of the glove and as inviting as a bull's-eye. I threw to that dark pocket. With each pitch it seemed to grow larger and larger until it was larger than the glove and then larger than Torre's chest protector and then larger even than Torre himself. Finally, it obliterated everything, and all I could see was that perfectly round dark pocket so ridiculously large and inviting that it was impossible for me *not* to throw the ball directly into it. And suddenly, for the first time in years, it was easy, really easy, unbelievably easy, and I wanted to laugh out

227

loud right there on the pitcher's mound. For nine innings I threw to that pocket. The batters hit ground balls and fly balls and, occasionally, a line drive someplace, and when the last batter was out I walked off the mound, grinning. Torre tucked his mask under one armpit and met me as I crossed the third-base line. He reached out his hand and said, "Now you look like a pitcher." I had pitched a two-hit shutout.

That night I called my brother to tell him the good news. "How many strikeouts did you get?" he asked.

"Two."

"Two! What's wrong?"

"Nothing," I said. "I wasn't trying for strikeouts. I'm a pitcher now, and it's really easy."

In my next start I beat the Indians, and then I beat the White Sox and then the Senators and then I lost to the Indians and then I beat the White Sox again.* Each victory came easier than the last, and even my one loss was less difficult than any loss at McCook or Davenport had ever been. I was simply knocked out of the game in the fifth inning after giving up three straight hits, the last one a double off the left-centerfield scoreboard by Max Alvis. I left the game strangely satisfied. I felt no recriminations and suffered none from my teammates. There had been no disgusted shouts—"Throw strikes!"—as I walked batter after batter, because in five innings I had walked

* * *

*These teams were filled with future major leaguers. The Senators (now the Twins) had Jim Kaat, Joe Bonikowski, Bill Pleis, Lee Stange, Dan Dobbek, Don Mincher; the Indians had Sam McDowell, Sonny Siebert, Al Luplow, Doc Edwards, Larry Brown, Ty Cline, Max Alvis; the White Sox had J.C. Martin, Al Hershberger, Joel Horlen, Joe Hoerner, Don Zanni, Gary Peters, Gerry Arrigo, Jerry McNertney; and the A's had Bill Bryan, Tom Satriano, Jack Aker and Ken Sanders. I'm sure there were other future major leaguers in the FWIL that year, but I don't remember their names. On the Braves that year, there were only six players who never made it at least for one inning to the major leagues.

only one. I had struck out two and given up seven hits. The hits were what beat me.

When I reached the dugout my teammates greeted me with the kind of commiseration I had never received at Davenport or McCook. "Tough luck, Pat . . . Didn't have good stuff today. . . . You'll get 'em next time."

I nodded thanks and sat down. Was that all there was to it? I just didn't have good stuff today? That was simple. Fathomable. I understood it in a way I never understood what had happened at Davenport and McCook when I had always had good stuff, great stuff, and yet game after game never had anything to show for it. Except walks, of course. And boos and losses and frustration. And strikeouts. I had had strikeouts, too. I had had Jim Hicks on one knee and later, saying, "Man, there oughta be a law against you, know what I mean? Make it ee-legal to throw a baseball *that* hard!" Such moments had brought me great satisfaction, and with it the knowledge that I had at least the potential to become someday an overwhelming pitcher like Sandy Koufax. Someday . . . maybe . . . after more frustration . . . too much, maybe. So much that at Davenport it killed my satisfactions. It *was* too much, I decided. Consequently, when I reached Bradenton, I was only too willing to swap them all—satisfaction, potential and, most importantly, frustrations—for the immediate and more muted easy wins and easy losses.

And if in bargaining off those frustrations I was also bargaining away my potential, would never see Jim Hicks on one knee again, well, so what. I would learn to find in my pitching subtler satisfactions. Pitching to Max Alvis, for instance, with the bases loaded and one out, I run the count to three-and-two before tossing a straight change-up that he grounds sharply to short for an inning-ending doubleplay. Another time I am pitching to Don Mincher with the winning run on third base.

229

Mincher, six feet, six inches tall and 250 pounds, is the kind of powerful but wild swinger I'd always loved to challenge with fastballs. I lead him off with a slow curve, which he looks at for a called strike. I follow with a straight change-up that catches him striding so anxiously that he has to let it pass for strike two. Now, telling himself to be patient, Mincher waits for another off-speed pitch. I throw a fastball down the middle of the plate. He looks at it a split second too long, and before he can tell himself to swing, it has already crossed the plate for strike three. Even as I walk off the mound satisfied, knowing that I have just pitched to Mincher as perfectly as one can ever pitch to a batter, I realize it was not the speed of my fastball but rather its element of surprise that overwhelmed Don Mincher.

I discovered in many things that autumn satisfactions I had never known before. I loved our morning workouts, which began on wet grass under a cool, springlike sun. We warmed with the sun; the others playing catch along the firstbase and thirdbase lines while the pitchers had ferocious games of pepper behind home plate. The batter in those pepper games faced the homeplate screen 15 feet away and slapped the ball toward the pitchers spread out along the screen. We backhanded one-hoppers with the timidity of unnatural fielders, then flipped the ball behind our backs to another who tossed it back to the hitter. We began those games casually, with laughter and many errors, but as the sun warmed and loosened our limbs and sweat began to pour down our reddening faces, we grew more intent and we lost our timidity and awkwardness and the games took on a flawless rhythm—slap, backhand, flip, toss— that increased in tempo, the balls coming at us sharply now, and then more sharply, and finally the hitter, caught up in the rising tempo, was swinging with all his might and we were

230

fielding vicious shots with the naturalness one acquires in self-defense and then firing the ball back to the hitter with all *our* might. The games went on without an error or a missed swing for long stretches, and always they came to an end when the hitter caught sight of Ben Geraghty emerging from the clubhouse and then smacked the next pitch over the homeplate screen into the street beyond and we all trotted to the outfield to begin shagging balls during batting practice while awaiting our turns to pitch in it.

I loved to pitch batting practice as much as I had dreaded it at Davenport and McCook. There it was an excruciating ordeal. I would throw three, four, five pitches in a row off the plate, and after each one the batter would grumble to himself, his hands growing slack around his bat, and I would try harder to throw a strike, and then harder, and without realizing it would begin throwing the ball faster, so much faster that when I finally did throw the ball over the plate, the batter either swung and missed or else was too stunned even to swing. Boiling now, I would shout, "Hit the goddamn ball!" He would shout back, "Throw strikes!" and I would fire the next pitch with all my might and the batter would just drop his bat and walk away from the plate. I would stand there, a madman, and no one else would step up to hit until Travis or Steiny replaced me with another pitcher.

But it was different at Bradenton. I would throw strike after strike at a good hitting speed, and each batter would hit four or five line drives and then run the bases, satisfied. I would throw to five batters and then, exhausted and drenched with sweat, walk off the mound toward the clubhouse, where I would change my shirt. As I did, someone always called out to me, "Atta boy, Pat! Helluva job!" and I would move toward that clubhouse as if on a cloud.

I got along well with my Bradenton teammates. I was a part

231

of their early-morning pepper games; and someone always stood alongside of me and passed the time in the outfield; and later, during games, I sat in the bullpen with Whitlow and the other pitchers to take the sun and talk pitching and listen to Whitlow's yarns and laugh at the antics of Bobby Botz.

On the day Whitlow told us about the sun's healing powers, Bobby made a great production of unbuttoning his fly, while saying, "Will it strengthen this limb, Whit?" Another time Bobby put a cherry bomb under the glove of our shortstop, Ronnie Liptak, just as he was stepping into the batter's box with the bases loaded. Liptak took a practice swing and then, hearing a small explosion, turned to see his glove high in the air, its fingers dropping from its pocket like petals falling from a daisy. We roared at the expression on Ronnie's face, and as we roared—as I roared—I warned myself to be careful, not to blow it this time, not to get too close and reveal that strange lack of mine. I ribbed no one. I laughed at others' jokes but initiated none of my own. I seldom acted first, but instead watched from the fringes and reacted to others' activity. I no longer spoke rashly, as I truly felt, but now replayed my every thought a dozen times to make sure that, once expressed, it would offend no one. Still, I was not deliberately aloof. I was not assuming an attitude as I had at Davenport. How could I? Unlike my teammates at Davenport, my teammates at Bradenton were all exceptionally talented, and either older or more experienced or had been more successful than I. No, it was simply that, like most adults, I was learning how to hide.

What had begun at Davenport as a romantic attempt to be aloof was now a very real desire to become a private person. Away from the ball park I truly did prefer to remain alone in town rather than join my teammates at the beach or at the dog track in Sarasota. And yet, at the ball park I felt a part of things,

232

too. My success permitted me this luxury in the same way my lack of success at Davenport and McCook had always denied it to me. I learned, however—even as I played in those pepper games, even as I laughed with the others—to hold something in reserve. I learned never to completely lose myself in any satisfactions, even as I was savoring them, and if this tended to diminish those satisfactions, well, at least it didn't destroy them as my previous rashness had always done.

For the first time in my career I enjoyed going on road trips with my teammates. They were pleasant drives along the Gulf Coast of Florida to St. Petersburg or Clearwater, 30 minutes to the north, and Sarasota, 10 minutes to the south. We never stayed overnight in those towns, and we drove to them in cars rather than buses.

I usually rode with Phil Niekro and Bruce Brubaker. The three of us, wearing our uniforms, jammed into the two seats of Bruce's new Corvette with the top down, and Ben Geraghty in front of the clubhouse shaking his head in despair as we peeled away from the curb and roared off toward the Sunshine Skyway. The Skyway, to the north, was a long, low bridge— a highway, really—that spanned Great Tampa Bay for almost 20 miles. We passed over that bridge at 80 miles an hour. The warm wind from the bay and from the speed of our open car was like a pillow pressed against our faces. We had to struggle to draw a breath, and when we spoke we fairly shouted to be heard over the rushing of the wind and the roar of the car's exhaust, and, even then, our voices always seemed to be trailing behind us. Along the bridge old men and young boys fished over the railing, and every so often Bruce had to swerve to avoid a fish that had eluded its captor and was now flapping out its life on the highway. The bay was to our right and left. The water close to the bridge was a dark greenish-grayish-blue.

233

It grew lighter and lighter in the distance until very far away where it touched the horizon it appeared white from the sun glancing off it.

I remember returning from Clearwater late one afternoon near the end of the season. The Skyway was deserted except for an occasional old man still fishing over the railing. The wind from the bay was much stronger now, and it pressed cold against our faces. Around us we could see the waves grown choppy in the twilight. The water close to the bridge was very dark, while a little way offshore it was almost black, then tinged with red, and finally, far out on the horizon, the bay was aflame from the huge, round vermillion sun resting on it.

When we left the Skyway and entered Bradenton the wind died suddenly and it grew warmer. We reached the clubhouse at twilight and found Dixie Walker in the bullpen barbecuing spareribs on a blackened iron grill. Dixie had stayed behind with a few players for special hitting instruction and then, anticipating the team's return, he'd set up his grill.

The smell of burning pork and fat and sweet sauce was everywhere. Dixie, still wearing his uniform under a high-waisted white bartender's apron, hovered over his ribs, basting them with a paintbrush. By the time the ribs were cooked the rest of the team had arrived. Without bothering to change or shower, we began to eat the sweetly burned pork. Ben Geraghty sent two players into his office after some beer, and we then drank the warm beer and ate more ribs until it was pitch black, except for the charcoal embers still glowing in the grill. When the ribs and beer were gone and our hands and faces were sticky with sauce, we went into the clubhouse to shower and change into street clothes.

After the others took off in their cars, I walked toward town. I was filled with food and beer and a kind of joy I had never known, but which I was positive could never be equaled or diminished by anything that would happen to me from then on.

I was feeling too good to return to my room or sit in a bar, so I stopped for some coffee at a drugstore in town. As I nursed my cup at the counter, I replayed in my mind the sources of my happiness. I saw again that dark, round pocket in Torre's glove, and I watched in fascination as it grew and grew. And then I saw Max Alvis grounding into a double play and Don Mincher caught in mid-stride, and then I saw the fastball that had surprised Mincher and the motion that had delivered it, and then I flashed forward very quickly to the recent moments in the bullpen with my teammates.

"Hello, Pat."

I turned around to see Sheila. She was holding her two young children by the hand. Their faces and clothes were dirty. Sheila looked dirty. Her once spotless dress was wrinkled and stained, while her hair, pinned in a bun, fell in matted wisps about her face. She looked as if she had not washed off her makeup in days, but just dabbed new makeup over the old each morning. Lost in my reveries, I almost didn't recognize her, and then I did, and still I was annoyed at her intrusion into my private moments of happiness.

"Do you mind if we sit down with you?"

"No, go ahead." She sat beside me and her children sat beside her. She asked me how I'd been and if I'd seen Nan lately, and then, before I could answer, she asked if I could lend her a dollar.

"Things haven't been going too well," she said with averted eyes. I was embarrassed for her. I opened my wallet and found only a ten. I handed it to her.

"Oh, no! I can't take this! Just a dollar will be okay."

"No, take it," I said. I wanted her to go away. "I don't need it. Go ahead."

She took the bill and stuffed it into her purse. Then she stood up and took her children by the hand. "I really appreciate this, Pat. Really. I'll pay you back."

"Sure. Don't worry about it." After she'd gone I returned to my coffee and my reveries, but they were no longer satisfying. I put a quarter by my cup and left. By the time I got back to my room I was upset and angry, and I didn't know why.

A few nights later I returned to my room slightly drunk. I opened the door and flicked on the light. Sheila was sitting on my cot.

"I hope you don't mind," she said. "The door was open."

"No, of course not." My head was swimming. "I never lock it. There's nothing worth locking up." She forced a smile. She was wearing the same wrinkled dress, yet she looked different. Her face was clean of all makeup, except for a light touch of lipstick, and her white skin shone like porcelain. She had unpinned her hair and brushed it so that it glistened reddish-brown as it fell on either side of her beautiful face. It *was* a beautiful face, so beautiful and innocent-looking with its large, black and now slightly frightened eyes, the eyes of a tensed animal, that I could not stop my head from swimming. She shifted her weight on the cot and crossed her legs Indian fashion. I could see under her dress now. She was wearing black panties. She made no attempt to hide them. As I stared at them I noticed the slight curve of her belly, and I remembered that she was pregnant. Then I saw in my mind's eye her soiled children and my head began to clear.

"I wanted to thank you again for the money," she said. And, after a pause, "But I can't pay you back. I don't have it."

"Forget it. It was nothing. Really. You don't have to pay me back.

"But I want to," she said. "I want to repay you in some way . . ."

236

Everything was sharp and clear to me now. "I don't want anything from you, Sheila," I said. "I really don't."

"Are you sure?"

"Positive." Her shoulders dropped a bit and her eyes lost their intensity. She got up from the cot and walked toward the door. As she passed me she turned her face away. When she reached the door she hesitated a second, her back to me, and then turned around. "Are you sure?" I nodded. She tried to smile, then said, "Thanks, Pat," and left.

Late into the night I lay on my cot in the darkness staring at the ceiling. I could not sleep. I knew I should feel satisfied with myself, and yet . . . I didn't. I felt depressed and strangely weary, as if I'd done a kindness beyond my years and in doing so had left behind a part of myself to which I could never return. It was not the kindness that depressed me but the perception that had initiated it. That perception had been an unwanted burden. It had *imposed* that kindness on me. It did not matter whether or not I wanted that perception, or where it had sprung from. It only mattered that, for the first time in my life, my perceptions were understandable to me so that I was bound by their dictates. I was no longer free to act on the whims and impulses of my youth.

# ··· 7

I N the spring, the real spring, I drove to Waycross in a new white Chrysler. It had fins like wings and red plastic seats. Its dashboard was a glass globe filled with dials that glowed at night with a blue phosphorescent light. The light reflected off my face and filled the car. I drove as in a blue nimbus.

The back seat and the trunk of the car were packed with my belongings and those of my wife of six weeks, who would remain in Connecticut until I summoned her to our as yet unspecified summer home. We were both 19.

At Waycross I was given a private room in barracks number two. I hooked up my new stereo system (a wedding present) so that its music could be heard in the long, open part of the barracks where the others slept side by side on cots. I had brought only two records. At night I played "The Lion Sleeps Tonight" and in the morning, to the delight of an Alabama farm boy named Clay "Cotton" Carroll, I played "In Them Ole Cotton Fields Back Home."

During the first week of spring training I worked out with Austin of the Texas League (AA). With my teammates, I did calisthenics, ran wind sprints, played pepper, threw easily off a warm-up mound and, in general, just stretched out the muscles in my arms and legs in preparation for the second week's games. After practice I slept for an hour or two and then drove through the swamp, turned left onto the highway and headed toward Waycross to have supper. A few miles from town I

238

stopped at a roadside bar no bigger than a two-car garage. Its dirt parking lot was filled with new convertibles with out-of-state license plates, souped-up old Chevys and Fords and a dozen or so battered pick-up trucks. Through the cab window of many of those trucks, hanging like a trophy or an heirloom, I could see a rifle.

Inside, the bar was noisy with ballplayers and farmhands and millhands and drifters, most of whom were drinking draft beer served in glass mugs that were stored in a freezer. Each mug withdrawn from the freezer was coated with ice so that when you drank from it your hand stuck to the glass and the icy beer took your breath away. The bartender withdrew a new mug with each reorder of beer. Besides the iced mugs, the bar offered only a bare concrete floor, a pool table, a pinball machine and a juke box. The words from that jukebox were from songs I'd never heard before or since: "I'm going down to Waycross, Georgia, goin' down to Miller's cave." Or "Jimmy Jones was the snowman's name. He put all the other local lovers to shame. He had good looks and a big fine car, and he even had a good-lookin' mother-in-law."

The ballplayers gravitated to the pool table and pinball machine while the owners of the souped-up cars and pick-up trucks stood at the bar sprinkling salt in their beer. Some of them ate dried strips of beef jerky so leathery they had to bite down hard and, with a vicious yank of the head, tear off a piece just as little boys tear off pieces from a licorice braid. Others ate pickled pigs' feet and hard-boiled eggs that had been floating in a cloudy brine in the glass jar kept on the bar until the bartender had reached in with a long fork, speared one and served it, dripping brine, on a paper napkin. The men at the bar wore cowboy boots and levis and straw hats. They were beefy men with overhanging bellies and sun-reddened faces that looked as mean and inscrutable as a hawk's. Every time they heard a loud noise or laughter from the ballplayers they glanced over their shoulders—not to share in our amusements, but with a look of edgy anticipation, as if waiting eagerly for one of us to say or do something to which they could take offense. Fearing trouble, I never stayed long.

After a few beers I returned to my car and drove into town across the railroad tracks that divided Waycross into black and white communities. On one side of those tracks was a dirt road and on the other side a paved road. I turned onto the paved road and parked my car in front of Ma Carter's house.

Like the house I'd visited in Keokuk, Iowa, it was a sagging, gray, Victorian structure with a roofed-over front porch. The porch was littered with about a dozen men—farmers in overalls, diesel truck drivers in khaki, businessmen in suits, ballplayers in Bermuda shorts and gray t-shirts. All were in various states of sprawl—sitting on the porch steps, leaning against the pillars, standing on the porch, half-sitting and half-standing on the porch railing. They were mostly strangers to one another. No one spoke except a few ballplayers who talked softly together.

At exactly five o'clock a large, black woman stuck her turbaned head through a partially opened screen door and said, "It's ready." The men, eager now, hurried into the dining room and sat down at long benches on either side of a picnic table sagging under the weight of a dozen plates and bowls heaped with food. Steam rose like charmed cobras from each of these. There were bowls of mashed potatoes with lumps of butter melting on their crests, candied sweet potatoes sprinkled with brown sugar, onion slices like so many bull's-eyes, wedges of tomato and stewed tomatoes and sweet-and-sour rhubarb and black-eyed peas and wild rice and whole carrots and okra and corn and turnips and every conceivable kind of vegetable, all fresh. And there were plates of hot corn bread and sourdough

240

biscuits and homemade white bread and even slices of store-bought bread that nobody ever touched. Occupying the center of the table, was a white platter piled high with chicken breasts and legs and thighs, all crisply fried.

The moment each man took his place at the table he grabbed his fork and, half-rising from his seat, reached out for the chicken, stabbed a piece, dropped it onto his plate, then reached out for another. When satisfied with his fair share of chicken he would turn his attention to the vegetables. Throughout dinner someone was always half-rising from his seat, stretching across the table to spear another carrot or sweet potato, and dropping it on his plate. Everyone ate in silence, heads lowered, jaws working speedily, and then a bit less so, and then even less until finally they stopped. When someone rose to leave he was promptly replaced by another who had been waiting impatiently on the porch for a place at Ma Carter's table. Men ate and left and were replaced in a continuing stream, and no one spoke a word. Around them, black women in white linen dresses filled glasses with iced tea and coffee and replaced empty bowls with full ones and then disappeared through a swinging door into the kitchen. If anyone bothered to look behind that swinging door, he'd glimpse a huge black stove covered with steaming pots that were being watched over by an old white woman in a butcher's apron.

For dessert there was homemade ice cream and apple pie and peach cobbler, as well as fresh strawberries and blueberries and blackberries and boysenberries all served in bowls of thick cream. Finally, there were half-moon slices of watermelon so large they had to be eaten with two hands. Each of us ate until his jaws ached and his stomach could hold no more, and then we rose, belched and headed toward the screen door. Near the door stood a small table on which rested two coffee cans. Each man dropped a dollar and a quarter in one can to pay for his meal and then emptied his loose change into the other for the waitresses' tip.

On Sunday Ma Carter served a brunch of pancakes and waffles and French toast, sausage and country ham and thick bacon slices, scrambled and poached and fried eggs, hot and cold cereal, apricot and orange and tomato and apple juices, and hot biscuits together with a dozen kinds of jams and jellies, freshly whipped butter and hot coffee so bitter it had to be diluted with cream by all except the hardiest souls.

I remember the first game I pitched that spring, although whether it was against Jacksonville or Cedar Rapids or Yakima, I'm not sure. I remember it was still cool in March in Waycross and I had to warm up a long time in the bullpen. I remember, too, that I did not feel right as I threw. My motion felt awkward. I had no rhythm. There was a point in my pitching motion when all the parts of my body—throwing arm, shoulders, back, hips, legs—should have been exploding in unison toward the plate. On this day those parts were out of sync. While the rest of my body was lunging forward, my throwing arm lagged behind. It was as if my arm was reaching back, too late, to grasp something it had forgotten. When both feet were planted in my follow-through and my body's rhythm was all but spent, then my arm began moving toward the plate. I released the ball without benefit from the rhythm that had been built up by the rest of my body. It was as if I were standing flat-footed and merely flipping the ball with my arm. Even as I threw I could feel what was wrong. But my arm had a will of its own that day and I could impose nothing on it. I bounced balls in the dirt and flung them over my catcher's head. And none of those wild pitches even faintly resembled the fastballs I'd once thrown in Davenport, Iowa.

I pitched to 12 batters that day and did not retire one. After

242

every walk and wild pitch and base hit, I cursed and glared and kicked the dirt as I'd so often done at Davenport, and then, quite to my surprise, it suddenly occured to me that what was happening at this moment was somehow different from anything I had ever experienced before. This thought startled me, like a strange and unexpected pinch hitter. I paused a moment between pitches and tried to focus on this different thing. When I finally did recognize it all rage left me and a sense of panic set in. It started as a flutter in my stomach and rose, a solid lump, to my throat. I could not swallow! For one terrifying second I thought simply of breathing, of finally catching a breath, and only when I had was my mind free to dwell on the other thing. I'd forgotten how to pitch! I had lost control over all those natural movements—arm motion, follow-through, kick—that had been merely reflex actions for so many years. I tried to remember, saw only bits and pieces, shattered fragments of a thing once whole. I sifted through the fragments, tried to fit one to another, could not remember how to make my throwing arm move in unison with my lunging body. I could not remember how I'd once delivered a baseball with a fluid and effortless motion! And even if I could remember, I somehow knew I could never transmit that knowledge to my arms and legs, my back and shoulders. The delicate wires through which that knowledge had so often been communicated were burned out, irrevocably charred, I know now, by too much energy channeled too often along a solitary and too fragile wavelength.

Terror-stricken, I looked through the homeplate screen and saw the scouts and managers sitting in their deck chairs, shaking their heads in disbelief. A cluster of ballplayers was forming around them, growing larger with each pitch as word spread from diamond to diamond. Behind them all was the rotunda —that cylindrical brick building rising high above the diamonds. On its flat roof I could see four Braves' executives—Birdie Tebbetts, John McHale, John Mullins, Roland Hemmond—pointing me out to one another. I began my motion, tried in midmotion to remember, felt my arm jerk uncontrollably toward the plate. And then I saw the ball rising over the homeplate screen, over the heads of those behind the screen, higher still, over the top of the rotunda and the heads of the men standing behind it, the men glancing up, startled, and then following the ball with their eyes until it came down on Diamond Four. For a split second everyone—players, umpires, scouts, managers, executives—stared at the ball resting on the infield dirt behind second base, and then they all looked up at the point where the ball had passed over the rotunda, and then, in unison, they turned toward me, blank on the mound. Someone laughed, and then others laughed, too.

I lost it all that spring. The delicate balance I had so assiduously created at Bradenton collapsed. Just like that. One moment it was a perfectly solid-looking structure—satisfactions, potential, success, talent—and the next it was nothing but rubble. The only thing left standing was a new and impenetrable frustration.

Each game I pitched that spring was, like the first, an embarrassment. Standing on the mound, I tried to remember. The bright sun receded in the sky, grew small and distant, dissolved. Staring plateward, I saw at the end of a long, narrow tunnel, a minute fresco—batter, catcher, umpire. I began my motion, heard from a great distance the shouts and nervous shifting of my fielders, pumped, raised both hands overhead, curiously felt no exertion, was moving as if in a dream, without effort, disconnected. I raised my left leg and turned it toward third base, paused—perfectly balanced on one leg, an odd-looking bird, still and blank—and then my body moved toward the plate,

244

and later, my arm. The ball traveled a great distance through the dark tunnel and I lost track of it. Moments later, sensing its return, I raised my glove and caught it, without feeling. I began my motion again, threw the ball, caught it, threw it, caught it, threw it. At times I was vaguely conscious of my fielders moving after it, and then, of myself moving, too (always the pitcher, even in a dream) drifting toward third base, straddling the bag now, aware of a runner moving toward me. He moves in agonizing slow-motion, his features twisted, his chest heaving and, curiously suspended over his right shoulder, a sunspot—the ball! The runner and the ball are approaching very fast now, growing larger and larger, are almost upon me when, with a ferocious grunt, the runner leaps into the air, momentarily obscuring the ball. He hits the dirt—whoomph —and slides. The ball, suddenly huge before my eyes, explodes in my glove, which instinctively slaps at his spikes, too late. "Safe!"

Amid the billowing dust, I am conscious now of the sun's glare and my labored breathing and my hot, coarse-flannel uniform dripping sweat and the heavy ball in my hand and the nauseating, oily-leather smell of my glove and the pressing shouts and whistles of my teammates and, finally, walking back to the mound, of the weariness of my limbs.

In camp that spring I became "the bonus baby who forgot how to pitch." I took to my room and locked the door. I played my records at full volume and hid behind the noise. I no longer drove into town for a beer or dinner at Ma Carter's. I took all my meals in camp. I ate either very early, before the others filled the cafeteria, or else very late, after they had eaten and gone. I seldom left my room in barracks two. I passed the time standing for hours in front of the mirror on the wall. I practiced my motion in pantomime. I threw a thousand pitches a day in front of that mirror. At first I went through my motion as quickly as if I was pitching in a game, because I hoped to slip naturally into a once familiar grove. Then, when that did not work, I went through my motion with great deliberation, step by methodical step, looking always for that point where everything started to go wrong. But all I ever saw reflected in that mirror was my own image. It hypnotized me. In midmotion my mind would drift, and by the time I forced it back I'd be in my follow-through.

No amount of throwing before that mirror, or in games, or on a warm-up mound with old "Boom-Boom" Beck beside me extolling the virtues of the fadeaway, halted my pitching decline. It generated its own momentum and I could do nothing to stop it or even slow it down. After each game in which I performed, I slid further down through the Braves' farm system—from Austin to Jacksonville to Cedar Rapids to Yakima to Boise and, finally, to Eau Claire, Wisconsin, of the Class C Northern League. I broke camp with Eau Claire, an act of kindness by the befuddled Braves' front office.

I reached Eau Claire in late April with my wife, who had joined me at the end of spring training, after a three-day drive from the southeastern corner of Georgia to the northwestern corner of Wisconsin. The land, like Nebraska, was barren of trees, but not flat. It was rich farm and dairy country of gentle undulations that had been divided into perfect square-mile plots of corn and wheat and oats and hay and grass and freshly furrowed dirt that was almost black. From the crest of one of these undulations (not even a hill, really, just a rise) one could see a gigantic patchwork quilt of green and gold and chocolate squares, the quilt rising and falling over a softly rumpled land.

Eau Claire was a neat, nondescript little city of about 30,000 people, most of them of Swedish or German ancestry. At one end of the city was a public park built on and around a hill. The base of the hill—the park's entrance—was ringed by a

246

narrow stream crossed by only a single bridge. Across the bridge was an open area with picnic tables, swings, seesaws and jungle gyms. Higher up the hill, the park grew thick and lush with trees and shrubs and rocky gardens. At the top of the hill, at the center of another open space, was a huge, cold, stone facade—the entrance to the city's only lighted baseball stadium and the home of the Eau Claire Braves.*

Carol and I lived in a single room with a tiny kitchen on the second floor of an old two-family house. The room was so small that once we pulled the bed out of the sofa (a Castro convertible of undecipherable vintage) it was no longer possible to cross from one side of the room to the other without walking on top of the bed. In the morning, if I woke first, I had to step carefully over my sleeping wife in order to get to the kitchen. The kitchen, which was just wide enough for two people to slip by each other, contained an ancient gas stove, a sink, some wall cabinets, two fold-up chairs and a one-by-three-foot folding table that dropped out of the wall at will.

It was there that Carol prepared the first meals of our early married life. I remember, especially, the first one. She had remained at home to prepare a late supper while I went off to pitch my first game of the season. I was hurt to think she felt it of greater importance to prepare our first meal than to see me pitch, although I knew she had never been much impressed by my talent. I remembered the first time we met, in my senior year of high school. When she asked my name, I lowered my eyes and, through modestly furrowed brows, said distinctly, "Pat Jordan." Nothing! She had never heard of me! All the while we dated, I waited impatiently for the day when she

• • •

*Hank Aaron began his baseball career as an 18-year-old second baseman with the Eau Claire Braves in the early 1950s.

would acknowledge my greatness. Why else would she be interested in me? Finally, someone told her I was a baseball star. But this did not impress her much. She knew nothing about baseball, found it amazing that someone would actually pay me a large sum of money, as she put it, "Just to play a game."

"You don't understand," I said, and dismissed her ignorance. But now in Eau Claire it disturbed me that, unlike most baseball wives, mine knew nothing about the game I devoted my life to. She took her cues solely from my enthusiasms and despairs. Whenever I pitched decently enough (a rarity that year) I had to tell her so, and only then would she smile and say, "That's nice, dear." And when I was knocked out of the box in the first inning (a more common occurence) and she saw my dejection, she commiserated, saying, "Well, it's not your fault. It's hard to do good when you only play a little bit. . . . Why doesn't your manager let you play as long as the other pitchers?"

On the night of my first starting assignment I pitched less than an inning. It was like Waycross. After I was relieved, I had to sit on the bench in the dugout in 30-degree weather (it was always cold in the Northern League) until the game ended two hours later. When I returned to our apartment at midnight, I found the table set, dishes gleaming, napkins folded and a single candle, unlighted. Carol was sitting by the table, her hands folded in her lap, her eyes pink-rimmed. On the counter next to the stove was a mound of freshly peeled but uncooked potatoes and a long, thick, raw steak.

She sniffled, shivering all over as if just emerging from cold water. "I couldn't light the oven," she said, finally.

"What!"

She held up a pack of matches with only a single match left. "I tried, but it wouldn't catch!"

"Jesus, Carol, I'm starved!" She began to cry (the failed

wife), and between sobs to plead forgiveness. Her martyred husband, returning from a hard night's work (less than an inning?) to find a barren table, decided, on a whim, not to grant it.

"If you can't cook, I'll eat someplace else," I said and turned toward the door. She clutched at my arm, caught it. "You can't leave me!" she screamed. "You can't! Please! Don't leave me alone!" Her eyes were glazed like a trapped animal's, and, for an instant, she frightened me. "I'll try again! *Please!*" She grabbed the book of matches and worked to light the last one. She struck the match over and over again, but it would not light. She stopped, finally, saying, "Please don't leave me alone," and then, exhausted, she sat down in a chair—a strange, frightened, hysterical girl . . . my wife! At 19! Soft and pale, with translucent skin. You could see through her, so easily . . . bluish veins and blood vessels, faint fibers in exquisite parchment.

She bruised easily, cried often that first year after she had stepped—smiling, trusting and innocent—on board a sinking ship with its mad captain. A thousand miles from home for the first time in her life, she was burdened with nothing but my black moods day after day, while I, obsessed with my disintegrating career, seldom gave her a thought. She was just there, hovering around my despairs, at times a pleasant diversion, at other times a burden. To her, I was her husband, the sole source of comfort and despair, and she wondered, secretly, if this was the way it was supposed to be? Always?

After two disastrous performances in Eau Claire I was relegated to the bullpen. Two weeks later I was the tenth pitcher on a 10-man staff. I mopped up in the last inning of lost causes, and, even then, often had to be relieved because I could not get three outs. During the next month I appeared in six games totaling 15 innings, was credited with two losses and no victo-

249

ries, and had an earned run average above eight.

Only three incidents stand out in that first month. I remember pitching an inning in Duluth, Minnesota, and later being asked by a Duluth player, "Aren't you the guy from Davenport? The one who could really bring it?" I nodded, embarrassed. "What happened to you? Your motion's all fucked up." Another time, I remember pitching to Lou Brock in St. Cloud, Minnesota.* At the time, Brock was leading the league in hitting with a .380 average. I struck him out on a soft, floating fastball. He swung so far ahead of the pitch that he asked the catcher if it was an off-speed pitch. At the end of the inning I sat down in the far corner of the dugout and cried. My teammates glanced over at me in disbelief. I cried uncontrollably, and my manager had to send another pitcher to the bullpen to warm up and pitch the next inning.

A third time, I remember a game in Winnipeg that began in weather so cold—19 degrees above zero—that we had to build small fires on the dirt floor of the dugout to keep our fingers from going numb. We huddled around the fires, simian man in gray flannel, and at the end of each inning sent one of our tribe to forage twigs and bits of paper in the open area behind the outfield fence. Because I was the player least likely to be used in that game, I was the one sent out to forage.

By June I no longer pitched, not even the last inning of hopelessly lost games (which were many, since the Braves were in last place). I spent each game in the bullpen. I warmed up constantly, inning after inning, trying to recapture what had once been as natural to me as walking. I became more obsessed

• • •

*I recall only six teams in the Class C Northern League that year: Winnipeg, Canada (Cardinals); St. Cloud, Minnesota (Cubs); Duluth, Minnesota (Tigers); Grand Forks, North Dakota (Pirates); Aberdeen, South Dakota (Orioles); and, of course, the Eau Claire, Wisconsin, Braves.

250

and frantic as I threw, and my motion became even more distorted. I was pushing the ball now, like a shot-putter, and I remembered, without irony, Dennis Overby pushing the ball in spring training after his arm went bad. But there was nothing wrong with my arm! I could have understood a sore arm, dealt with it, accepted it eventually. What was happening to me was happening in my head, not my arm. Whenever I began to throw a ball, my head went absolutely blank, and afterwards it buzzed with a thousand discordant whispers.

After awhile in that Eau Claire bullpen, no one would catch me anymore, neither our third-string catcher, nor any of my fellow pitchers, all of whom thought me mad, but comically so. I threw alone, without a ball. I stood on the warm-up mound, pumped, kicked and fired an imaginary baseball toward the plate. Behind me, my teammates sat on a bench gesturing at me with their heads and laughing.

I hadn't pitched in a game for two weeks when the Braves' minor league pitching coach, Gordon Maltzberger, passed through Eau Claire. Maltzberger spent the spring in Bradenton with Milwaukee and Louisville, while Boom-Boom Beck worked with the lower minor leaguers in Waycross. During the season, however, Boom-Boom returned to his home, while Maltzberger moved up and down the Braves' minor league system, stopping a day or two in Palatka, three days in Eau Claire, five in Cedar Rapids, a week in Jacksonville and 10 days in Louisville before beginning from the bottom all over again. He was a prim, fussy man in his late forties, who had pitched briefly in the major leagues during World War II. He wore horn-rimmed glasses and had thin lips always pressed so tightly together tha a hundred tiny lines had formed like stitch marks around his mouth, which made him resemble a prissy, taciturn spinster.

At Eau Claire, Maltzberger spent his time giving encouragement to those pitchers pitching well and avoiding those, like myself, who were not. In the bullpen one night, I asked him to help me with my motion. "I'll get to you in good time," he said. I grabbed his forearm. "But you've got to—now!" I said. He looked down at my hand on his arm. I let go. "I'll get a catcher," I said. He did not hear me. He was still looking curiously at his arm. He shook it out away from his body, as if shaking off an insect. Then he walked back to the dugout, showered and left that night for Cedar Rapids.

Three more days passed. My manager, Jim Fanning, had not spoken to me in a week. He passed me with a nod and quickly averted eyes. Finally I confronted him in our deserted clubhouse one night. I demanded that he pitch me. "I haven't pitched in two weeks!" I said. I could hear my shrill voice and feel the tears sliding down my cheeks. It embarrassed me. Still, I could not stop. "Everyone pitches but me! When am I gonna pitch?"

He, too, looked at me curiously. Then warily. His features clouded—narrow eyes, long sharp nose, lipless grin, all slanting upward toward his temples like the features of a fox. He was a trim, good-looking man in his thirties who would grow trimmer and better looking with age. By forty he would resemble one of those well-tailored gentlemen sipping an expensive scotch in the pages of *The New Yorker*. A catcher in the Chicago Cubs' farm system, he had never risen higher than the American Association (AAA). There he was a bullpen catcher, who made good use of his idle time. He pasted newspaper photographs of prominent players in action on plywood and cut out their silhouettes. During each game, young boys hawked these mementos in the stands for one dollar.

Fanning called his business "Jim Fanning Enterprises," and, in truth, he was an enterprising man. Even at Eau Claire he had the distracted air of a man who had no intention of remaining a lowly minor league manager for very long. Sitting at the far end of the dugout during our games, he seemed always to be contemplating strategy—not for those games, but for his career. His players knew this. "Jim's gonna be a big man someday," they prophesied. "He don't belong in a uniform."

They were right. Today, Jim Fanning is the general manager of the Montreal Expos. I saw him a few years ago in the ballroom of the Lord Baltimore Hotel during the Orioles–Pirates World Series. The ballroom was filled with hundreds of baseball executives who had just finished dinner and now, over scotches and bourbons, were proposing trades to one another. They scribbled names on paper napkins with felt-tip pens, then hurried to another table and presented the names to a rival executive. Jim Fanning sat alone at an oval table sipping from a glass and sucking on a long cigar. In his forties now, he looked impeccably trim and distinguished in a navy blazer, gray slacks and black patent-leather loafers. While he sipped and smoked, various men came up to him, presented their napkins and waited. Jim thought for long moments, contemplated strategy while blowing smoke through puckered lips toward the ceiling, then nodded. When he was alone, finally, I went over and introduced myself.

"Remember me, Jim?" I said, standing before him. "At Eau Claire in '61?"

He grinned at me and, without rising, shook my hand. "Sure I do, Pat. How you been?" And then, really remembering, his features began to cloud exactly as they had that night years before when I'd confronted him, hysterically, in our clubhouse On that night he had said, "Sure you're gonna pitch, Pat. Just calm down. I was gonna start you in Winnipeg on Sunday."

We left for Winnipeg, the first stop of a 13-day road trip, after a Saturday night game in Eau Claire. It was midnight when we finished storing our bags in the backs of three identi-

253

cal station wagons (black 1958 Chevys with a screaming Indian painted on each front door) and then got inside (three players in front, three in back) and drove off toward Winnipeg, 12 hours to the northwest. Sitting by the window in the front seat, I remember watching the highway unroll before our headlights like a beckoning white-striped carpet. We drove for hours with nothing to see but the highway and the black, limitless Minnesota woods. And then, about an hour from Fargo, North Dakota, we saw a brilliant white light in the darkness, and we stopped to eat at a truckers' cafe. The cafe glowed like a star in the center of a vast open space dotted with dimly lighted gasoline pumps. The area was crowded with small-cabbed, big-bellied diesel trucks, some of them parked off in the darkness, others being gassed up at the pumps, still others hissing steam, grinding gears and roaring off down the highway.

When we finished eating and returned to the car I sat in the middle of the front seat, my knees jammed up to my chest because of the drive shaft hump, as we crossed the flat, open plains of North Dakota. Pat Sherrill drove and I sat beside him. Around us, the others slept, their heads resting on one anothers' shoulders. Whenever they woke with a start they looked around, embarrassed, and tried to go back to sleep sitting straight up. After awhile they began to list again, their heads drooping in stages, and before long they were sleeping just as before.

On my right shoulder I could feel Rico Carty's heavy, bristly head and his hot breath, while in the rear-view mirror I could see the intertwined bodies of Jerry Hummitzsch, Jim Snyder and Larry Allender.

Allender was a tall, handsome youth with a cowboy's angular face and glistening black hair he was perpetually combing into a D.A. He looked forward to our trips to Winnipeg because of

254

that city's reputation for having three single women to every man.

Most of our pitchers hated to pitch in Winnipeg because of its cold weather, but once Larry discovered that those games were televised, he never failed to volunteer to "take one for the team," as he put it. Before every inning he combed his hair in the dugout, slipped on his cap with care and proceeded to the mound, where he walked the first batter he faced. He always walked the first batter, it seemed, and then held him close to first base with long, repeated, darkly handsome glances over his left shoulder directly into the camera behind the coach's box. That night strange girls would be prowling through the corridors of our hotel looking for the room of "number 27, the guy who pitched today."

Sleeping on Allender's shoulder in the car was Jim Snyder, an earnest, chunky, blonde, 22-year-old Mormon from Southern California. Since he neither drank liquor, danced nor smoked tobacco, Snyder had little in common with most of his teammates, although he did have a common bond with Allender, I discovered, when his wife told my wife that they "just loved to party." On this road trip Carol was staying with Peggy Snyder, who, as usual, would be trying to convert her to the only true religion, Joseph Smith's. Although I smoked, danced and drank liquor, I had no great attraction to those vices and would gladly have surrendered them if Carol had been converted to the Church of Jesus Christ of the Latter Day Saints.

Leaning ponderously against Snyder was Jerry Hummitzsch, a six-foot, three-inch, 230-pound Iowa farm boy we had nicknamed "Baby Huey." He had large ears sticking out from a small head of closely cropped hair like spring grass, and a massive body, half muscle, half baby fat. As a rookie pitcher of 21, he showed an excellent fastball, decent control and absolutely no curveball. Still, he was one of our more successful pitchers, and within a year he would be pitching for Austin of the Texas League (AA). By then he had developed a modest curveball, which, with his fastball, made him one of the Braves' brightest prospects. The front office expected him to pitch the following year with Louisville of the American Association and the year after that with Milwaukee. But while still at Austin, Jerry was returning from a fishing trip one night when his car ran off the road and he was killed.

In the front, I could not sleep. I was too cramped in that middle seat (I could feel the muscles in my calves fluttering) and I was too excited about the prospect of finally pitching again. But most of all I could not sleep because Pat Sherrill was driving. He drove transfixed, his eyes glassy and wide and his hands gripping the steering wheel so tightly that his knuckles were bloodless. He never let the speedometer dip below 90. Whenever he saw an approaching bend in the road, the tip of his tongue would dart back and forth across his lips and he would hunch forward over the wheel in anticipation. He'd plow into that curve at 90 miles an hour, the rear end of the wagon beginning to drift, sliding as if on ice into the opposite lane while the front end pointed toward the woods and we were navigating that curve sideways, tires screeching and the stink of burning rubber everywhere. Halfway through the turn, Pat would nail the accelerator to the floor, spin the steering wheel to the left, and the rear end would snap back and the front end would straighten out and we'd roar down the highway without ever having dipped below 90.

Pat loved to drive. He refused every offer of relief on those 12-hour trips, told us he had driven with his wife and baby in a two-seat Triumph from their home in Sonora, Texas, to Eau Claire without stopping, except for gas and food and to make love to Linda in the front seat while the baby slept in the tiny

256

compartment under the back window. That drive helped build up his stamina for his true vocation, he said, which was not to become a major league third baseman (under which assumption the Braves had given him a $20,000 bonus) but a race car driver on the NASCAR circuit. His idol was not Eddie Mathews but a wild and, then, unknown young racer also from Sonora named A. J. Foyt. Whenever Pat got the chance he practiced driving techniques taught him by "Ole A. J." He especially looked forward to these exhausting drives to Winnipeg, which tested his endurance, and to more driving pleasures at the Winnipeg Stadium.

The stadium was a perfect oval, like a football stadium. It was surrounded by a high wooden wall and a concrete sidewalk running along the outside of that wall. The sidewalk ringed the stadium and was just wide enough for a car to drive on. After each game, Pat forced us all to wait with him in the car until the last pedestrian had departed. Then he eased the station wagon onto the sidewalk and, while the rest of us pleaded with him, he floored the accelerator and we went spinning around that oval on two wheels at his favorite speed of 90 miles an hour. We cursed and screamed at Pat to stop, hung onto the door handles for our lives, and were certain that looming up around the next bend would be some poor soul whose startled expression, just before he was splattered across our windshield, would be with us the rest of our lives. But Pat never even heard us. He just licked his lips and sweated, taking pleasure in his driving until he was physically drained. Then he would jerk the steering wheel to the right and the car would fly off the sidewalk, momentarily suspended in midair before its suspension sagged and its belly whacked the ground. Tires spewed pebbles everywhere and the car spun onto the highway, as always, without missing a beat.

Pat was to be my roommate in Winnipeg on this trip. We

had roomed together once before. I remember returning to our hotel room late that night, slightly the worse for drink, and opening the door to find him naked, sleeping on his head, the balls of his feet high against the wall. The next morning he told me he practiced yoga. "Helps me relax," he said with an involuntary wink of his left eye. He had an assortment of such winks and twitches and shakes of the head. Unless driving, he could not sit still, not even in our dugout during a game. Hands on hips, he paced back and forth across our vision, whistled shrilly, yelled out in a cracking falsetto, "Atta Babe!" and made a thousand tiny spitting noises with his lips, "pppttt." Drained of saliva, he continued to spit. Whenever he got up to bat and grounded out or flied out, he raced full-speed toward first base, rounded the bag into foul territory and continued at full speed back to the dugout. Just before reaching it, he'd hit the dirt with a beautiful hook slide, kicking dirt in our faces, and then pop up and step into the dugout. At the end of every inning he was the first player to leap out of the dugout and run full speed to his position—which amazed his teammates since he was such an atrocious third baseman we wondered why he wanted to rush out there just to make errors. The Braves had given him a bonus in spite of his fielding, not because of it. He had the potential, however, to be a great home run hitter. He was a powerfully built six-footer with long, muscular arms and a barrel chest. We called him "Chesty" because of the unique way he fielded ground balls. He'd puff out his chest like a bully, let the ball bounce off it, bend down, pick up the ball and throw it to first base. He seldom used his glove except to protect himself against vicious line drives. His glove seemed to confuse him, like a strange growth at the end of his hand that he'd never learned to manipulate. He was the first infielder I ever saw who backhanded ground balls hit directly at him.

*     *     *

We reached Fargo at dawn. Pat turned right onto Highway 29 and we drove directly north toward Canada. We drove for hours without seeing anything but the endless gray Dakota plains and an occasional farmhouse off in the distance, and when at mid-morning we crossed the Canadian border into Manitoba Province, still the land did not change. We reached Winnipeg at noon, went directly to our hotel rooms and fell asleep, fully clothed, on the bed. I woke two hours later, stiff and malodorous, and went downstairs to the coffee shop for breakfast.

We arrived at the stadium at 3:30 P.M. for a five o'clock game. We dressed into our uniforms in the clubhouse off the left field foul line and then walked across the diamond toward our dugout along the firstbase line. The Cardinals were taking batting practice, so some of us stopped at short or second base to chat with players we had known from other leagues, other years. We would take no batting practice after our exhausting drive, only infield practice. The others broke out the bats and balls from the canvas sacks and began games of catch and pepper. I stepped down into the dugout, sat on the bench and waited (the starting pitcher's privilege) for Jim Fanning to toss me a new ball and tell me to warm up. It was a simple routine, yet one that never failed to thrill me—and certainly never so much as at that moment. The manager opens a small box, withdraws a new ball from white tissue, spits on the ball (partly for luck), rubs dirt in with the spit (the ball no longer white now, but the color of rich cream), tosses it to that day's starting pitcher and says, with a wink, "Go get 'em, Pat!"

Jim Fanning tossed me a ball and told me to go to the bullpen. "But don't warm up yet," he said. I sat in the right field bullpen and watched our team take infield practice. I grew anxious as game time drew near. Finally, one of my teammates came sprinting toward me. I stood up, flexed my shoulders,

259

touched my toes twice. It was Hummitzsch. He tossed me a catcher's mitt. "Jim wants you to warm me up," he said. "He can't spare a catcher right now."

"But I thought . . . he told me I was starting . . ."

"I only know what he told me," Hummitzsch said, and stepped onto the mound. I caught him until he was warm, each pitch a blur through my tears. When he returned to the dugout I remained in the bullpen for a few minutes, and then I walked across the outfield to our clubhouse. I changed into my street clothes without showering, packed my blue canvas bag with "Braves" stenciled in white at both ends, and walked to the bus stop. I took a bus into town, got my other bags at the hotel and took a Greyhound bus from Winnipeg to Eau Claire.

I reached the Eau Claire bus terminal at nine o'clock in the morning and found my wife there, crying. "I didn't know what had happened to you," she said. "Everyone's looking for you. Jim Fanning called. He said you ran away. . . . I didn't know. . . . I thought you'd left me, too. . . ." She began to laugh and cry at the same time. "I had this ridiculous vision. You were running like a madman through Canada, you were in your uniform. . . ."

That night John Mullins, the farm director, telephoned. He told me that for jumping the club I was suspended without salary from the Eau Claire Braves. I told him he was too late, that I had suspended the Eau Claire Braves from my career.

"Don't be a smart-ass," he said. "We're reassigning you to Palatka in the Florida State League. You get your ass down there within two days or I'll see to it you don't get your final bonus payment."

We left at six o'clock in the morning. I drove for 34 hours, stopping only for food and gas, but, unlike Pat Sherrill, not to make love to my wife by the side of the road. We did not speak for hours. Carol alternately slept and stared out the window at the steadily changing land, and again must have wondered what kind of man her husband was.

I thought about my career. I thought about it when we were driving around Chicago on the Tri-State Tollway and when we were driving straight south through Indiana on a badly chewed up two-lane highway, and when we passed through Evansville with its thousands of roadside gas stations and, late in the afternoon, when we turned east into Kentucky with its vast stretches of grassland being nibbled by sleek horses. I was still thinking about it when we passed through Owensboro with its beautiful white-pillared mansions set far back off the road, and when we turned south again and headed toward the mountains around Nashville, Tennessee.

We reached the first mountain late at night in a dense fog. While Carol slept, I fell in behind a long trailer-truck moving slowly up the grade. The truck moved slower and slower as the mountain grew steeper and steeper, and then it was barely moving at all and the driver was shifting gears feverishly and the truck was lagging between each shift, sliding backward before the gears finally caught and it began moving forward again. I snapped alert; saw in my rear view mirror the road disappearing in the fog and off at the side of the road the mountain falling away into blackness. I was sweating now and my back ached from being held so rigidly as I leaned forward over the steering wheel. Suddenly the truck stopped, the square back end of its trailer looming huge in my windshield. I jammed on the breaks just in time. The truck then slid a few feet before stopping again. I looked in my rear view mirror; it was filled with the headlights of another trailer-truck. The truck in front exhaled a blast of smoke, lurched forward and disappeared. I released the brakes, pressed the accelerator pedal too hard and my rear wheels began to spin. Then they caught

261

and the big Chrysler leapt over the top of the mountain and went speeding down the other side. I stabbed at the brakes repeatedly, but the mountain was so steep that we continued to hurtle down into the fog amidst the smell of burning brake linings.

I was still thinking about my career when we reached Chattanooga at dawn and a little later when we crossed into Georgia, the land of red clay. Carol, who'd been sleeping against the door, lifted her head and mumbled, "Where did we stop last? What state is it?" and then fell back to sleep before I could answer. She was still sleeping when I drove around the outskirts of Atlanta with its glass skyscrapers in the distance and, up close, the unpainted wooden shacks of the Negro slums. She did not wake until mid-morning, when we were deep into the South of two-lane black-tops and fetid swamps and a white-hot sun and lone Negroes walking along the soft, sloping shoulder beside the road. One of those black figures waved to us as we whooshed past. I beeped the horn, too late.

On the outskirts of Cordele we stopped at a fruit stand and bought six peaches for breakfast. We ate the peaches as we drove toward Tifton. The juice dribbled down our chins and onto our clothes, but we did not care. We did not care that our breath was sour and our bodies rank with sweat and that our clothes stuck to our skin. We were inured to every sensation, to aching backs and cramped limbs and burning eyes. After 30 hours of driving nothing mattered but that we finally arrive. Carol did not even seem to notice (or, if she did, she no longer cared) that the Chrysler was hurtling along at over 110 miles an hour and that I was driving with one arm out the window and only one hand on the steering wheel.

We passed through Valdosta at noon, crossed the Florida state line and headed south toward Lake City, which we reached an hour later, and then turned southeast toward Lulu and Guilford and Lake Butler and Starke, where we saw a sign, "Palatka 39 miles." I was still thinking about my career. I had been thinking about it for 33 hours and I still did not understand it, what had happened to it, to me. As we approached Palatka, I decided that nothing had happened, nothing momentous, that is, nothing that would not be straightened out once I began pitching regularly again. That was all there was to it, I told myself, although I knew that the Braves did not share this belief. Why else would they have sent me to "The Elephants' Burial Ground?" That's what we jokingly called Palatka during spring training. It was the lowest of the Braves' Class D teams, a receptacle for aging veterans playing one last season; for all those faceless "Lefties" and "Studs" who were used to fill out a roster until midseason, when they were released; and for one-time prospects trying to make it back from calcium deposits and ripped tendons; and for others, like myself, who had somehow missed it along the way for a reason that was, as yet, unclear to anyone.

I lived in Palatka with Carol for eight weeks, and I remember it with almost the same clarity of detail I do McCook—although for a different reason. Palatka was the last place whre I played professional baseball. It was different from McCook. McCook was stark, desolate, exposed, surrounded by limitless horizons that left one breathless. Palatka, resting on the banks of the St. Johns River, was surrounded by dense tropical foliage, the limitless swamps and, overhead, a pitiless sun that smothered one's breath. It was always hot in Palatka, and it rained daily. The land never dried. All the wooden buildings rested on cinder blocks a foot off the ground, and yet even that did not prevent the moisture and the heat and the insects from eating away the wood. Warm, moist pieces of wood came off

263

in one's hand, so that it seemed one could peel away the walls of a building like an orange if he wished to. The town's main street was called Lemon Street. It was made of cobblestones. Weeds grew between the stones and out of the cracks in the sidewalks and at the bases of the concrete buildings, so that the vegetation appeared to be strangling the town as the swamp on the outskirts crept relentlessly in. There was a paper mill that supplied most of the blacks and poor whites with employment. Each morning at six o'clock they were summoned to work by the blast of a shrill whistle that woke the entire town. Shortly thereafter the town was blanketed by a lavender haze and a terrible stench that lifted only slightly at night when the mill shut down.

Palatka was a suffocating place, claustrophobic, and everything in it emitted an overwhelming sense of decay.

We came in on Lemon Street and drove slowly over the cobblestones past Pig's Bar-B-Q and the Wyn Dixie Supermarket and the old Howell Movie Theater, featuring Judy Holliday in *The Solid Gold Cadillac*. We stared out the windows at our new home and, in turn, were regarded by the townspeople. Mostly aged, they sat on benches that lined both sidewalks and faced the street. We passed through their gaze as through a gauntlet and came upon an unbelievably pure chalk-white building—the pool hall. The sidewalk at the base of the pool hall was splattered with white, too, as if both had been doused liberally with all the leftover talcum powder its customers had rubbed on their hands. We stopped before the St. James Hotel, the tallest building in town. In the lobby, old men dozed in faded armchairs, while overhead a huge fan churned so slowly I could count its blades. We registered with the grinning clerk. He wiped a handkerchief across his brow. "Hot 'nuff for y'all?" he said.

Fully clothed, we fell asleep on an old iron poster bed and did not wake from this, the longest of all road trips, until the following night. We then ate spareribs at Pig's and drove out to the ball park to watch my new teammates play. They were not called the Braves, I learned from the hotel clerk, but the Azaleas. "After the town flower," the clerk said. "They play their games in 'The Bowl'," he added with a touch of pride. "The Azalea Bowl." A slightly pretentious name for a Class D ball park, I thought, until we arrived there and I saw the name was not so much pretentious as it was ludicrous. The Azalea Bowl was similar to McCook's Cibola Stadium, except that Cibola, a speck on the plains, was a temporary, skeletal structure that looked as if it had been assembled yesterday from a few planks and metal braces and could just as quickly be disassembled tomorrow without leaving a trace. "The Bowl" (as the players leeringly called it) was a slightly more permanent looking structure at the edge of a swamp. It was enclosed by a 10-foot high fence that began behind the left field bleachers, went behind the homeplate stands and terminated behind the right field bleachers. The fence had been painted green years ago, but the paint had mostly peeled away and now the wood had begun to rot. The outfield was enclosed by a three-foot fence whose purpose seemed less to define home runs than to hold back the swamp. Thick green foliage hung over the wall, obscuring the faded names of restaurants and gas stations that had been advertised there. Long vines and tendrils crept under the wall onto the playing surface, so that often, when an outfielder chased a ball to the wall, those perverse vines would tangle in his spikes and trip him up. Each week it seemed the vines crept further onto the playing field and the swamp pressed closer, overrunning The Bowl just as it was overruning the town.

Carol and I arrived at The Bowl in the third inning of a game between the Azaleas and the Tampa Smokers.* We sat on the top row of the homeplate stands, which were only 10 rows high. It was a tiny ball park that seated less than 1000 people. On this humid night in July, however, there were no more than 100, most of them blacks laughing and cheering in the segregated bleachers along the left field foul line.

On the field, my new teammates trailed the Smokers 4–0, under dim lights and with the noise of the swamp as a backdrop (thrashings in the foliage and the caws of strange birds). In the fifth inning, with the Azaleas trailing 7–0, a snake slithered under the outfield fence and the umpires called "Time!" while our rightfielder beat it to death with a bat. By the seventh inning the Azaleas trailed 11–0, and the moisture from the swamp had crept into the outfield in the form of a low-lying gray mist. The outfielders, concealed from the waist down, waded eerily through the mist after fly balls.

The Azaleas eventually lost that game, and were, I discovered, one of the worst minor league teams ever assembled. They had assumed last place early in the season, only to bury themselves ever deeper into the cellar as the season progressed. Their fortunes had so turned against them by the time I appeared in July that players often refused to take the field. The team's leading pitcher, "Birdlegs" Perez, a Dominican Republic dandy with a cherubic face and a body like a stick figure, had lost seven games in a row. He refused to pitch anymore. He claimed he had calcium deposits in his elbow—the occupational hazard, he protested of delivering a 1000 different

•  •  •

*The Tampa Smokers were a farm team of the Cincinnati Reds. Other teams in the league were the Sarasota Athletics (Kansas City), Daytona Islanders (Chicago White Sox), Leesburg Orioles (Baltimore), St. Petersburg Yankees (New York) and Orlando Twins (Minnesota).

266

pitches (knuckleball, palmball, spitball, etc.) from a 1000 different angles (overhand, sidearm, semi-sidearm, etc.), none of which, it seemed to an impartial observer, were particularly effective.

The Azalea's leading home run hitter was Paul Cato, a portly, unshaven first baseman who looked like a sinister adversary of Eliot Ness. Paul refused to take the field one day after he'd placed his first baseman's glove beside the dugout, taken a lap around the park to loosen up, and returned to the dugout to find his glove stolen. "Enough is enough!" he was heard to shout before retiring to the clubhouse, where he sulked for the entire game.

The Azaleas' leftfielder, Tim Strickland, had been a teammate of mine at McCook. Tim was the shy North Carolinian who shook hands like an Italian film star and whose only spoken words all season were to the umpire: "You gook, you couldn't call a donkey fight!" After indifferent successes at McCook and the following year at Wellsville, Tim had become a star in Palatka. When I arrived in July he was leading the Florida State League in hitting, only a few percentage points ahead of Tampa's hustling second baseman, Pete Rose. Tim was not used to the pressure, and each day he grew more twitchy as Rose irrevocably narrowed the gap between them. He pleaded with his manager to drop his name from the starting lineup. He complained of mysterious ailments, clutching his stomach in pain or cradling his splitting head, and he accused Pete Rose of voodoo.

Finally, I heard that he cracked. He did not show up for a Saturday afternoon game at The Bowl. Evidently—according to reports—he wandered up and down Lemon Street muttering to himself. He accosted strange women, clutched their arms and rolled his eyes. They pulled free and hurried away. He invaded a dress shop, told a salesgirl he loved her, followed

267

her behind a rack of summer creations. They tussled, the rack tottered, dresses spilled over a customer. She flailed at them and screamed. Tim fled to his single room on the top floor of the St. James Hotel. He sat by the window and drank a case of warm beer. He drained each bottle in a single gulp and then tossed it out the window at a passing car. Bottles exploded on car roofs, scattered across the cobblestones. Someone telephoned the sheriff. *The town was under siege!* Tim was arrested. He went meekly, sat in a cell while the sheriff telephoned the Milwaukee Braves. A decision was made. Tim was escorted to the bus depot and put on a Greyhound heading north. That was the last we ever saw of him. Later, someone reported that he was in jail—an Army stockade, actually. He was a draft dodger, they said. He finished second in the FSL batting race. There was an asterisk after his name.

Louie Haas was our second baseman. He was a courtly 20-year-old native of Paducah, Kentucky, who had been given a $40,000 bonus three years ago and ever since had had difficulty compiling a batting average as substantial as his weight. He weighed 137 pounds. He was five feet, four inches tall and had the large brown eyes and hairless cheeks of a prepubescent boy. He dreaded every game at The Bowl. The fans berated him viciously—as they did all of the Azaleas, I was to discover. We served a cathartic purpose in the lives of those fans. Our lives, at the time, were even more despairing than their own, our failures each night more ludicrous and open to derision. The fans laughed and jeered at our inadequacies, which somehow (in their eyes) diminished their own, made their drab lives seem a little less drab. Even the blacks in the left field stands laughed at the Azaleas, the niggers' "niggers."

But the fans were most vindictive with little Louie. They resented his large bonus, which, even to the most inexpert eye, seemed unwarranted by any talent he exhibited on the diamond. Mostly, though, they just felt he was the least threatening of all the Azaleas and so the safest to heap their abuse upon. Unlike Cato, for instance, who glared ominously at any fan who dared criticize his cloddish footwork around first base. They questioned his manhood, accused him of lacking pubic hair, genitalia, until one night Louie could stand it no longer. A group of about four "good ole Southern boys" were sitting behind our firstbase dugout, jeering Louie's every move. They passed a paper bag back and forth, tilting their heads each time to drink from it. In the seventh inning Louie fielded a ground ball and, without a glance, fired it over Cato's head, over our dugout, into the midst of his hecklers. They dove for cover— the paper bag hanging in midair for an instant before it shattered on the stands. The ball ricocheted around the bleachers, barely missing the hecklers, then bounced onto the playing field. Louie picked it up, wiped imaginary sweat from his hand and shook his head. The hecklers rose warily and began mopping the drink from their clothes. They used the red polka dot handkerchiefs one associates with cowboys or farmers. Finally they returned to their seats and were strangely silent for the rest of the game.

When the last out was recorded in that first night's game, Carol and I remained seated while the few fans exited and the lights were clicked off. For a moment we sat there in total darkness. "My God!" I finally said. "It's gonna be a long two months." She nodded and then got up and returned to our car in the parking lot. I went to the Azaleas' clubhouse to introduce myself to the manager burdened with this corsage of withered talent. Myself included?

His name was Mike Fandozzi. He was a 36-year-old minor league veteran who had toiled for most of 18 seasons in towns like Wellsville, Boise, Yakima and Palatka. He resembled a diminutive Victor Mature. He had slick black hair, oily skin and a toothy smile that seemed even wider that his face. He was only five-feet, six inches tall, but he had the pronounced slouch of a seven-footer with a height complex. He was quick to smile or frown, and his winks, twitches and involuntary gestures were brought on, no doubt, by the play of the Azaleas. This was his first season as a manager (he also played the infield on occasion), and he feared that if things continued this way, it would probably be his last. Even while one talked to him he would dart furtive glances over his shoulder as if anticipating approaching doom or maybe just the hand of a Milwaukee executive, who would consign him permanently to his winter home in upstate New York where, during the off-season, his wife taught school and Mike played nineball and eightball and collected welfare checks. ("And what kind of employment are you suited for, Mr. Fandozzi?" says the caseworker, leafing through his list of jobs. Mike looks out the window at the falling snow, smiles his Victor Mature smile and says, "Mostly shortstop. But I can play a little second base, maybe third, too.")

I met Mike as he was stepping out of the shower. I introduced myself and extended my hand. He looked at it for a moment and then at me. "I know about you," he said. "I know what happened at Eau Claire. I don't want none of that shit here, you understand?"

"Sure," I said. "Don't worry. All I want to do is start pitching again."

"Okay," he said. "So long as we understand each other." He smiled brilliantly and stuck out his dripping hand.

"When am I gonna pitch?" I asked. He snatched his hand back.

"See! See! That's what I mean! I'll decide that. You just

keep your nose clean and be here every afternoon at 5:30. I'll handle the rest."

I nodded. He smiled again and stuck out his hand.

I was on the inactive list for two weeks. I arrived at the ball park each day at 5:30, dressed into my uniform, pitched batting practice, ran 10 half-hearted wind sprints, showered, dressed back into my street clothes and joined Carol in the homeplate stands. We watched about five innings of each game, or until we were sure Mike had noticed me, and then we snuck off to "Pig's" for supper and then back to our apartment where we watched television and made love.

We had had difficulty finding an apartment. Most landlords did not like to rent to ballplayers. We were "too transient," they said, meaning ballplayers in general, I thought. Later I realized they meant the Azaleas in particular, who appeared and disappeared in a mysterious stream throughout the season. But eventually we found a tiny house the size of a garage at the end of a dead-end street.

The house rested on a small rise and was obscured by a large weeping cottonwood tree in the front yard. The kitchen contained a battered refrigerator just cool enough to keep food from spoiling for six hours, and an old gas stove that continued to hiss even after it was lighted. The living room was bare and rugless, and contained only a few sticks of wicker lawn furniture (couch, coffee table, straightbacked chair) that had been exposed too often to the elements. The bedroom and the bathroom were off the living room. The toilet when flushed sent a trickle of water under the door into the bedroom. More than once we woke drowsily during the night to go to the bathroom and were shocked alert by cold water on our feet. Finally we learned to hold back the water by stuffing a towel against the crack under the door. The bedroom was rugless,

271

too, and as stark as the rest of the house except for a huge canopied four-poster bed in the center of the room. Carol immediately fell in love with the bed. "It's so elegant," she said. We made love often in that bed, hated to leave it, our oasis, in the morning. One night in the midst of an entanglement we heard a creak and the groan of sagging timbers, and then we were falling through space. When the mattress hit the floor we were momentarily stunned and then enveloped by a black shroud, the canopy. Carol began screaming hysterically. She flailed her arms, kicked me in the groin, and was still sobbing uncontrollably after we had extricated ourselves from the collapsed bed. Ultimately we located a few wooden crates and metal pails on which to rest the mattress before returning to bed. We slept carefully, made no sudden moves, conducted all future lovemaking with slothlike caution.

Of course we could have avoided such anxiety by simply putting the mattress on the floor and sleeping there, but Carol would not have it. She was too terrified of the bugs, she said. They were the size of goldfish. Black, crackly-shelled, palmetto bugs, they lived in the walls and ventured out only in darkness. When we returned home at night and flicked on the lights, we would catch them on maneuvers in the middle of the living room floor. The light momentarily stunned them. They froze. Carol and I began stepping on them. Their backs cracked like eggshells. They regained their senses quickly, scattering in disarray and waddling in crunchy, audible steps toward the walls. We stomped after them. Carol cornered one, raised her foot high and smashed her spike-heel through the floorboards. The condemned, given a reprieve, darted into the wall. Carol pulled her foot out of the floor and her heel broke off. She began to cry. "They're eating the house out from under us!"

The next morning I bought six aerosol cans of DDT. We sprayed every corner of the house until it was filled with mist and we began to vomit. We waited. Nothing. We waited all day and into the night and still nothing. We turned off the lights and were about to go to bed when we heard a thousand crunchy steps. I flicked on the lights and they scattered into the walls. I trapped a straggler in a glass jar, emptied a can of DDT into the jar and then screwed on the top. The jar clouded up and the palmetto disappeared from view. I waited—10, 15 minutes—and then unscrewed the top and turned the jar upside down. The palmetto fell onto the floor and darted into the wall. We went to bed with the lights on. Carol stuffed towels in the crack under the door leading to the living room and more towels under the door to the bathroom and then we lay down cautiously on our precariously balanced bed in our brilliantly lighted, hermetically sealed room and stared at the ceiling.

The two weeks passed slowly. I played pool in the mornings, drank lemon cokes on the benches that lined Lemon Street, then went fishing in the afternoon with Ron Pavia, the only other married Azalea besides Fandozzi and myself. Ron was a short, chunky, swarthy Portuguese from Cranston, Rhode Island, who so resembled a character in the cartoon strip "Yogi Bear" that we nicknamed him "Boo Bear." "Boo" and I went fishing every afternoon, although we never caught anything. We went first to a bait store where we bought 30 shrimp frozen in a pail of crushed ice, and then we went to a grocery store and bought six lemons and a package of Dixie cups and a few six-packs of Seven-Up, and then we went to a liquor store and bought a gallon of port wine, which we stuck in the pail with the shrimp. Finally we drove to the outskirts of town where the road passed over the narrowest part of the St. Johns River without benefit of a bridge railing. There we parked the car on a soft shoulder and sat on the edge of the road with our feet dangling over the river. We baited our hooks with shrimp and tossed them into the water, then poured some port wine over crushed ice, added a dash of Seven-Up, a squeeze of lemon and relaxed. It was always hot in the afternoon, so hot we could look down the road and see the black tar shimmering like liquid glass. To combat the heat we refreshed ourselves often with wine coolers. Soon we no longer noticed the heat, the sweat pouring down our necks, our heads nodding on our chests, the bamboo poles now weightless in our arms gone numb. Nor did we notice that we never got a nibble, that we never saw a fish, that after awhile we had even polished off our bait along with our wine coolers.

We fished like this daily, and we probably would have continued until the end of the season if not for an experience we had late one afternoon after we had finished the last of the wine. The sun was beginning to set and it had grown dark and cool, although by then we were too stiff even to notice. We had not moved a muscle in minutes, it seemed, when suddenly there was a splash and we saw, rising straight out of the water, twisting like a corkscrew as it rose, a huge ugly fish. It had hide like rusted armor and a mean, long-billed face like an alligator's. The fish kept rising and rising in slow motion, endlessly it seemed, until it had reached a height of almost six feet and its beady pop eyes were level with our own. We stared at it, Ron and I looking into the pop eyes of the garfish and he in turn scrutinizing us with a narrow squint. Then he opened his long-billed mouth, revealing rows of tiny thumbtack-like teeth and, with a single swipe, severed both lines before slipping silently back into the river.

We said nothing. We just sat there, holding the poles with our severed lines that no longer reached the water and staring at that point in space from which the garfish had just stared at us. Shortly thereafter we got up to leave. We threw the rest of the shrimp into the river, and then we threw the pail of ice in, too, and the empty bottles of Seven-Up and wine, and then, as an afterthought, we threw in our bamboo poles. We never dared mention what we had seen—what we thought we had seen—to anyone, not even to ourselves.

I was finally put on the Azaleas' active list toward the end of July, and a few days later I won my first game of the season. I pitched five innings against the Daytona White Sox before Mike had to relieve me with the tying runs on base. My relief pitcher retired the side and then pitched three more scoreless innings to preserve my first victory in almost three months. Nothing had changed in my pitching, really. I had given up three runs on ten walks, three hits and a wild pitch. I had struck out one batter. My motion was still a disaster, and my fastball and curveball were faint shadows of what they had once been. But I had had luck that night for one thing (now that I no longer needed it), and for another, I had begun to cease to care. It relaxed me. I no longer struggled to remember. I threw easily, without thought or anxiety over my lost promise. It was hard to be tormented by one's own lost promise at Palatka, where one was surrounded by so much lost promise. We laughed at each other's inadequacies.

One night Boo Bear, playing third base, kicked two routine ground balls into the thirdbase stands. When he returned to the dugout at the end of the inning, he sat at the far end of the bench, shaking his head in despair. Someone called down to him, "Atta boy, Boo, great hands!" Then laughed. We all began to laugh. Boo glanced sideways at his laughing teammates, his face dark and threatening, and then not so threatening, and then he was laughing, too. "Ah, fuck it!"

I laughed at myself also. For the first time. After my victory over the White Sox, Louie Haas shook my hand. "Nice motion you got there, fella. Smooth, really smooth."

"Just a little something I picked up along the way," I said, and we both laughed. Ironically, I was the most successful

275

pitcher on the club during the last few weeks of the season. I started every fourth game and often relieved between starts. In one sevenday span I appeared in four games totaling 23 innings, and I won two of them. When we left for Tampa on the last road trip of the season, I had a 4–4 record and was one of the few pitchers on the club with a .500 winning percentage. Despite such modest success, however, I was not fooled into thinking I had recaptured anything. I knew I was not throwing well, was getting by on luck, a little know-how and indifference. I realized that my pitching had deteriorated as much as it possibly could have at Eau Claire, and now, at Palatka, I was not making progress, I just wasn't getting any worse.

I thought about all these things as we drove toward Tampa on that hot afternoon near the end of the season. I wondered where I'd lost it, tried to discover that point where it all started going downhill. But it was like trying to read isolated, disconnected points on a graph (my argument with Torre, changing my motion in Bradenton, my nature), none of which, alone, indicated a direction. My inability to see it clearly was frustrating. I put it out of my mind, turned to Boo Bear beside me in the front seat. "Pour me one of those, Boo."

Ron had set up a small bar on the dashboard—wine, ice, Seven-Up, lemons—and he had already poured himself two coolers while I was daydreaming about lost promise.

"Aren't you pitching tonight?" he asked.

"Fuck it," I said, and he laughed. Boo poured me a drink, and a little later he poured me another, and then another and he kept on pouring until we reached Tampa, five hours later.

I started that game without a care in the world, and it didn't bother me a bit when I walked the first four batters, or when Mike came out to the mound to relieve me from the last game of my career, or when I walked into the dugout with an idiot's grin and my teammates burst out laughing.

I sobered up on the ride home that night, and wasn't grinning when we reached Palatka at four o'clock in the morning. I drove to our house and woke Carol.

"What's the matter?"

"Nothing," I said. "We're going home. Pack our things."

"But the season isn't over yet," she said. "You still have two more games."

"Don't worry," I said. "It's all right." We loaded the Chrysler with all our belongings and then, because we still owed a month's rent on our apartment, I coasted the car down the hill past our landlord's house. And then I turned the key and we drove off.

We reached Jacksonville at dawn and Brunswick a little while later, and then Savannah and Florence and Fayetteville. The towns and the time passed rapidly as I daydreamed about my career.

When we reached the city limits of Rocky Mountain, North Carolina, it was dark again. We moved slowly through traffic, past motels and gas stations and traffic lights, and suddenly it occurred to me, with a chill, that I had no career. What would I be without baseball? I could think of nothing. I stopped at a red light, an interminable red light. And it was then, for the first time, that I began to wonder . . . why?